AF580439

THE BEST OF

Canadian Pastels

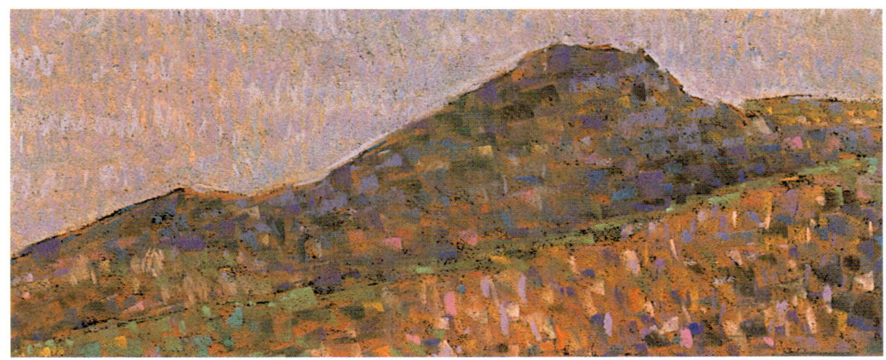

EDITED BY HERBERT ROGOFF

PASTEL SOCIETY OF CANADA
SOCIÉTÉ DE PASTEL DU CANADA

ART INSTRUCTION ASSOCIATES, SARASOTA, FLORIDA • DISTRIBUTED BY NORTHLIGHT BOOKS, CINCINNATI, OHIO

INTRODUCTION

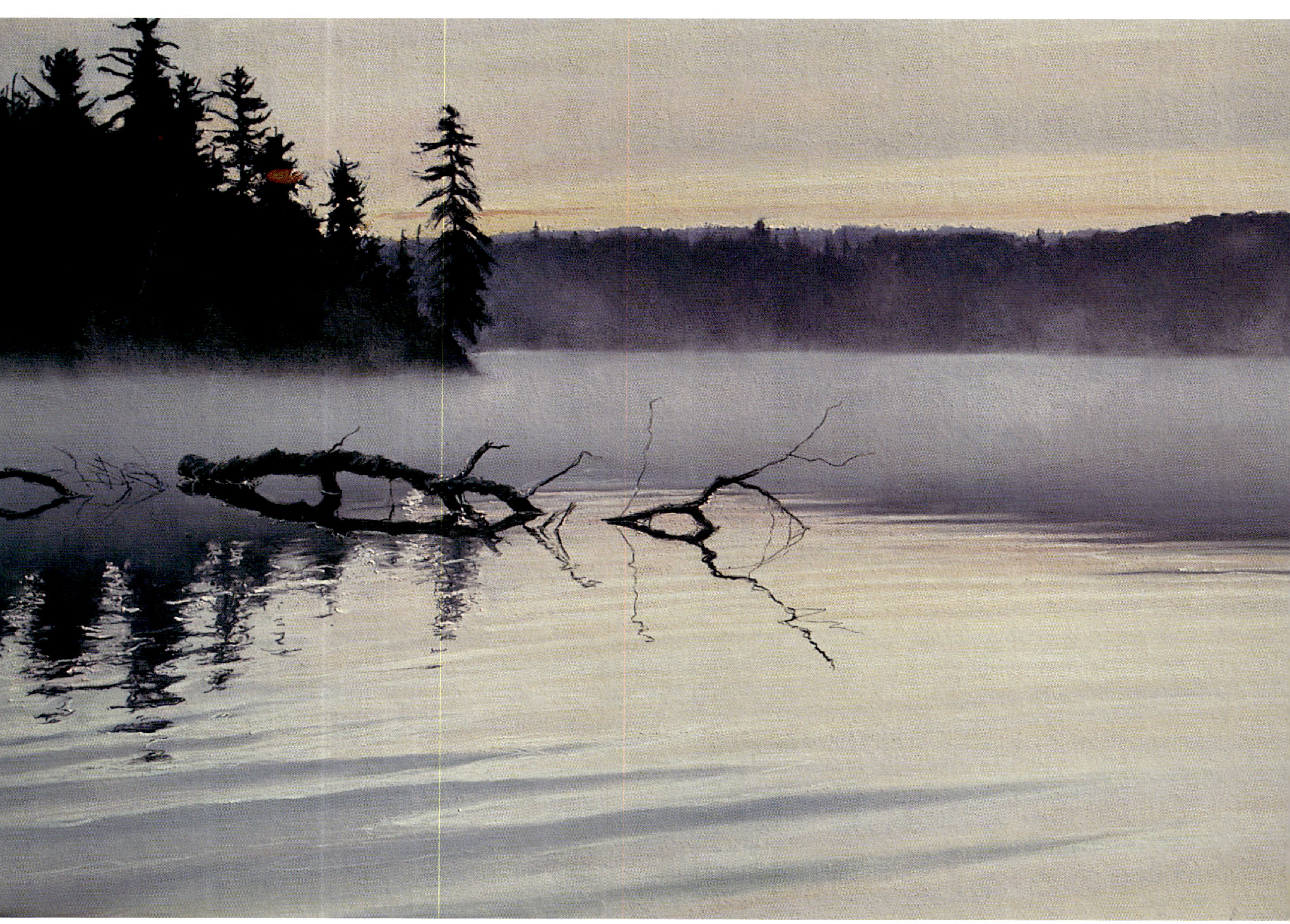

Dave Beckett

First Light

17" x 33", Mid-tone pastel paper

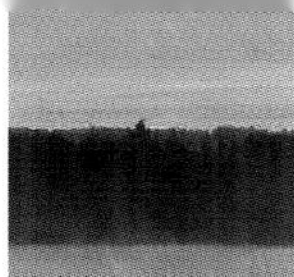

We are proud to bring you paintings by members of the Pastel Society of Canada. We do so with hopes that their appearance within these pages will inspire other pastellists as well as to inform aspiring artists who are curious about painting with this wonderful material. Before we go on to the many creations that we have chosen to reproduce in this book, we would like to write a few words about pastels and the characteristics of the medium.

Artists have used pastel crayons as a medium of expression for close to three centuries, and even earlier, according to some experts on the subject of cave paintings. Some of the prehistoric murals, they claim, may have been actually executed with some kind of colored chalk. While this remains speculative, we *do* know that pictures painted with pastels first appeared in Paris some time during the 1720's. We are fortunate that painting icons such as Jean-Baptiste Chardin, Edgar Degas, Mary Cassatt, and many others, have left us considerable contributions in the pastel medium that have been admired and studied for great numbers of years.

What are pastels? Basically, they are made of pigment and a binder— or vehicle – which converts dry powdery pigment into a moist lump that, through the process of extrusion, creates pastel sticks. After the sticks have been formed, they are baked in an oven, which evaporates the water-based binder, thus solidifying the sticks. The finished product, therefore, is a painting material of pure pigment.

While oil paints, watercolors, acrylic paints and pastels all are made with the same pigments (give or take a few), only the pastel binder evaporates. Linseed oil, which is used for oil paints, is necessary to keep the pigment in suspension. Gum Arabic, which is mixed into pigments to make watercolors, is needed to help the water-based paint stick to the paper. With acrylics, we have pretty much the same situation except that the plastic resin that's used to mix with the pigments is instrumental in making acrylic paints dry absolutely waterproof.

You can now see that pastel is the only medium that does not require the aid of any fluid binder. The sticks are compressed pigment that will adhere quite easily to any paper which has a tooth, or texture. And without the influence of an alien substance – the binder – pastel paintings will hold their color for a far longer period of time than any other painting material.

By this, we don't mean to imply that *all* pastel colors are permanent, that all of their colors will last forever. Pastel painters must be scrupulous about their choice of colors, using only those whose permanence has been time-tested. These colors are recognizable to everyone who paints: Burnt Sienna, Yellow Ochre, Cadmium Yellow, Cadmium Red, Ultramarine Blue, and all others that we have learned to trust in oil paintings, watercolors and acrylic paintings. Colors that the pastel painter has to avoid are those with fanciful names, ones that are not in the lexicon of the artist.

Despite the plus factor of its purity of color, it is important to know that pastel paintings can be quite fragile. After all, the color rests on the painting support in a powdery manner, and all sorts of terrible things can happen. You can overcome this liability by framing the painting under glass with a substantial mat to protect the painting surface from the glass. A number of artists choose to preserve their pictures by spraying a light coat of fixative over the surface and then framing it under glass. A word of caution – using fixative on pastel can be tricky. Too much spray may alter the colors.

In the final analysis, after painting a few pictures with this medium, you will discover that when properly cared for pastel paintings will last indefinitely.

And, now, without further ado, as emcees are wont to say, here is our show. Please enjoy our display from Canada.

The Editor

STILL LIFES

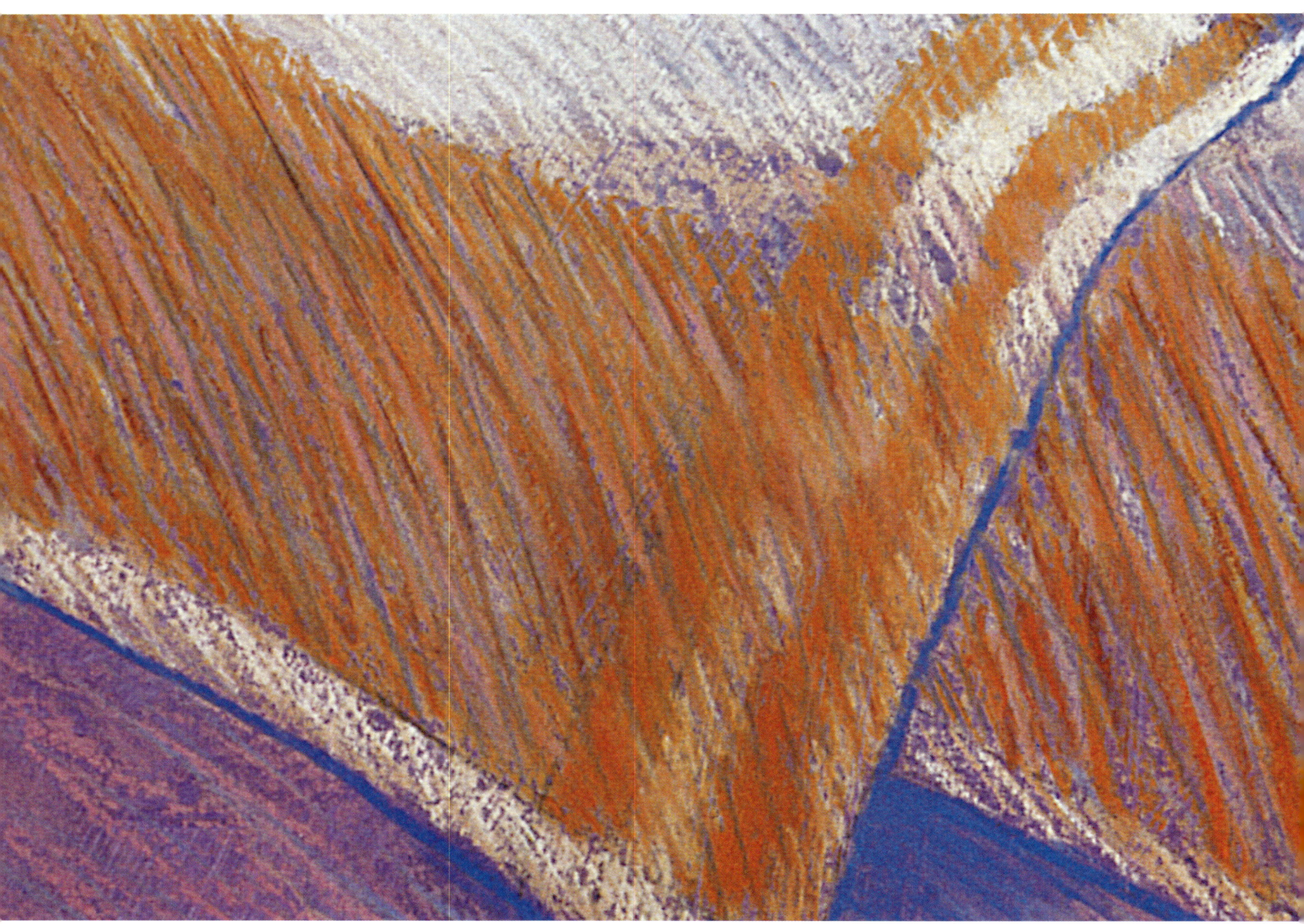

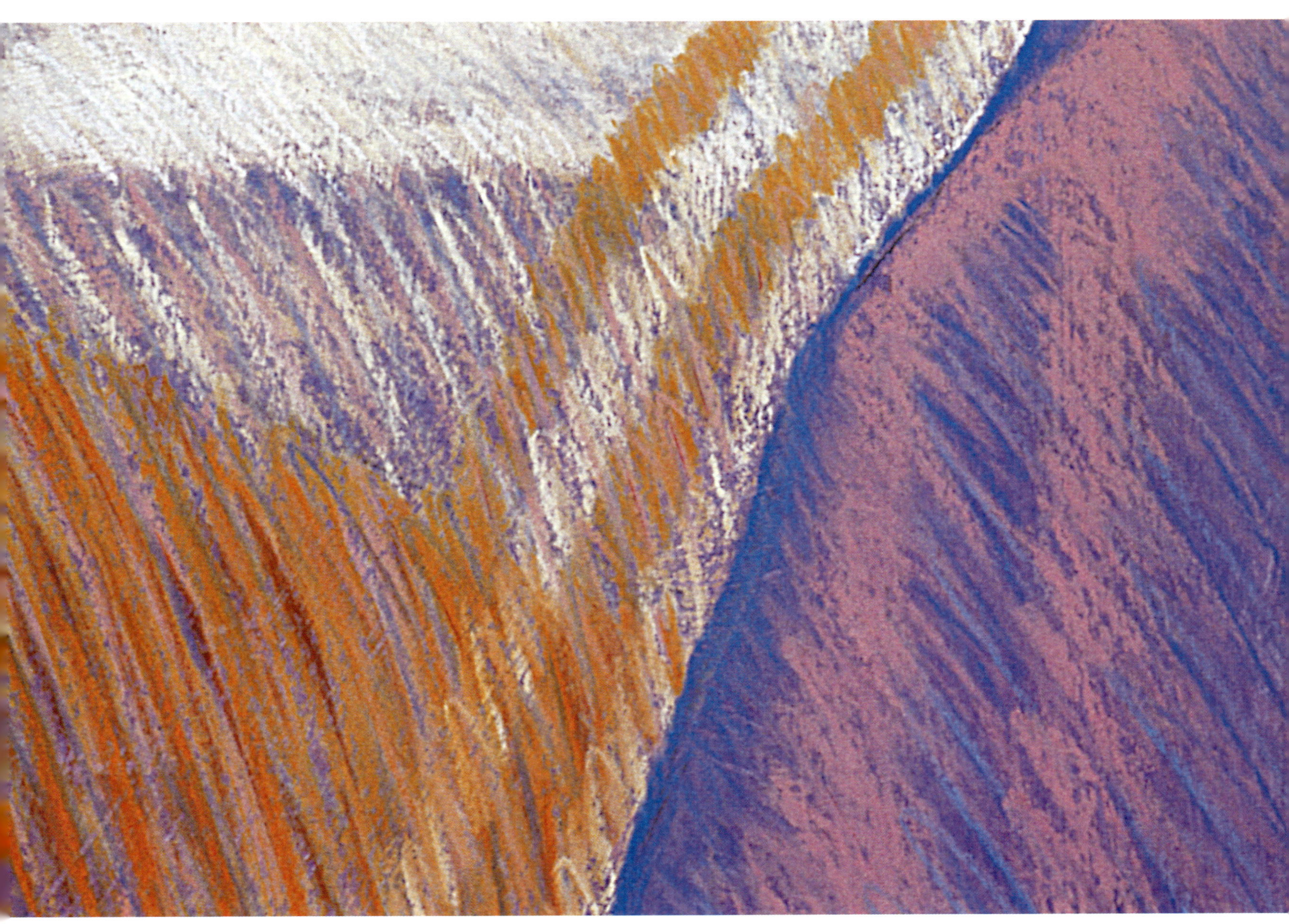

Rose Zivot

I study my reference photographs and begin planning and experimenting with color swatches used in every part of the painting. The initial outline is usually drawn in pale blue Carb-Othello or Conte. I prefer to correct and refine the drawing as I work each section of the painting. The background is always painted first because it helps me resolve all the other color relationships. For my florals, I often choose an intensely dark background, saturating the sandpaper with pigment so that no paper shows. Several layers of dark forest green or burgundy red, or deep blue, are covered with black and blended to give me a velvet setting for developing texture. Against this rich background, my flowers seem to sparkle and jump off the paper.

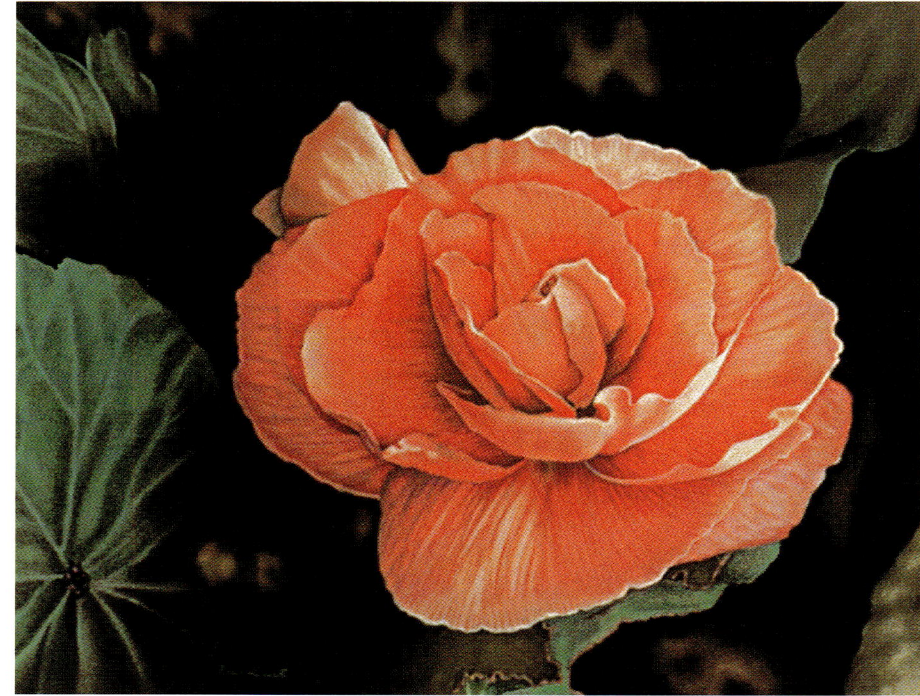

Corallina Begonia

24" x 28"
Fine sandpaper

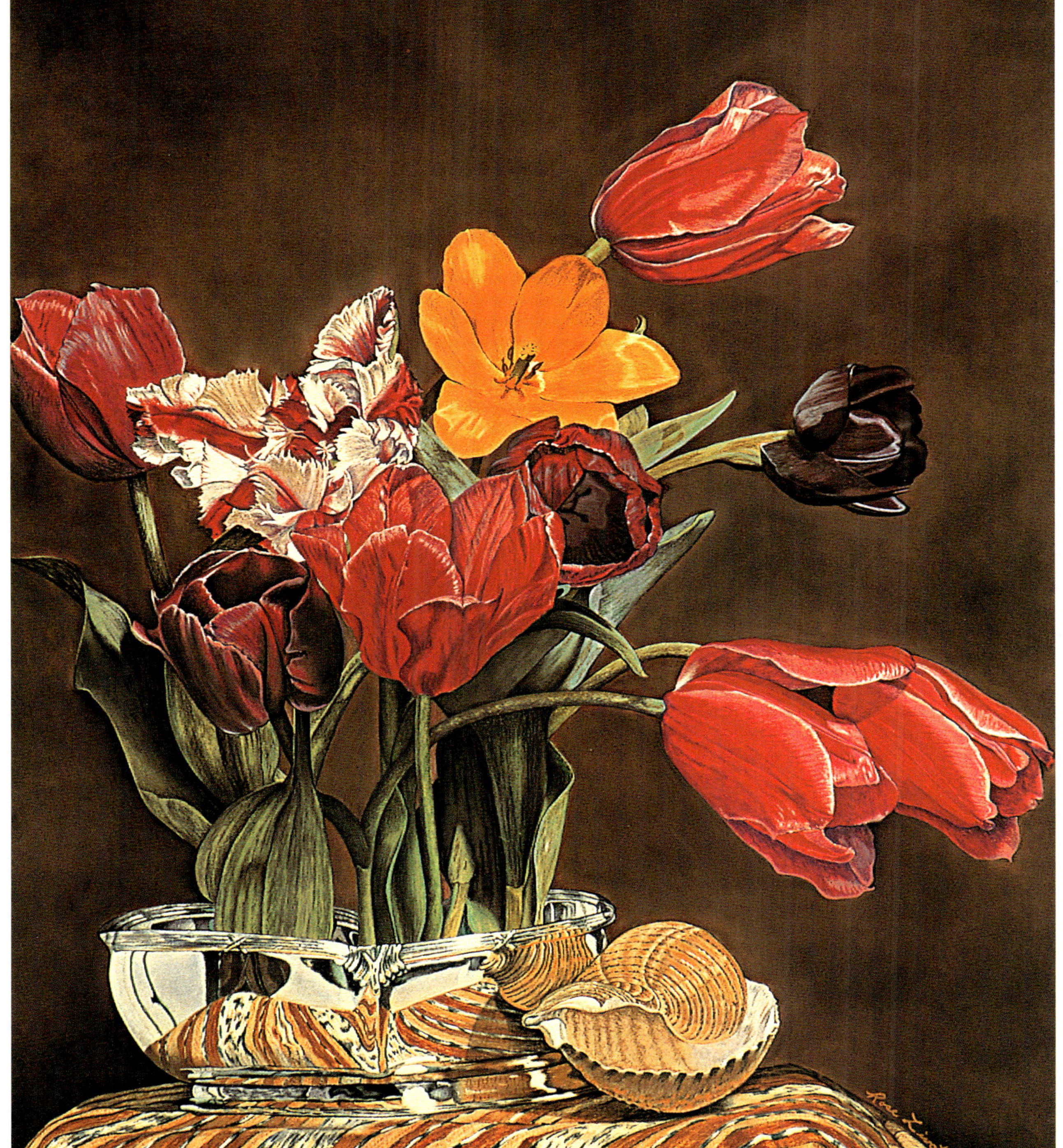

Tulips in a Silver Bowl

30" x 36"
Fine sandpaper

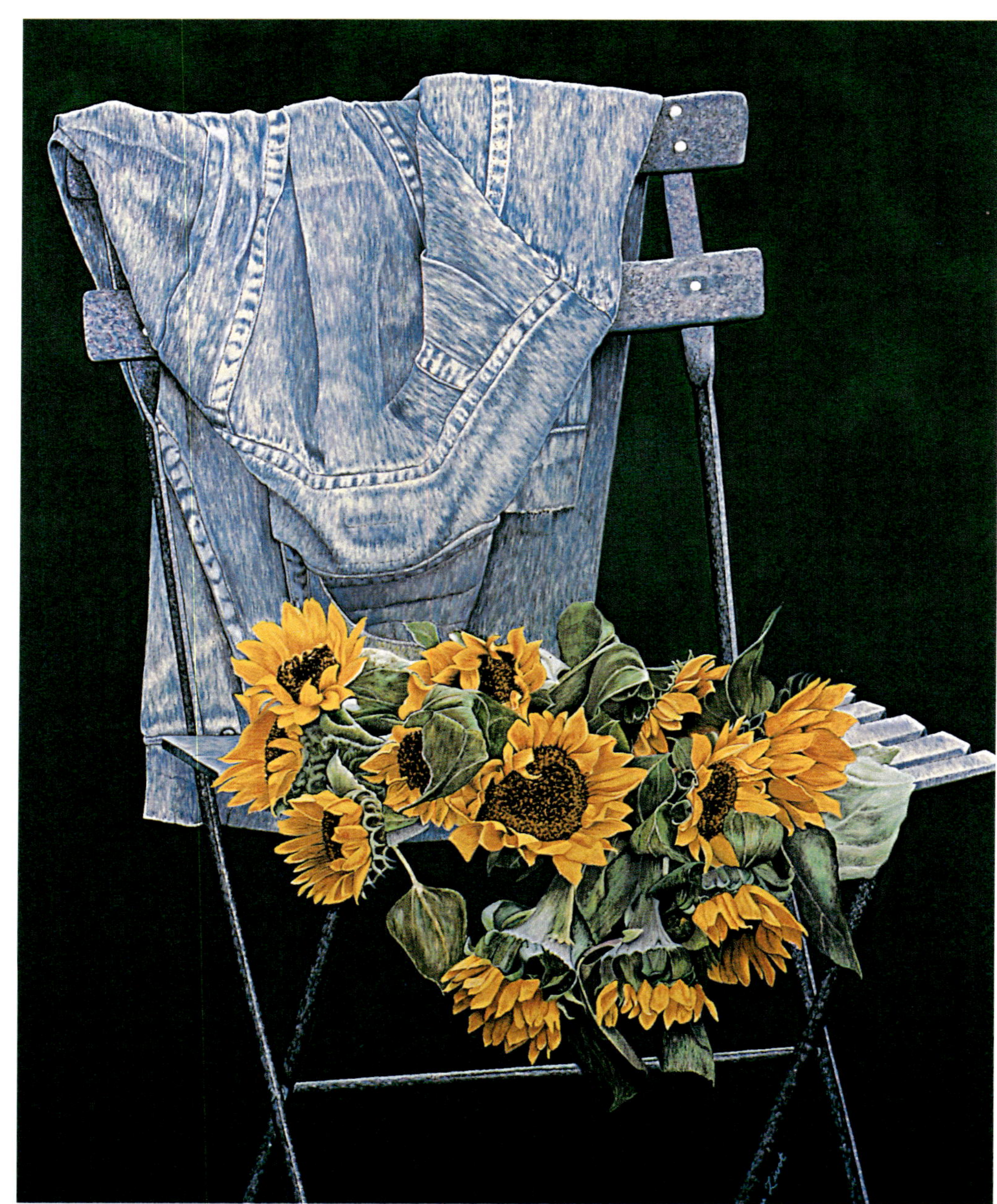

Rose Zivot

Just Picked

30" x 36"
Fine sandpaper

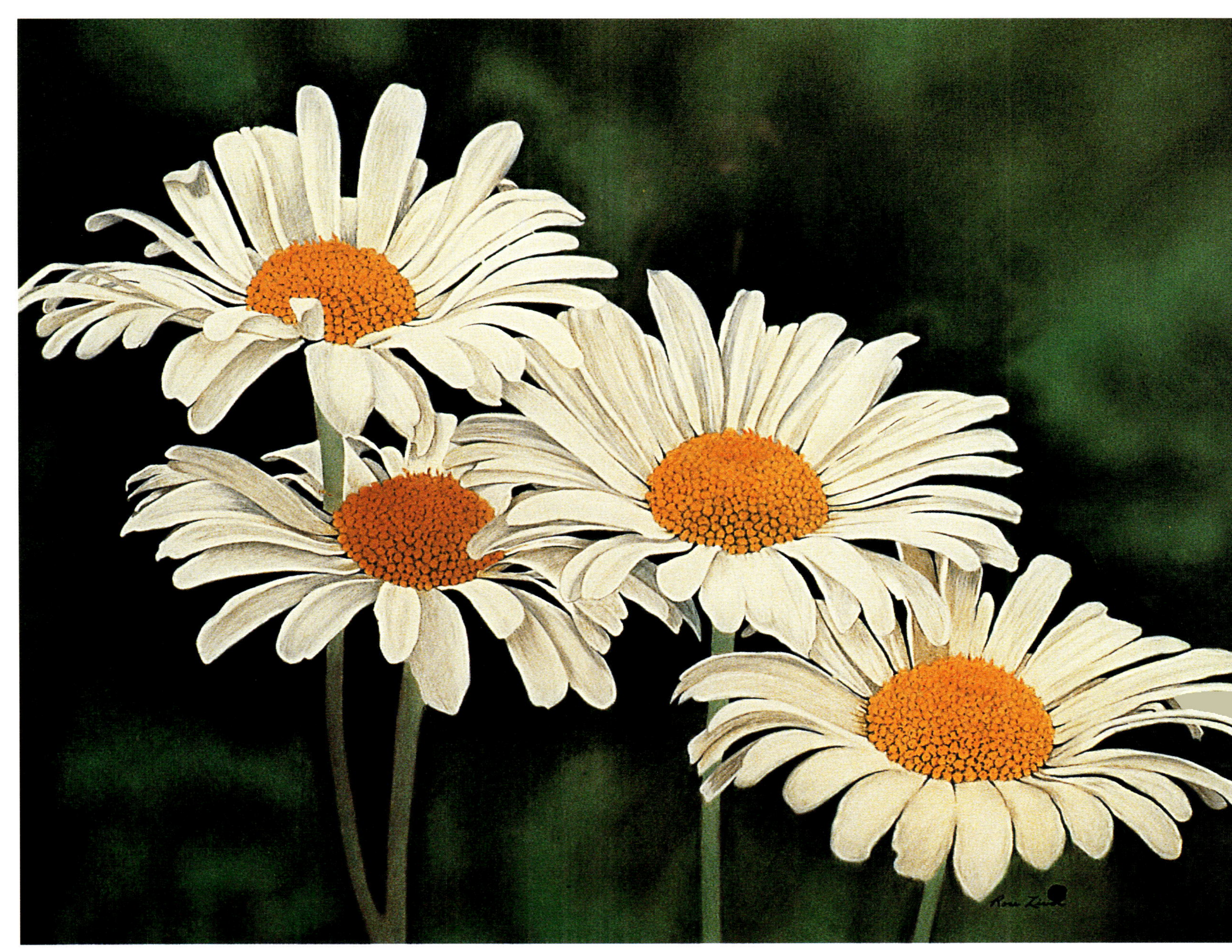

Rose Zivot

Don't Pick the Daisies

32" x 38"
Fine sandpaper

Barbara Amos

The inspiration for a drawing or painting usually comes to me at an odd moment, when I am involved in some daily event. A certain object or the particular way the light falls on something catches my interest and the next time that I am in my studio, I attempt to recreate it. Sometimes this comes together quickly, but just as often it is a lengthy process of arranging items, removing them, adding something else, setting up the lights, changing the lights, and so on. I was quite relieved when I read that it sometimes took Cezanne three hours to set up a still life. For me, this part of the process is intuitive. Eventually there comes a moment when everything comes together and I am curious about the aspect of drawing what I see.

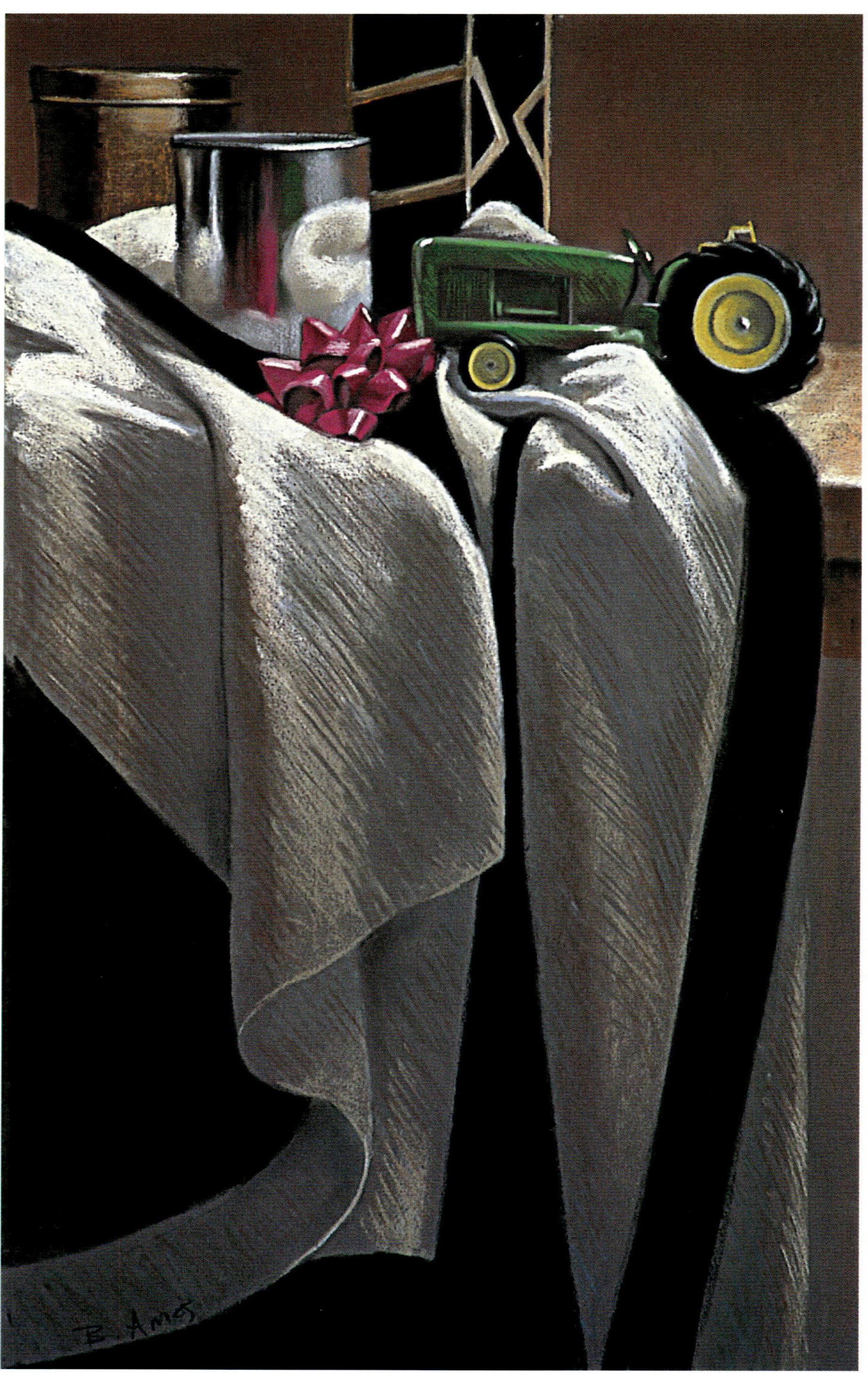

Tractor and Bow

18" × 29"
Gessoed cold-pressed
watercolor paper

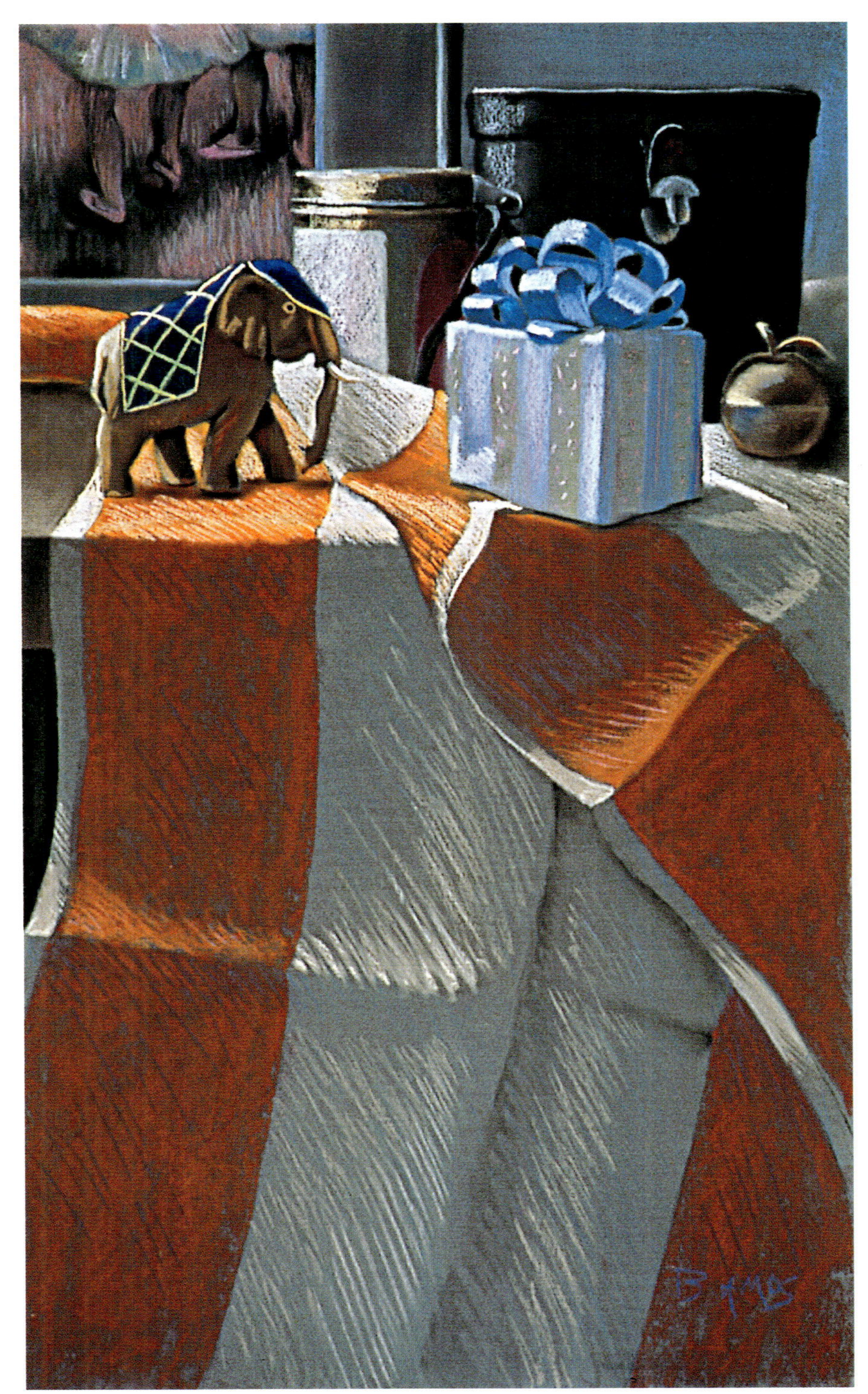

Elephant and Present

22" × 30"
Gessoed cold-pressed
watercolor paper

Barbara Amos

Mexican Plate, Vases, and Tape Measure

19" × 25"
Gessoed cold-pressed watercolor paper

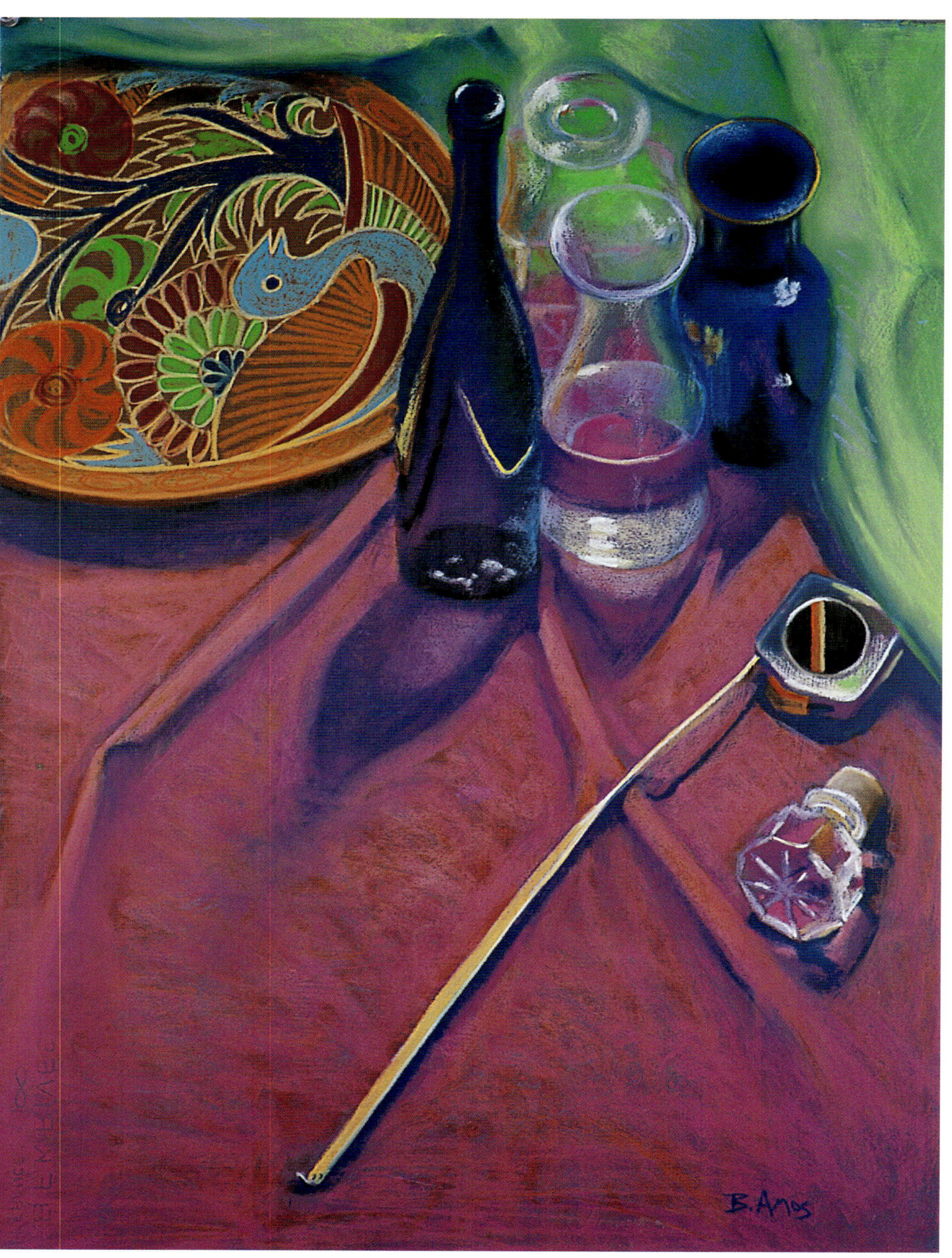

Barbara Amos

Teacups and Vases

22" × 30"
Gessoed cold-pressed
watercolor paper

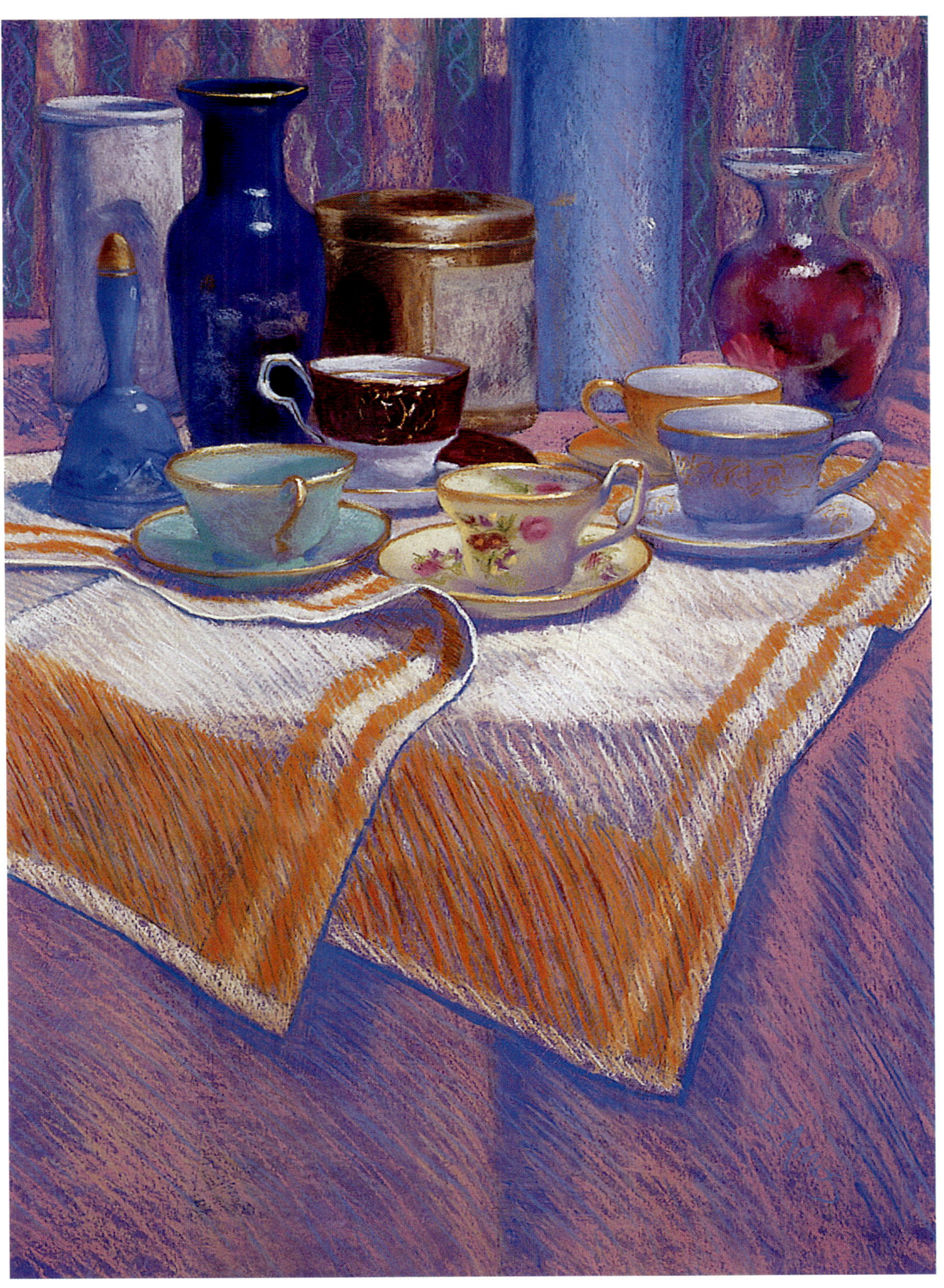

Horace Champagne

The ground that I choose to work on is an important factor in pastels. Textured surfaces trap the pigment best and the color of the paper or canvas can influence the overall mood of a painting where it is allowed to show through. I favor papers in shades of brown and olive green for my scenes of old Quebec City, and I turn to dark blue for Rocky Mountain landscapes. I find white paper too too garish.

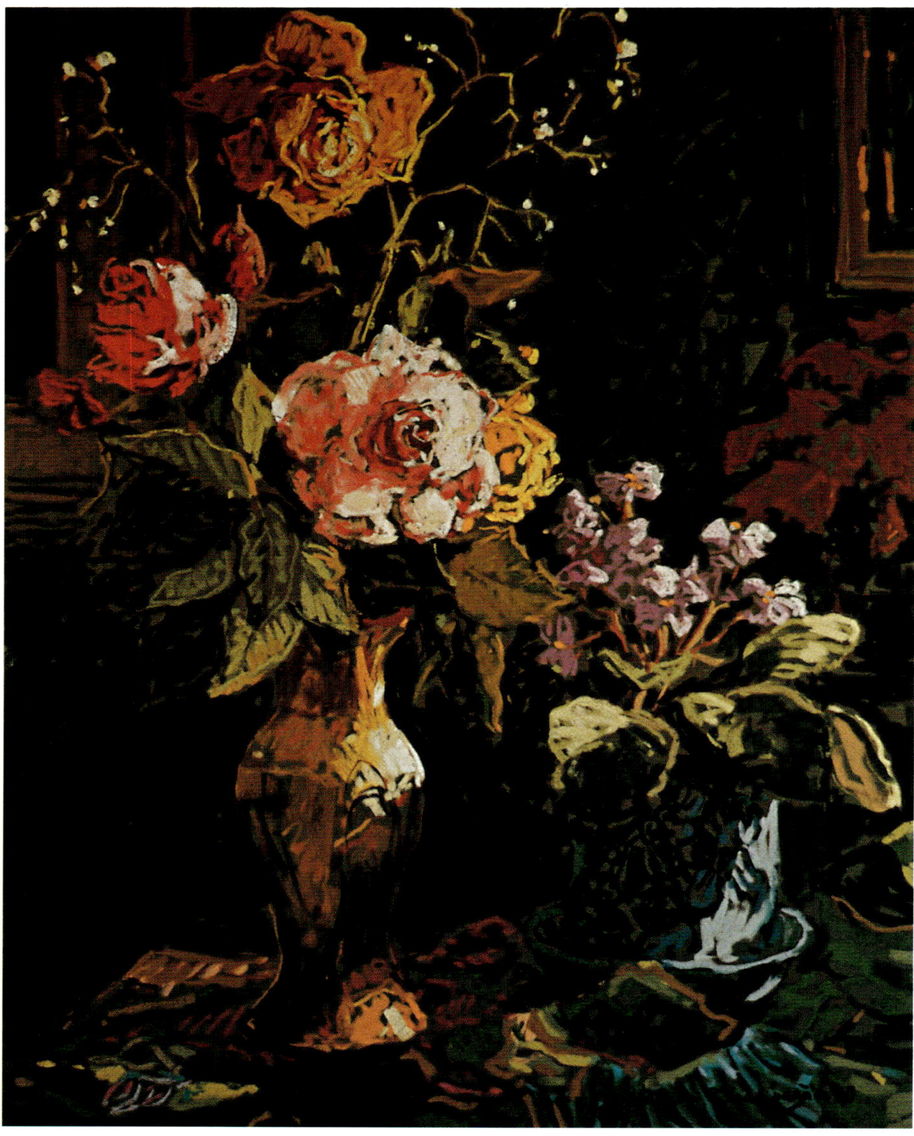

Roses, 1996

16" x 20"

Dave Beckett

I lay out my initial sketch in India ink with a brush after the general drawing is finished to my liking. I begin each piece at the top and work my way to the bottom of the painting. This not only allows me to keep the unfinished area clean but reminds me of the color values (background grays, foreground colors stronger). I use workable fixative only to darken some colors.

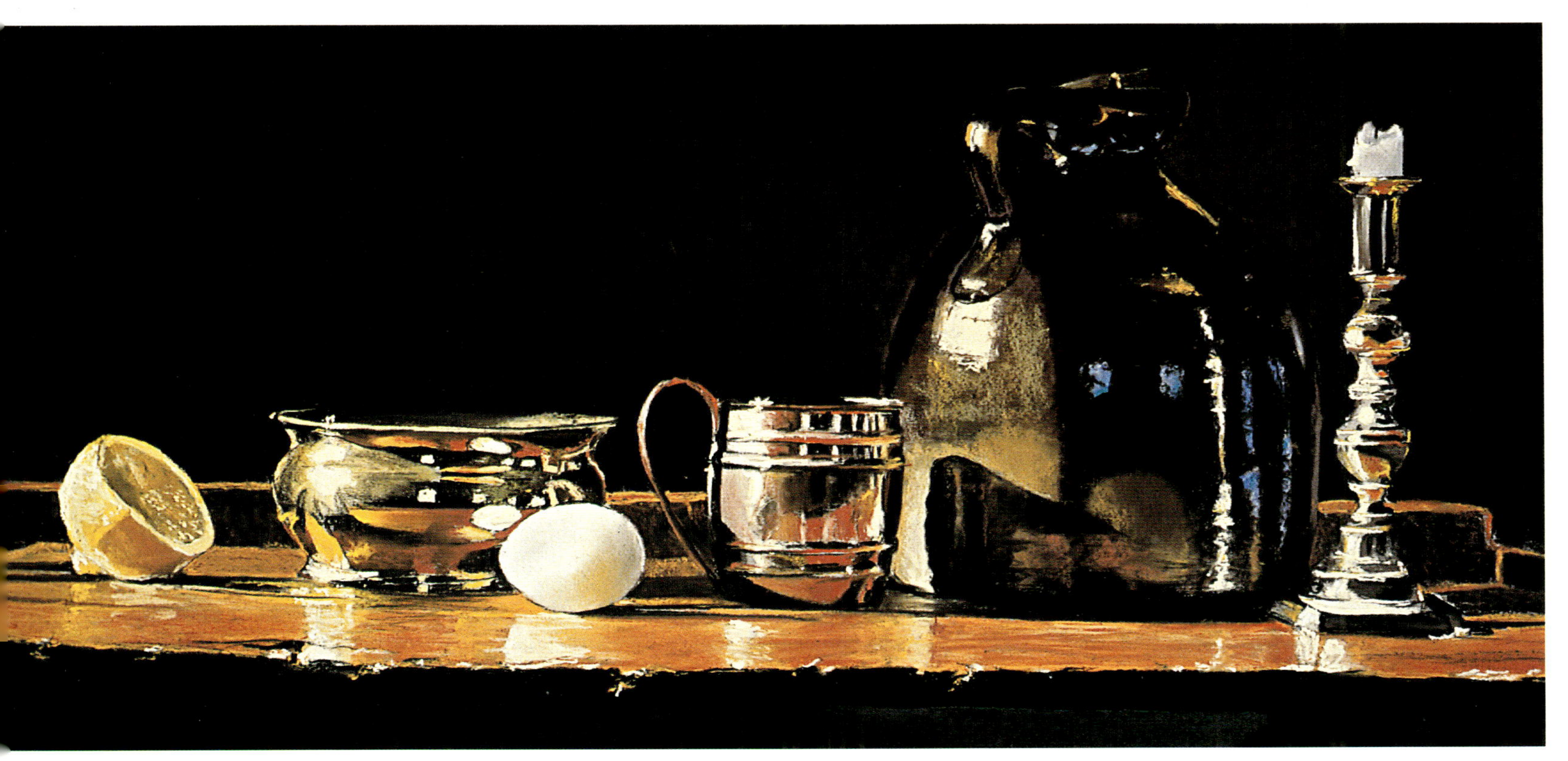

Remembrances

30" x 32"
Mid-tone pastel paper

Marija Petricevic

Pastel is a wonderful, spontaneous, direct and forgiving medium, capable of wide interpretation. It can be blended, crosshatched, scumbled, dotted, feathered or combined with other media. Its drawing line is versatile, its colors have impact and immediacy, and it can express a broad range of textures. I enjoy painting animals and people because each personality is a little different, and each painting is a new challenge. I try to understand the person beyond the appearance, capture the character and unique personality, and interpret that on paper or canvas. I begin to apply color with hard pastels, then switch to soft, making broad strokes with the sides. To finish the detail I use pastel pencils.

Flower in Desert

16" x 20"
Toned Sennelier paper

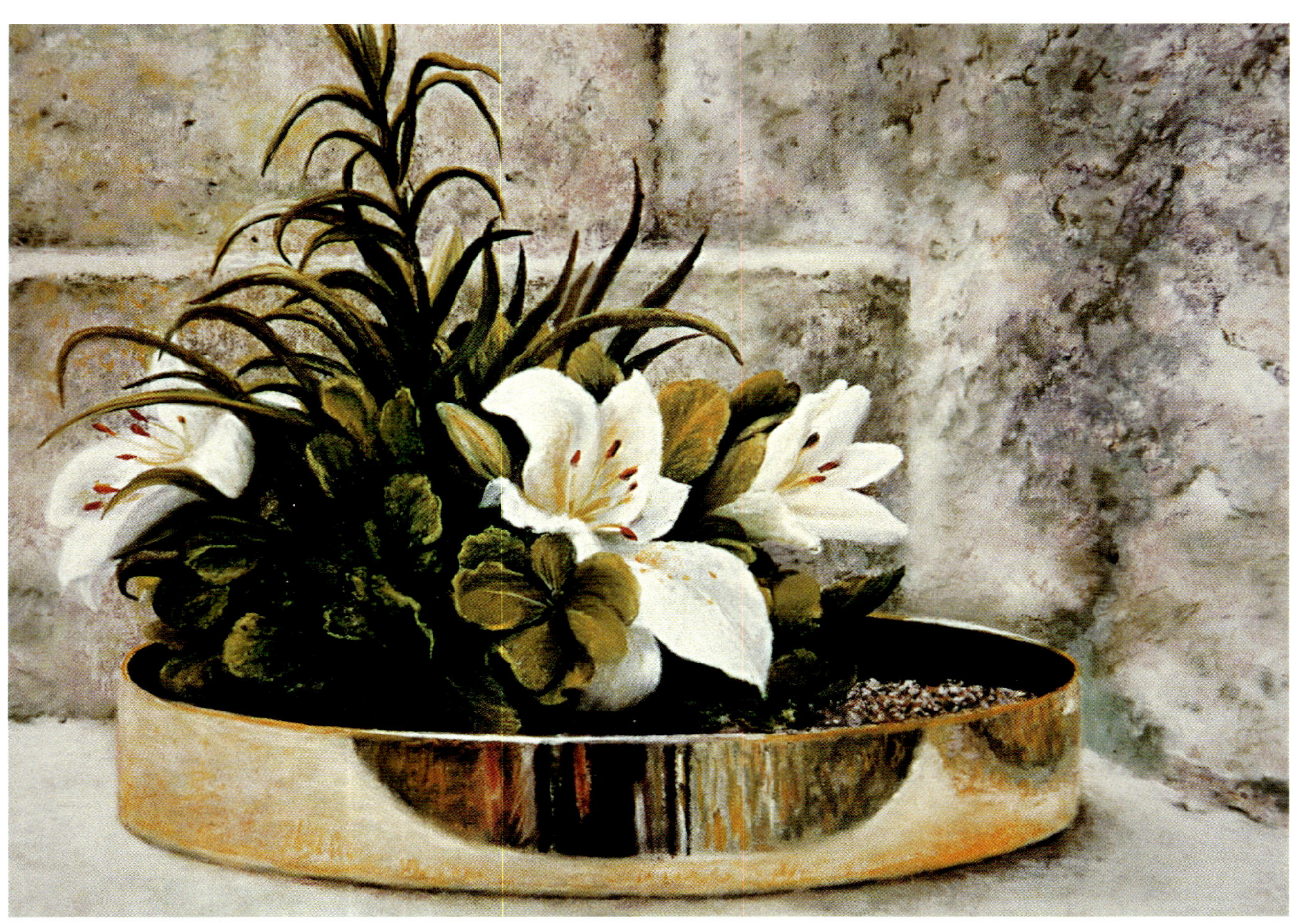

Geoffrey Jamieson

I sketched the subject in simple outline pencil on a sheet of layout paper. When the drawing was satisfactory, I traced it onto a sheet of tracing paper, using a black ink pen. Turning the tracing over, I covered the lines showing through on the reverse with a dark gray pastel. A light gray pastel paper was chosen and, on the smoother side, I carefully applied the tracing paper (pastel-covered side down) and traced along the ink lines with a pencil. The result was a gray pastel outline of the composition on the Canson paper. After selecting an assortment of pastels for use in the main areas, I began painting from the arrangement in the sun room. I applied the final details with pastel pencils.

The Three Graces

19" x 25"
Canson Mi-Teintes paper

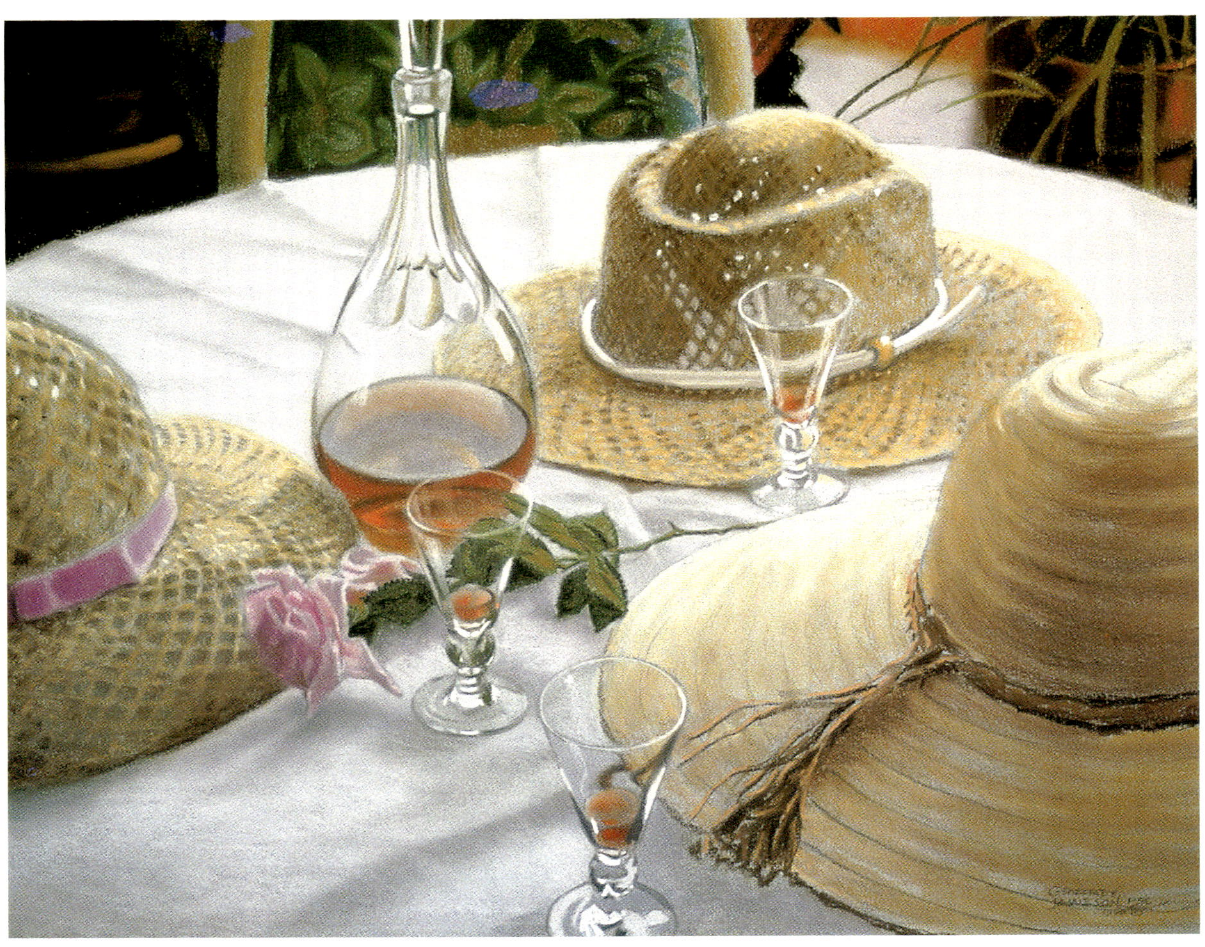

Marilyn-Ann Ranco

On a fine pastel paper (Sennelier, Canson Mi-Teintes), I quickly block in the overall design, establishing large shapes as well as the light and dark areas in charcoal or Burnt Sienna pastel. Next, I build thin layers of color with Rembrandt Pastels (semi-soft). Then, I finish the painting with tender pastels: Sennelier, Rowney or Schminke. For very fine details, I use NuPastels sharpened to a point or Conte Pastel Pencils. I hardly use fixative because I find it darkens the colors.

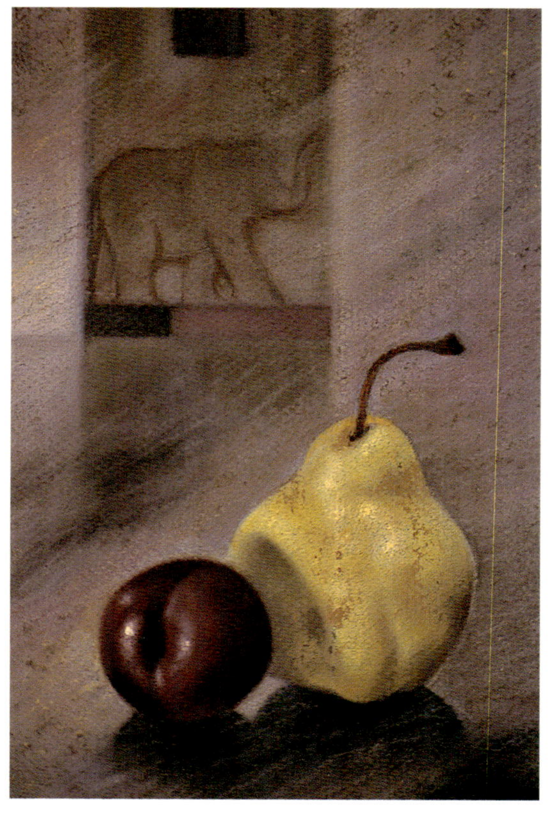

The Elephant

9" × 12 ½"
Pastel paper

Tulips and Peony

9" × 12 ½"
Pastel paper

The Vase from Italy

14" × 25 ½"
Pastel paper

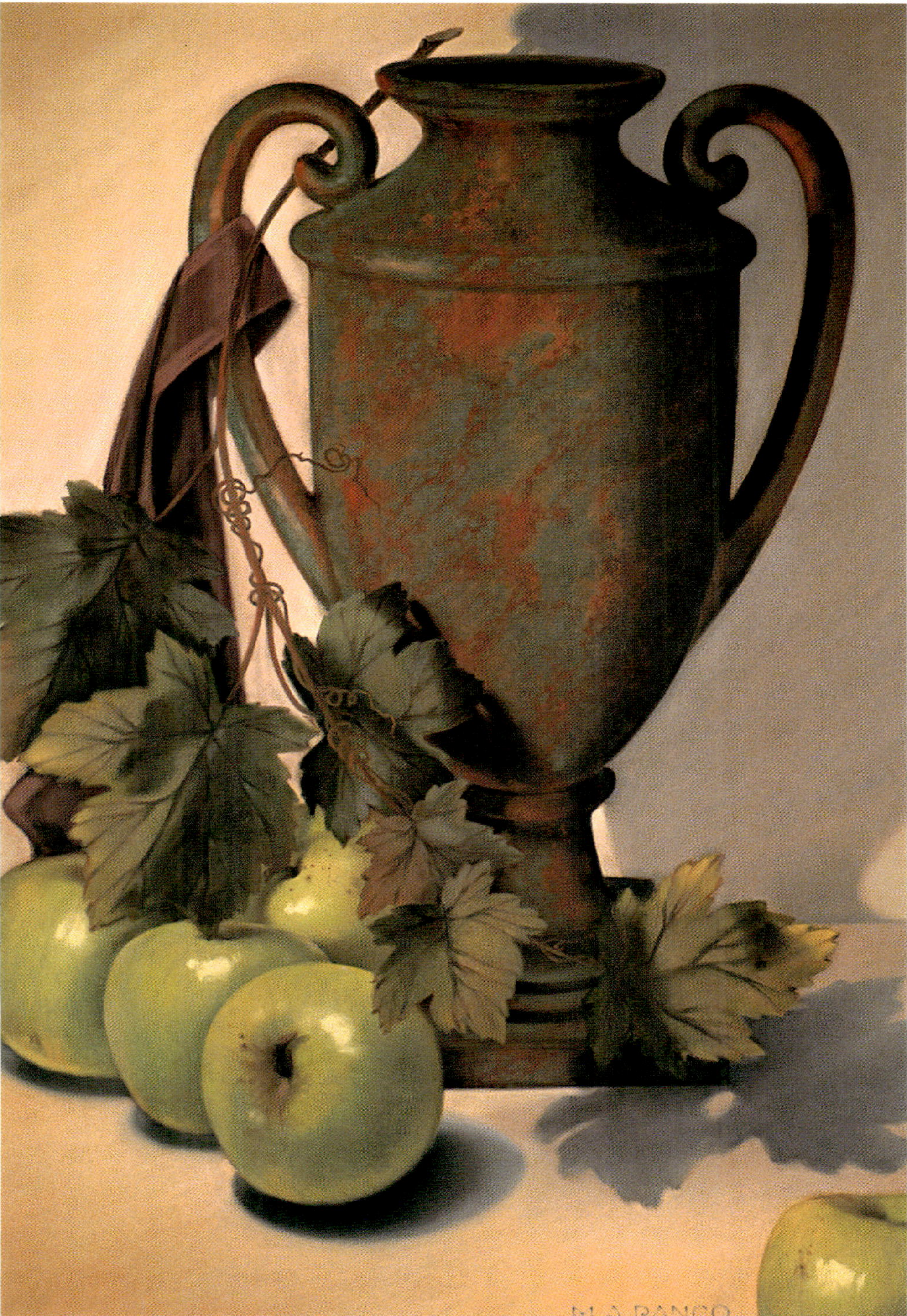

Charles Couper

As a still life painter (primarily), my procedure is usually to arrange a composition by selecting some distinctive object for a major emphasis and then embellishing it with others which have symbolic or color harmony potential. It is a trial-and-error procedure in which a plethora of options are considered. Many objects are tested in combination for color, balance, texture, shape and symbolic harmony, ultimately resulting in a simplicity growing out of complexity.

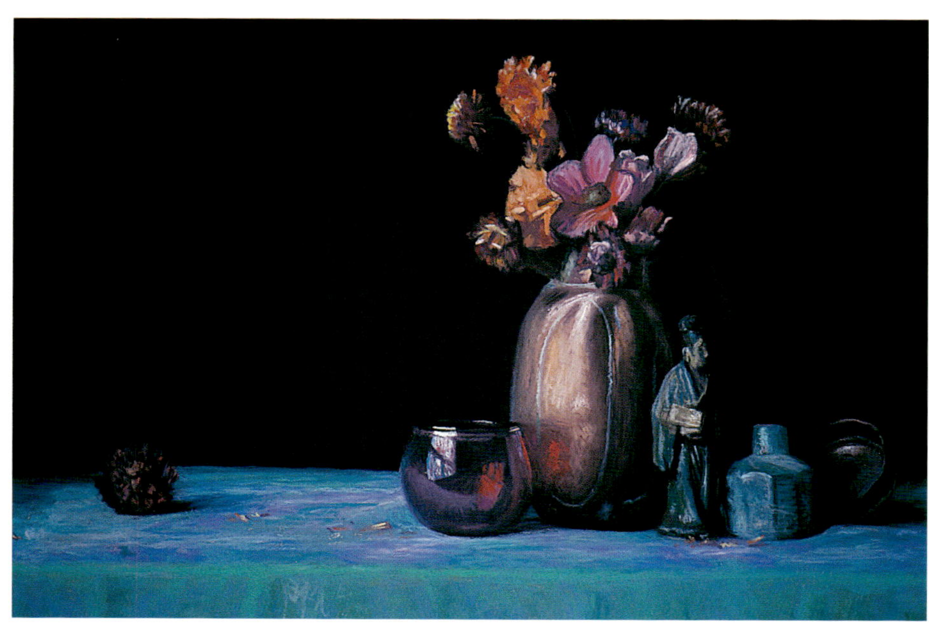

Arrangement in Rose and Green

12" x 16"
Sandpaper dry
mounted on foam panel

Copper and Tomarillos

12" x 16"
Sandpaper foam panel

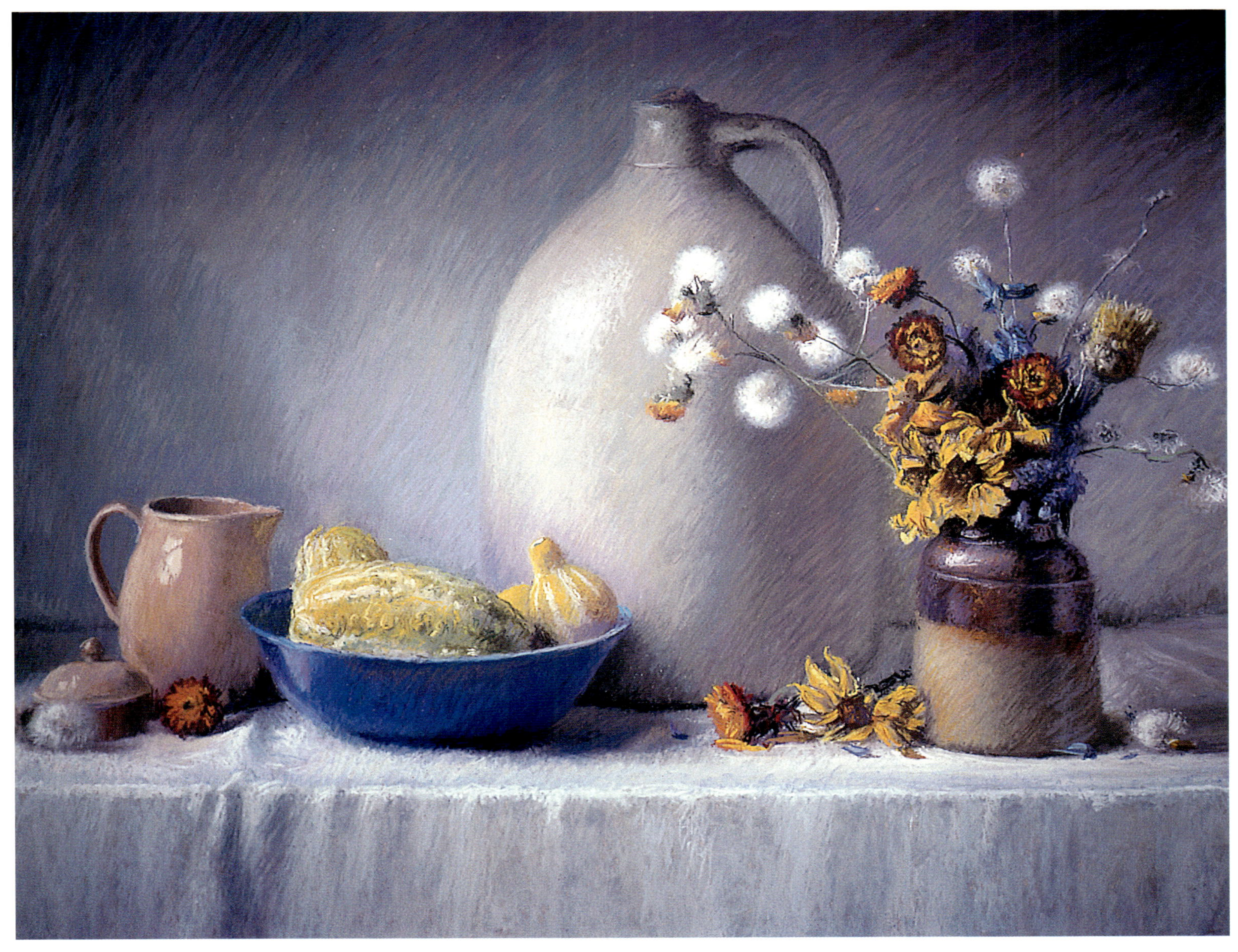

October Table

20" x 30"
Sandpaper foam panel

Joyce Dessert

I work mostly on acid-free Canson pastel paper and work only with pastels. I use both hard and soft pastels interchangeably: the hard to blend the soft. I spray with fixative when and if needed. I really enjoy my pastels and believe that anything that can be accomplished in other media can also be done with pastels.

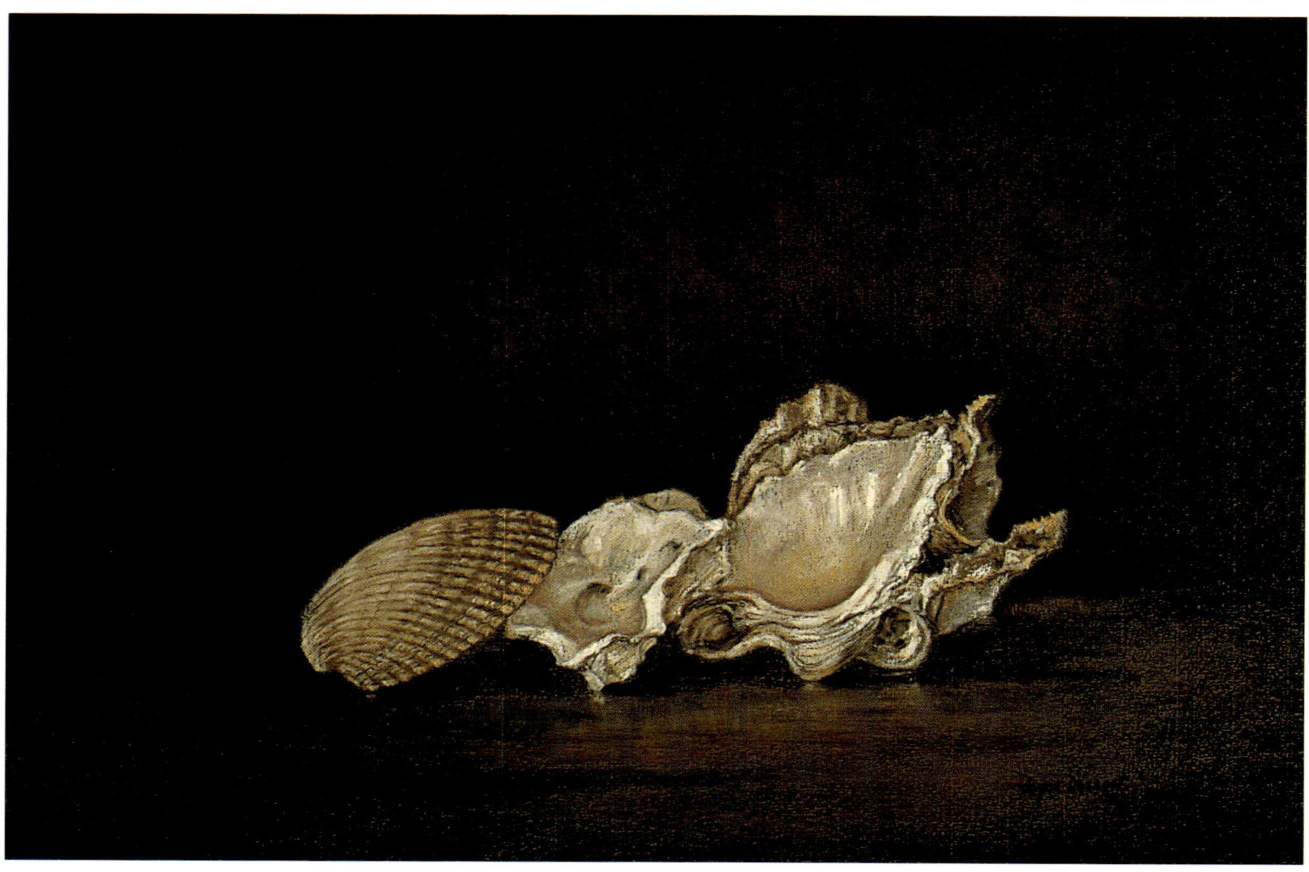

Shells

16" x 25"
Canson Mi-Teintes paper

George Balcan

A group of Montreal artists used to paint together each week. What started out as "stay for a cup of coffee" gradually grew into lunches and dinners and, sometimes, a birthday party. Harry was the eldest of our group, also the brightest and most fun. And that's why he got such a great party. What was left made a great study for a still life.

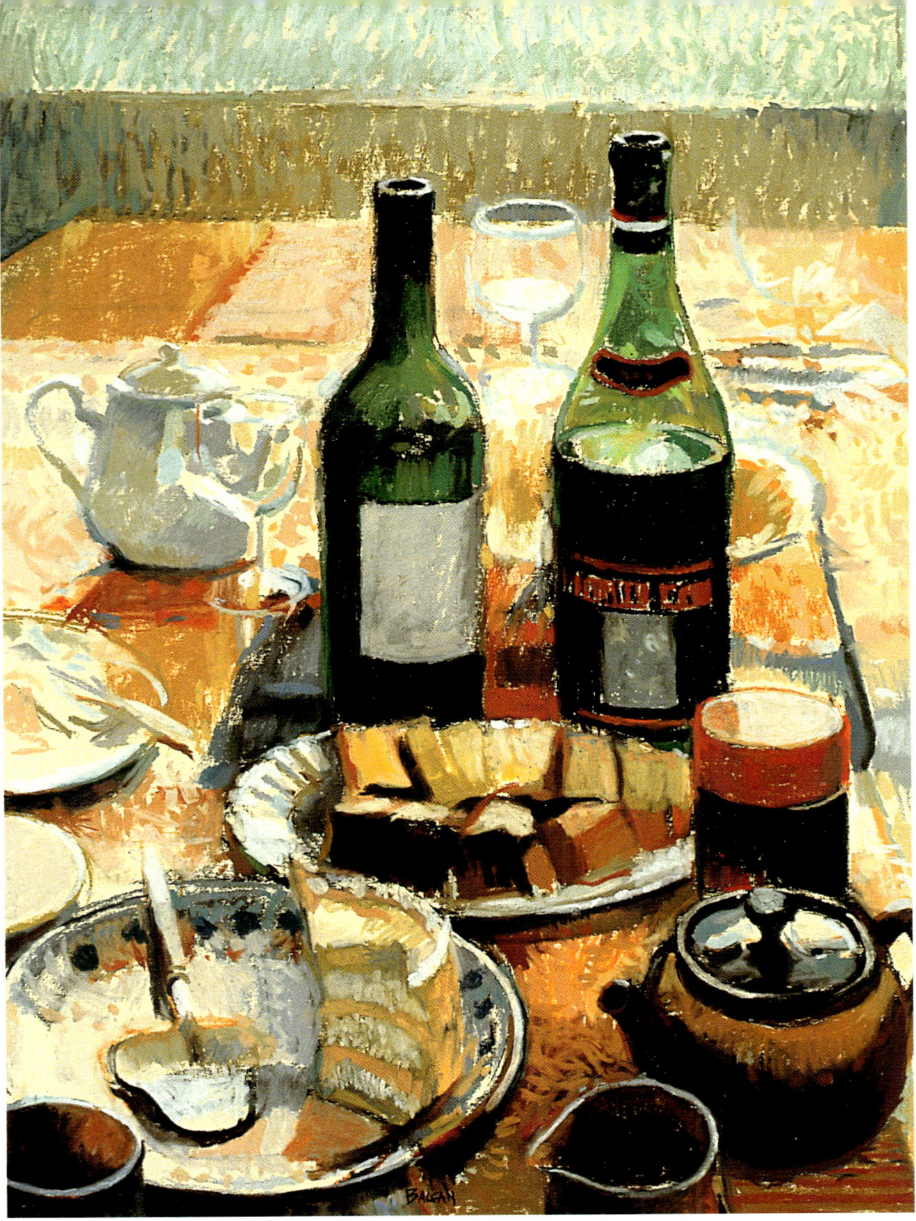

Harry's Birthday

18" x 24"

Anita E. Kertzer

After a pleasing placement, an undetailed sketch indicating proportions and an appropriate color scheme is chosen. I enjoy employing a rapid execution in order to capture both the spirit and the resemblance of the sitter. This method also applies to still life subjects without the limits of time restraint because the inanimate objects obviously do not move. No matter what the pastel painting represents, it is essential to me to avoid overkill; this deadens the final painting. I often remind my students that "it is important to develop a light touch. Remember, you are working with beautiful dust."

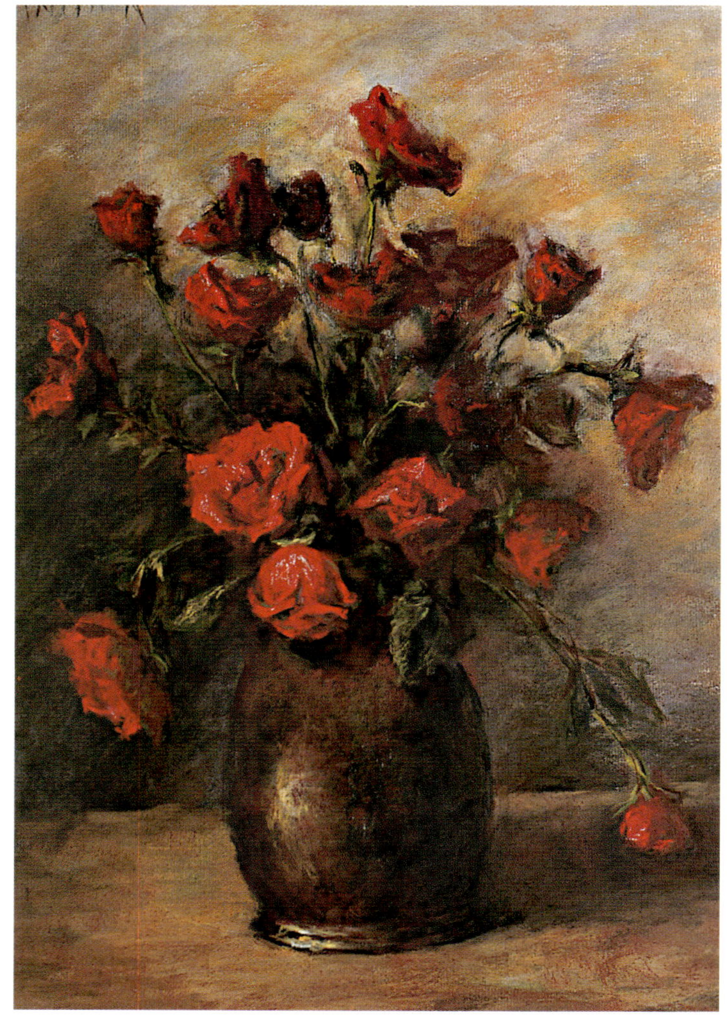

Red Roses

18" x 24"

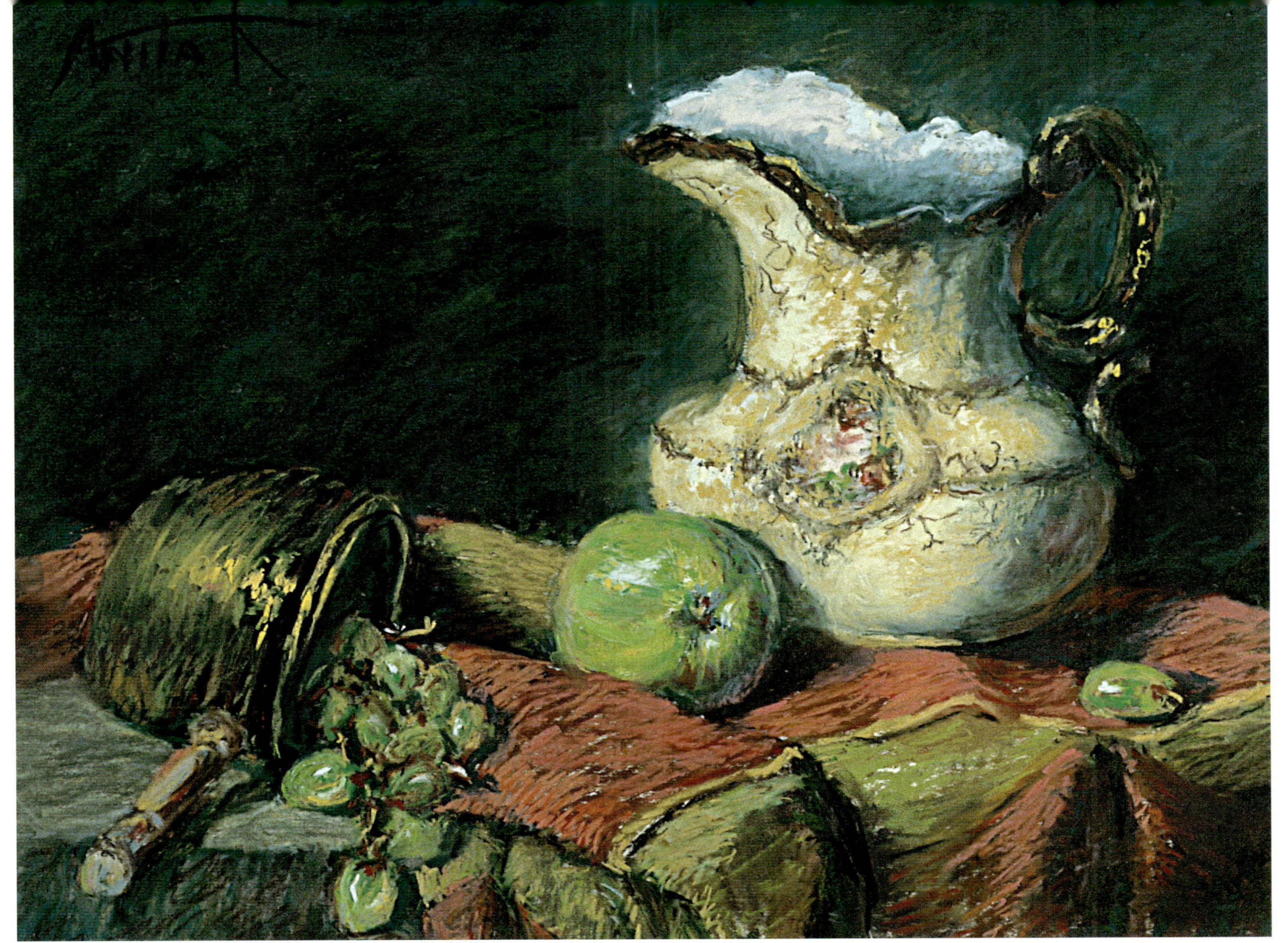

Heirloom

18" x 24"

Mireille Collet

Each component of my pictures is drawn using strokes of color complementary to the color in which it will be finally rendered. These strokes can still be seen when the painting is finished, allowing the colors to vibrate against each other. Only very soft pastel, like Sennelier or Schminke, is able to convey the dramatic contrast between strongly lit and shadowed areas. Only a few different colors are used to convey the emotion and the ambiance. The background is worked first so that it is easier to get a good idea of how the subject matter is progressing.

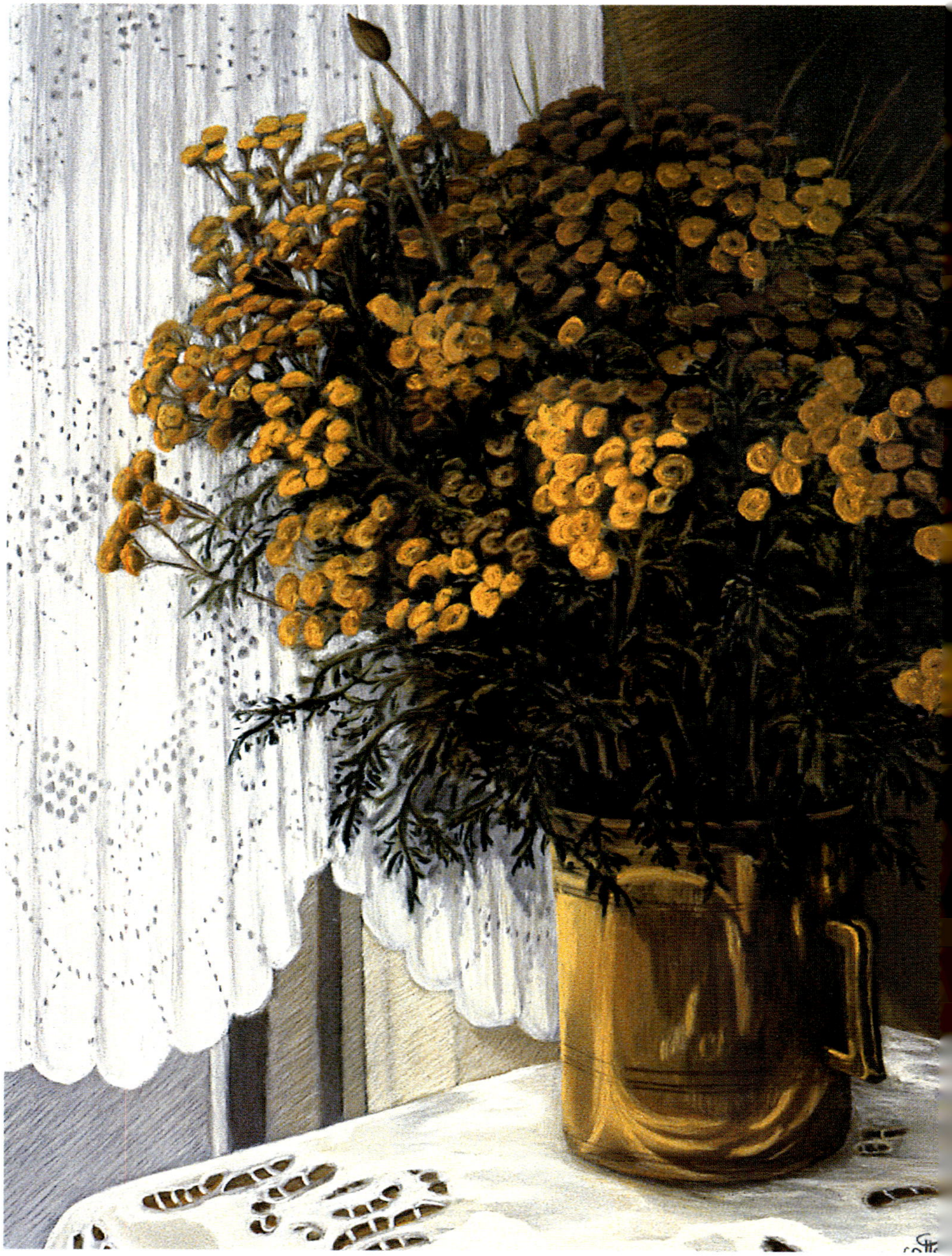

Bunch of Tansies

19" x 25"
Brown Sennelier sandpaper

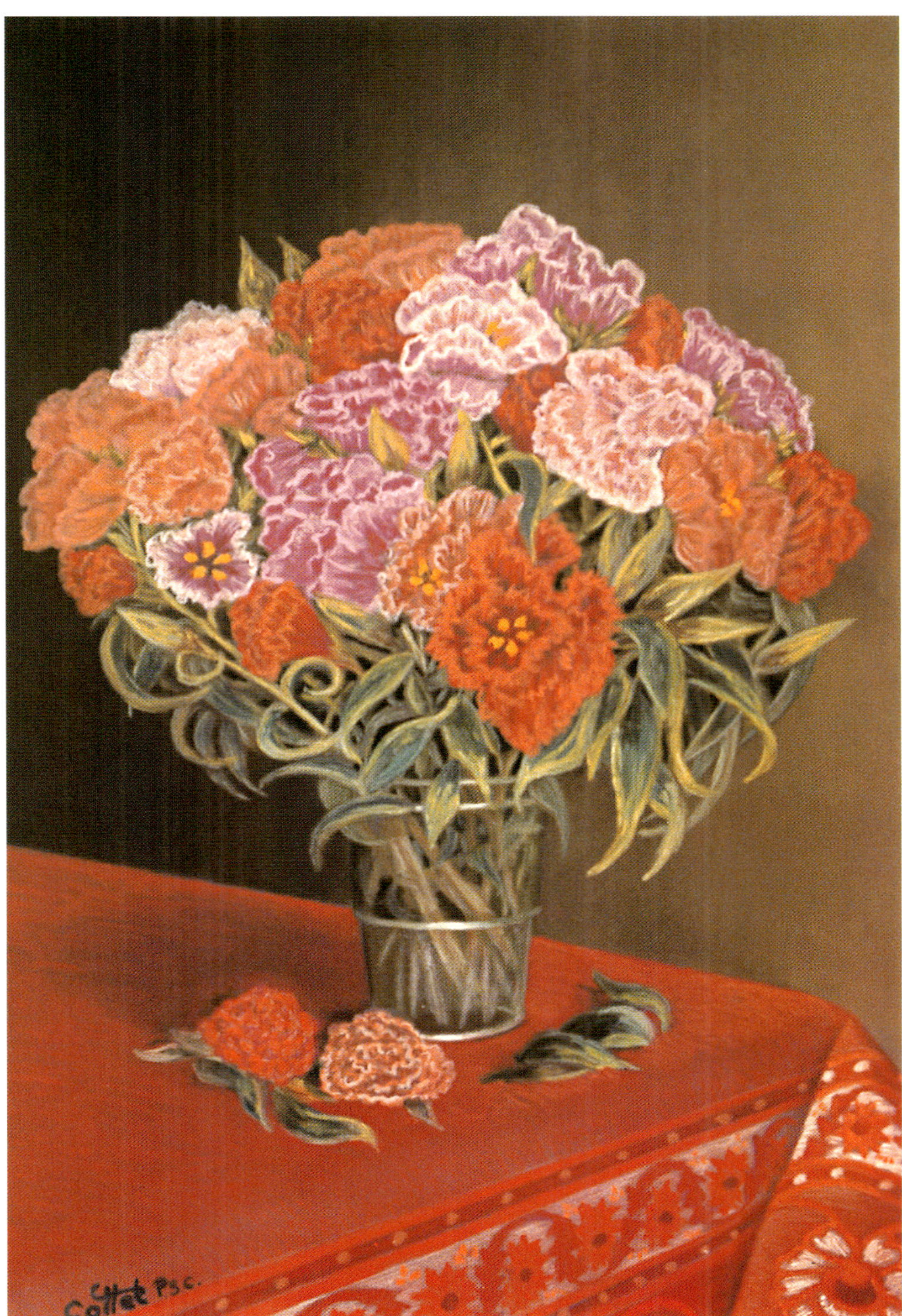

Bunch of Flowers on a Red Tablecloth

12" x 18"
Beige Sennelier sandpaper

Lois McKercher

This painting is a combination of my love for Canadian antiques, my patchwork cushions and fresh summer fruit. I painted this on a medium blue Canson paper.

Flopbench and Summer Fruit
18" x 22"
Canson Mi-Teintes paper

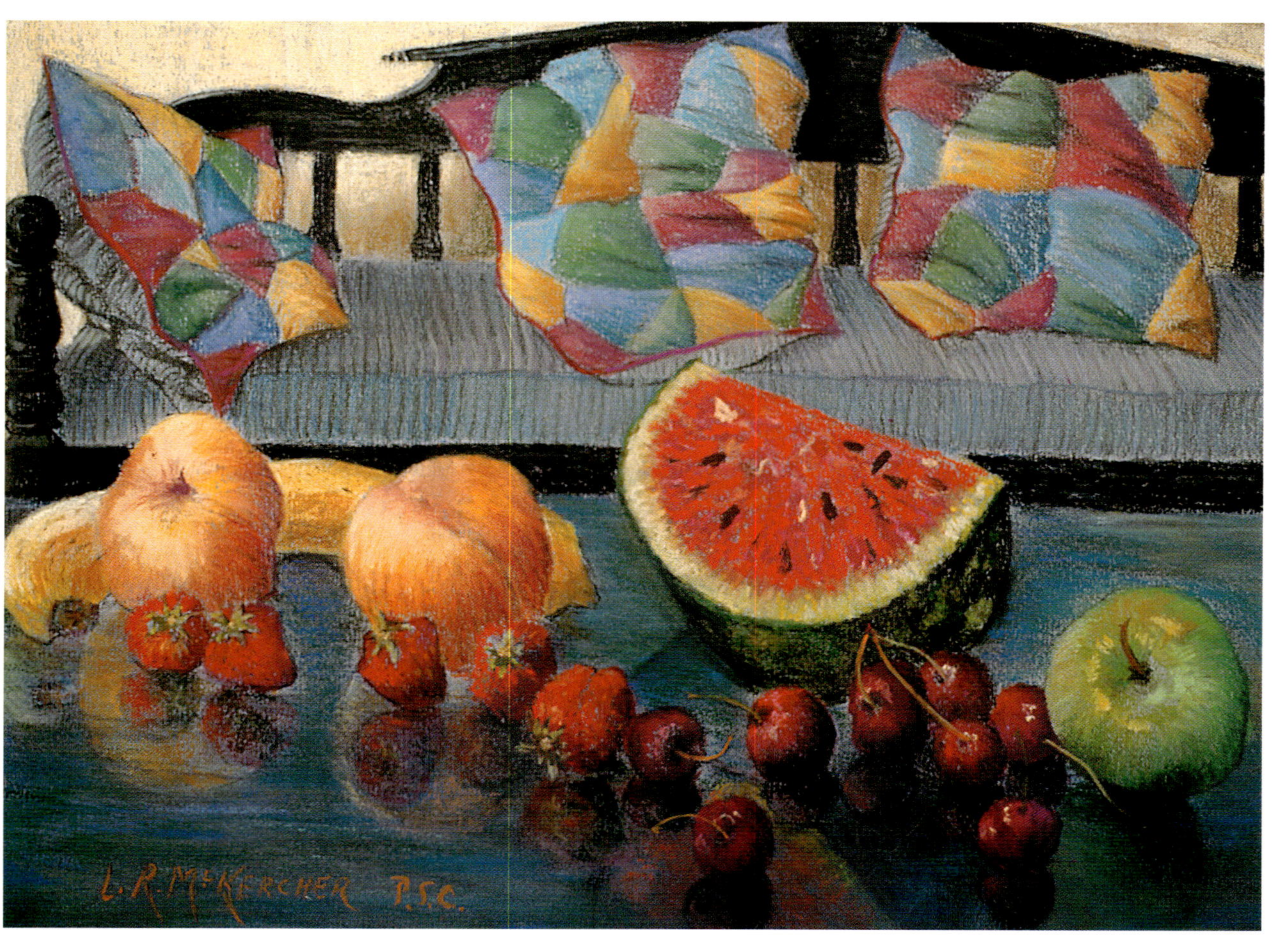

Loredana May-Brind

1st Spring Bouquet

18" x 24"

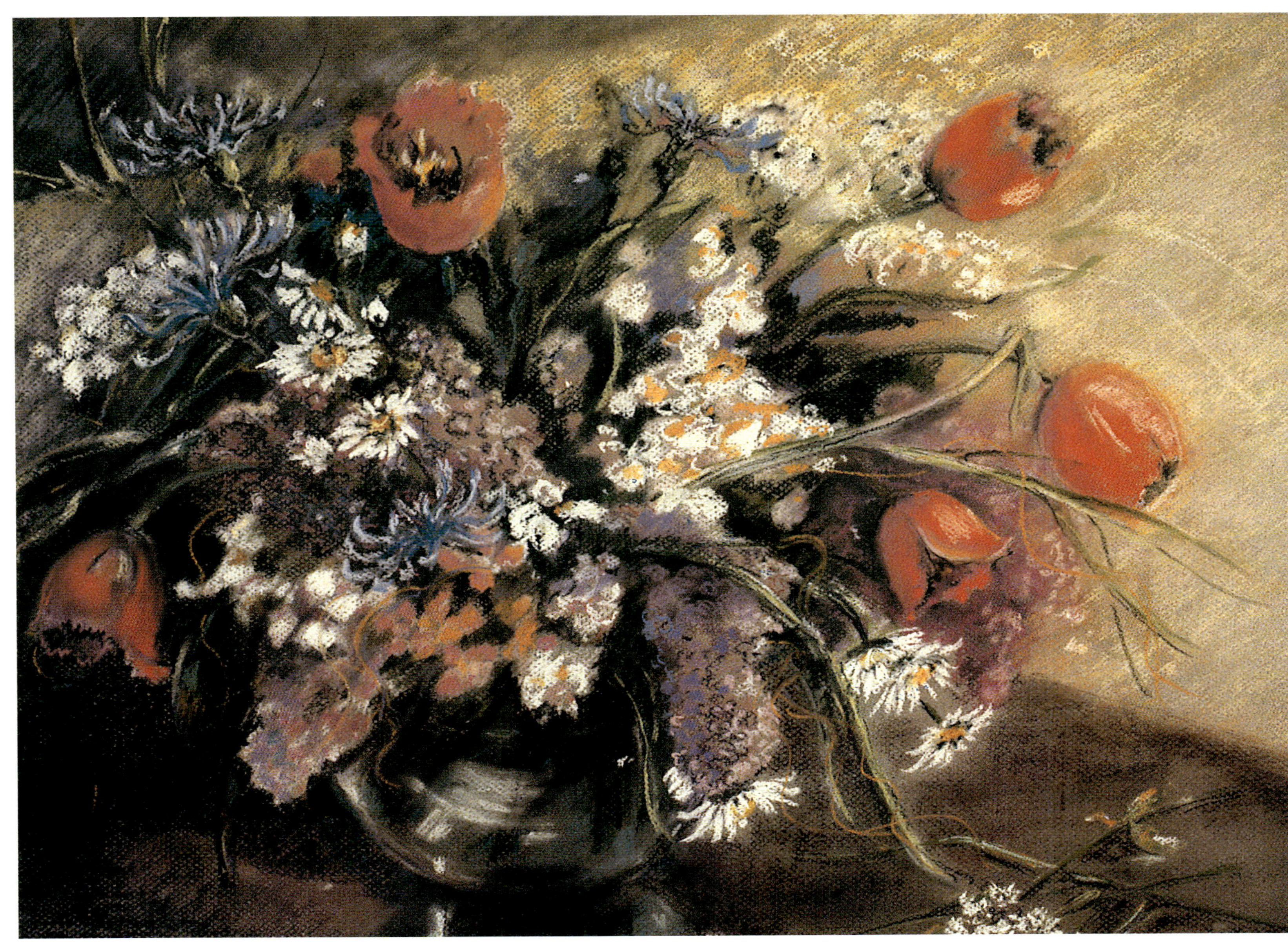

Wendy Trethewey

I find pastel to be the perfect medium for capturing texture and detail due to its glowing freshness. I work on a middle tone, neutral colored paper so it doesn't influence the colors of the pastels used. In most of my paintings, I let some of the paper work for me, to show through; this contributes to the medium's freshness and spontaneity. Strathmore and Canson are my preferred papers due to their resilience. I choose the smooth side to work on since it's easier to capture fine detail and texture. My palette includes soft pastels for large areas, NuPastel for firmer detail, Conte and pastel pencils for fine lines. To lessen the pastel dust fallout, I turn the painting (taped to a board) upside down and give the board a few sharp knocks.

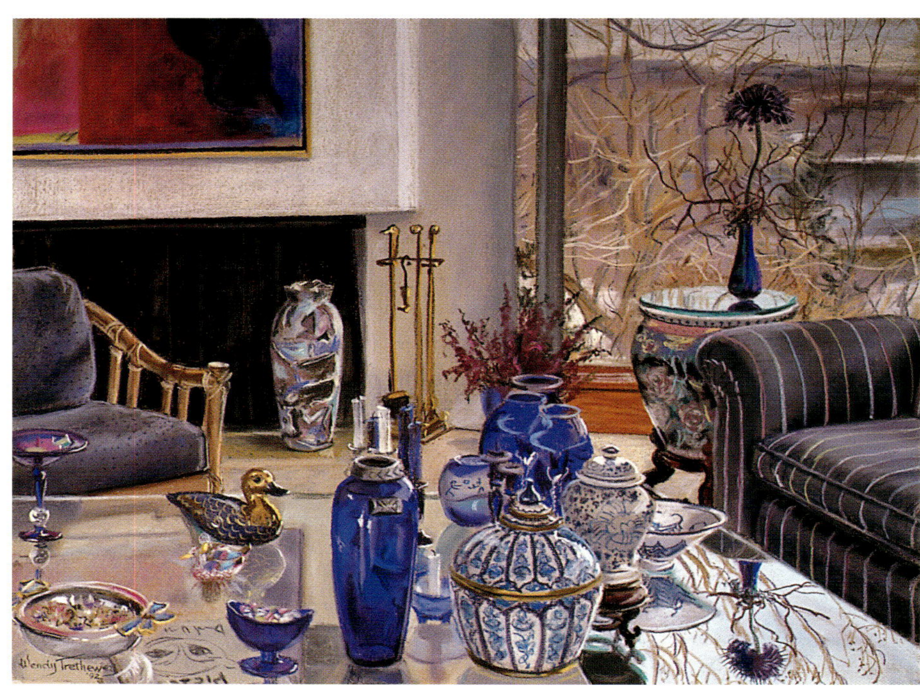

Tabletop Collection

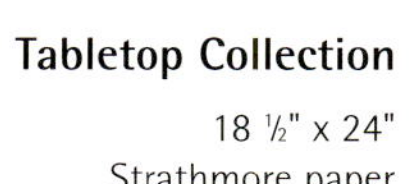

18 ½" x 24"
Strathmore paper

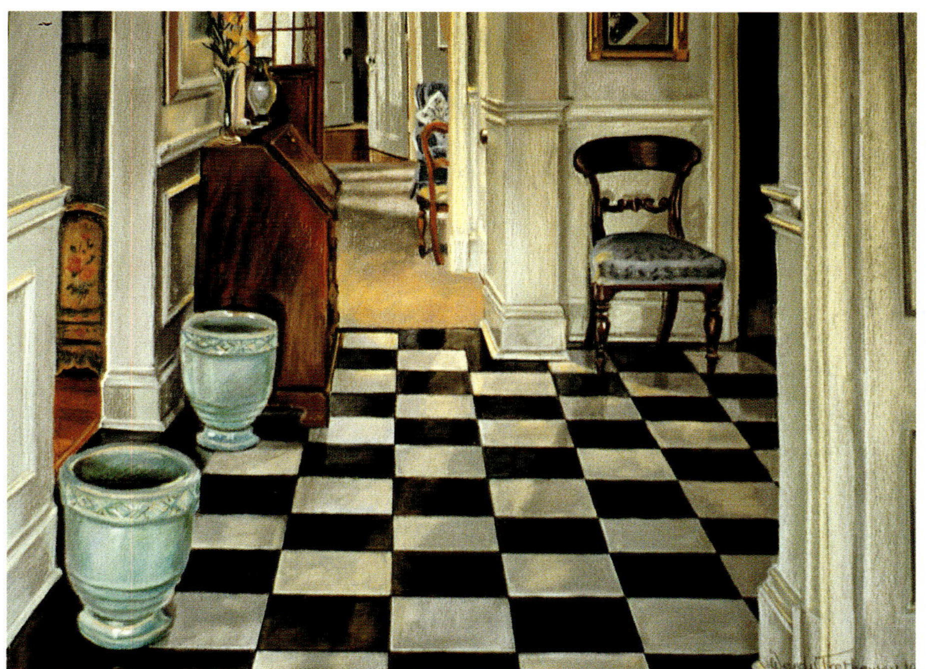

Foyer

19" x 26"
Strathmore paper

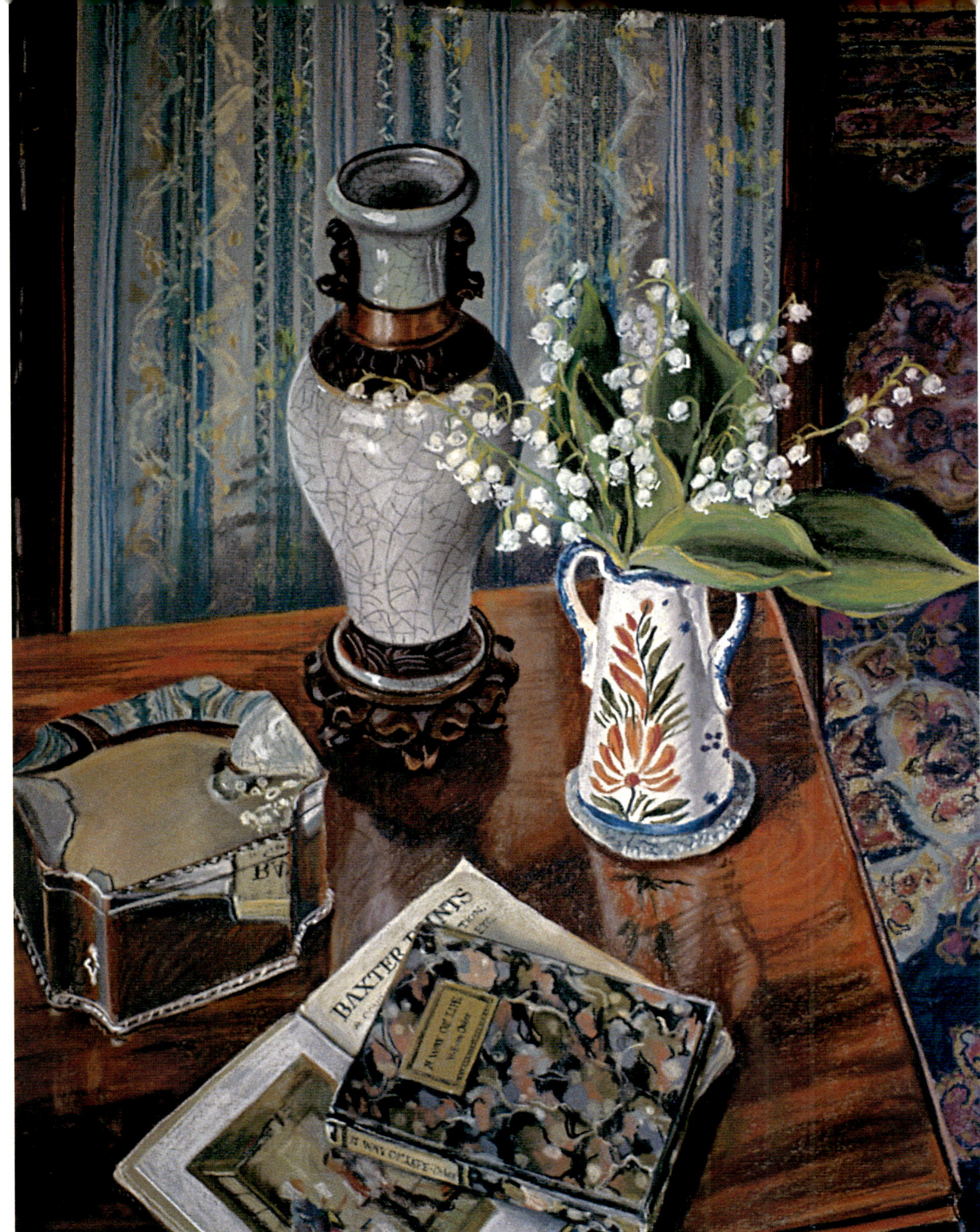

Heirlooms

18 ½" x 24 ¾"
Strathmore paper

LANDSCAPES

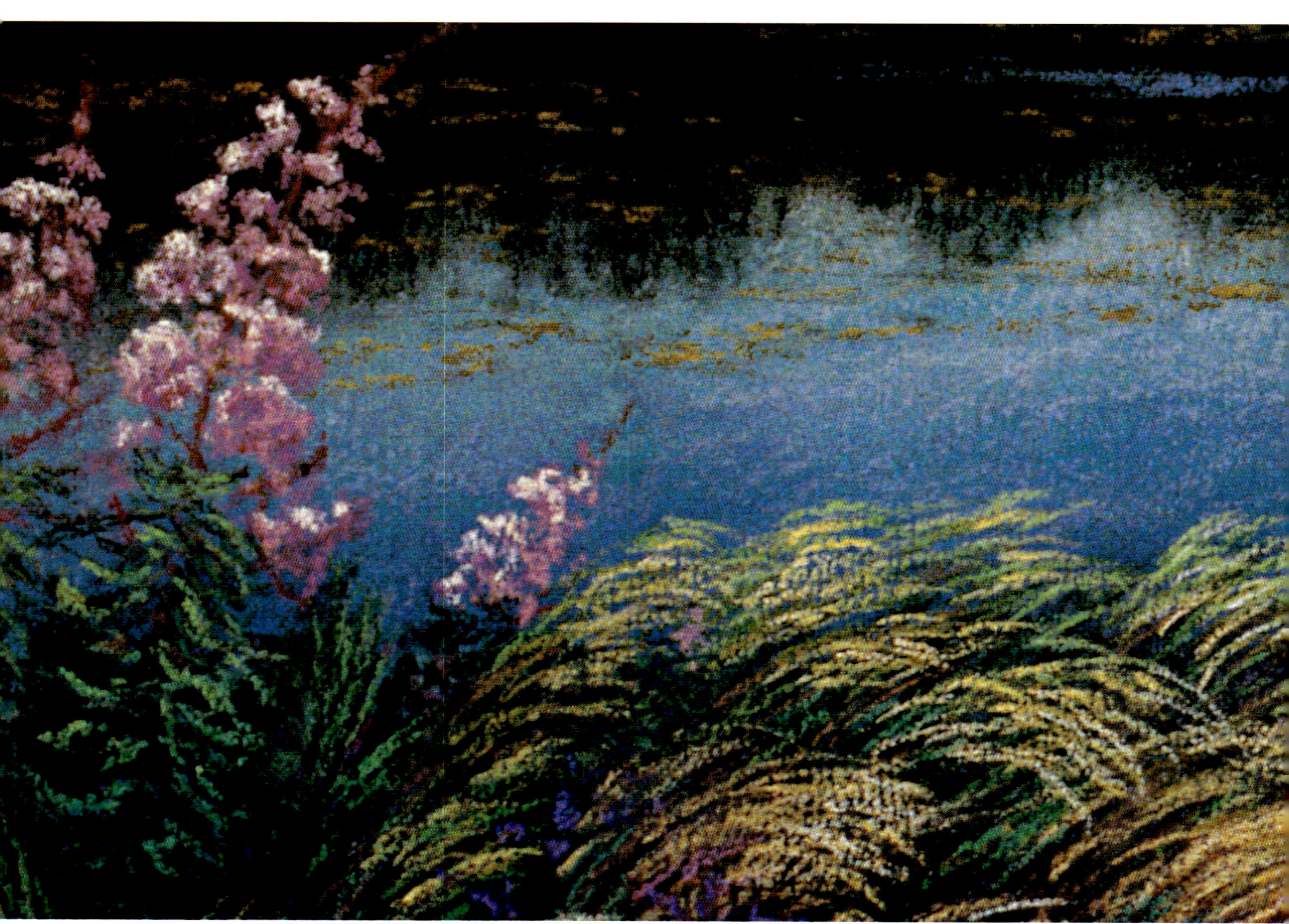

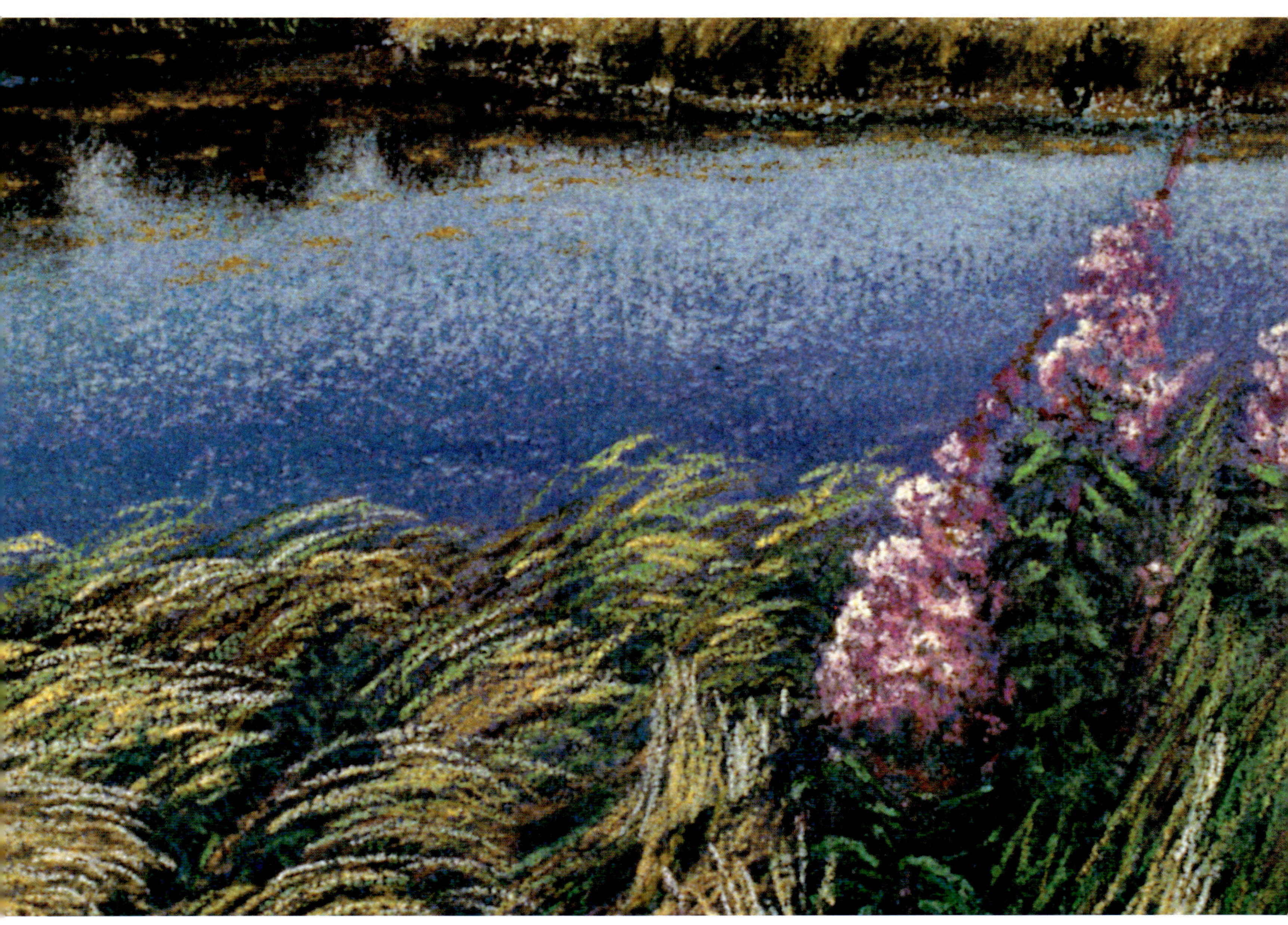

Dave Beckett

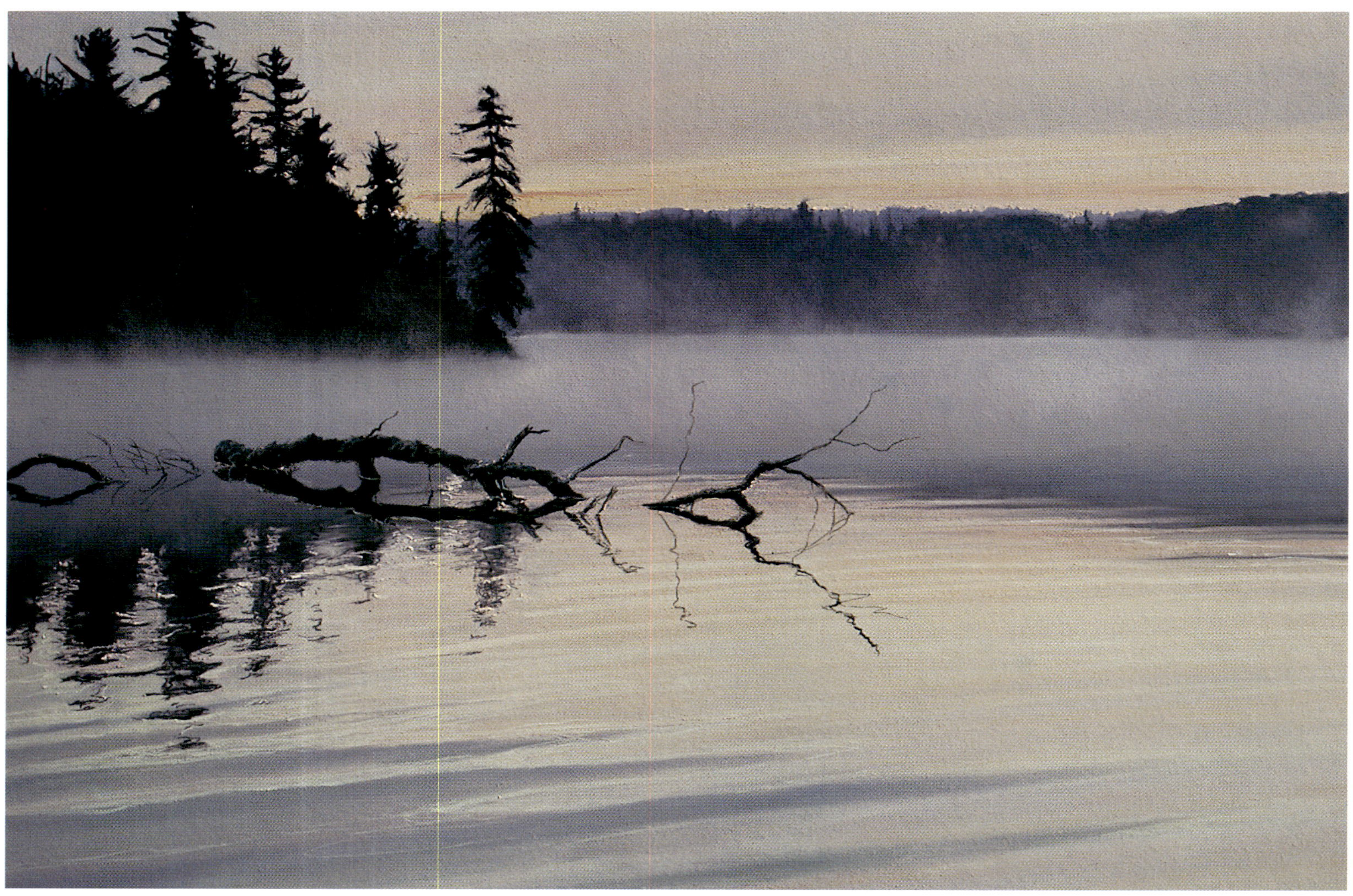

First Light

17" x 33"
Mid-tone pastel paper

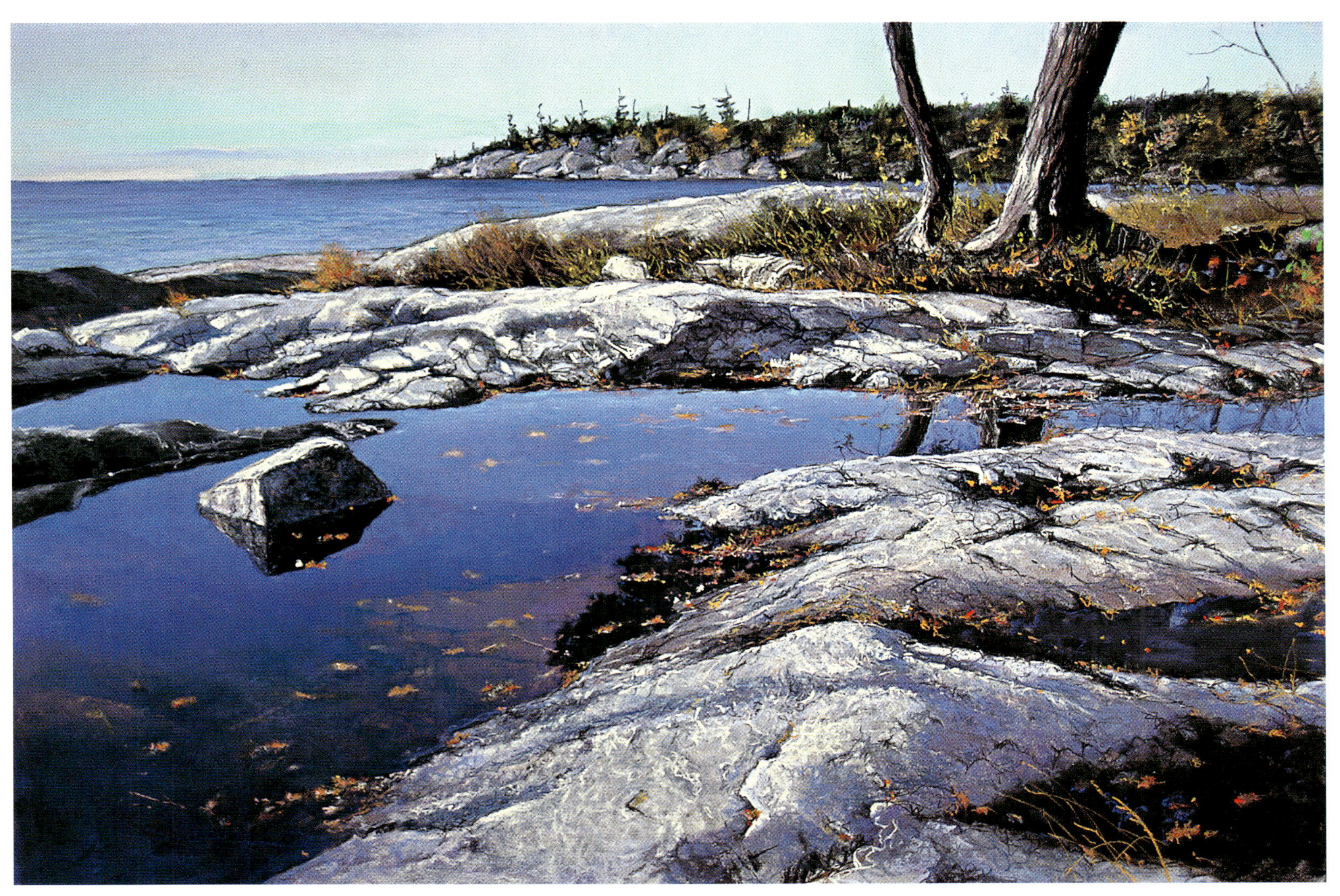

Tranquil Reflections

23" x 34"
Mid-tone pastel paper

Dave Beckett

Silent Waters

32" x 43"
Mid-tone pastel paper

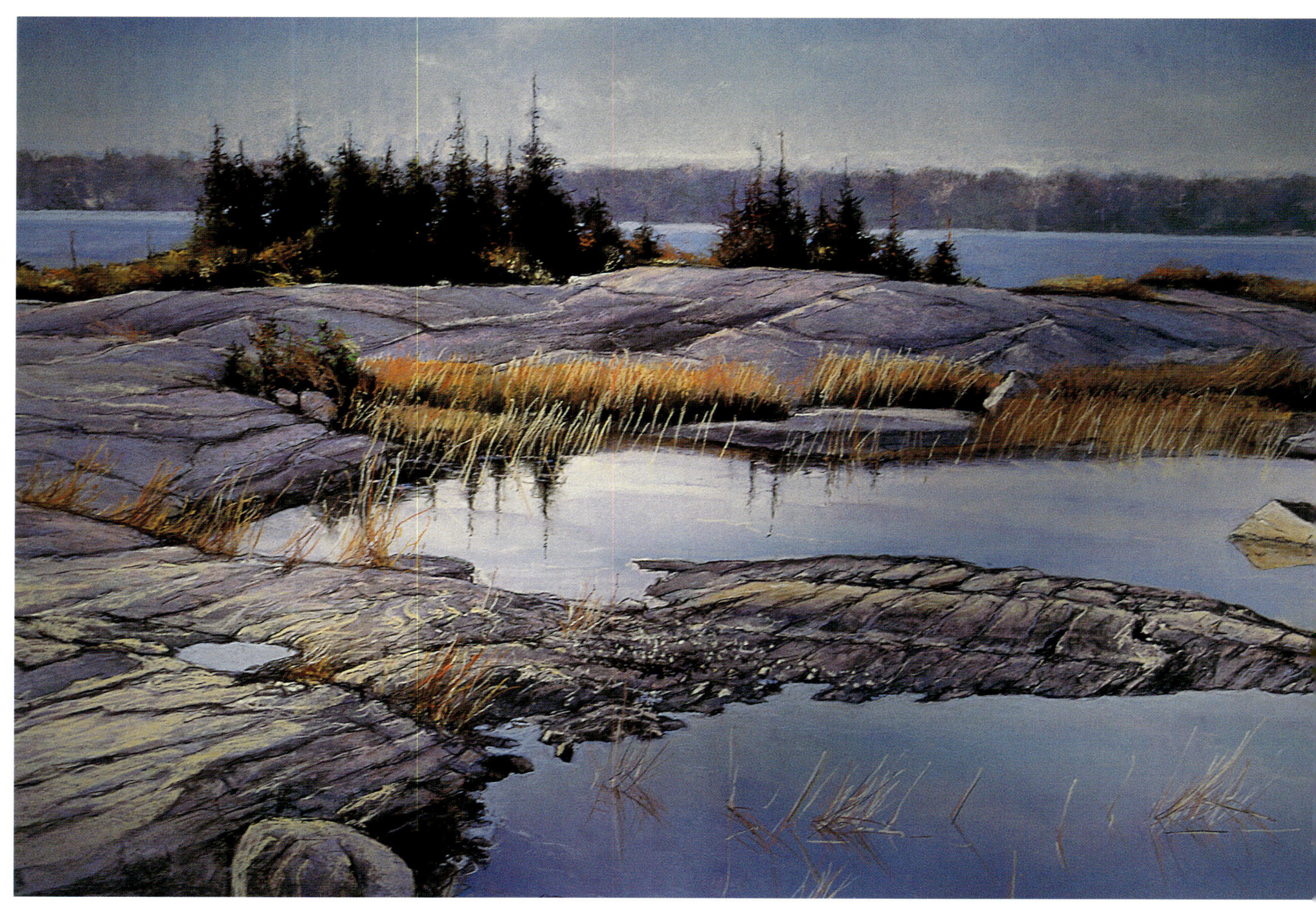

Jean Pilch

All of my paintings pictured here were done with pastel pencils which integrate the bold, clear and opaque color of pastels with the opportunity to produce fine detail. This drawing approach involves careful preservation of hard edges, as well as layering and blending of color through the use of stumps and even Q-Tips. All of the paintings are studio work based on my own reference photography. My objective is to combine technical precision with strong design elements to present an edited but convincing realism.

Fall Accents

17 ½" x 29 ½"
140 lb. Arches hot
pressed watercolor paper

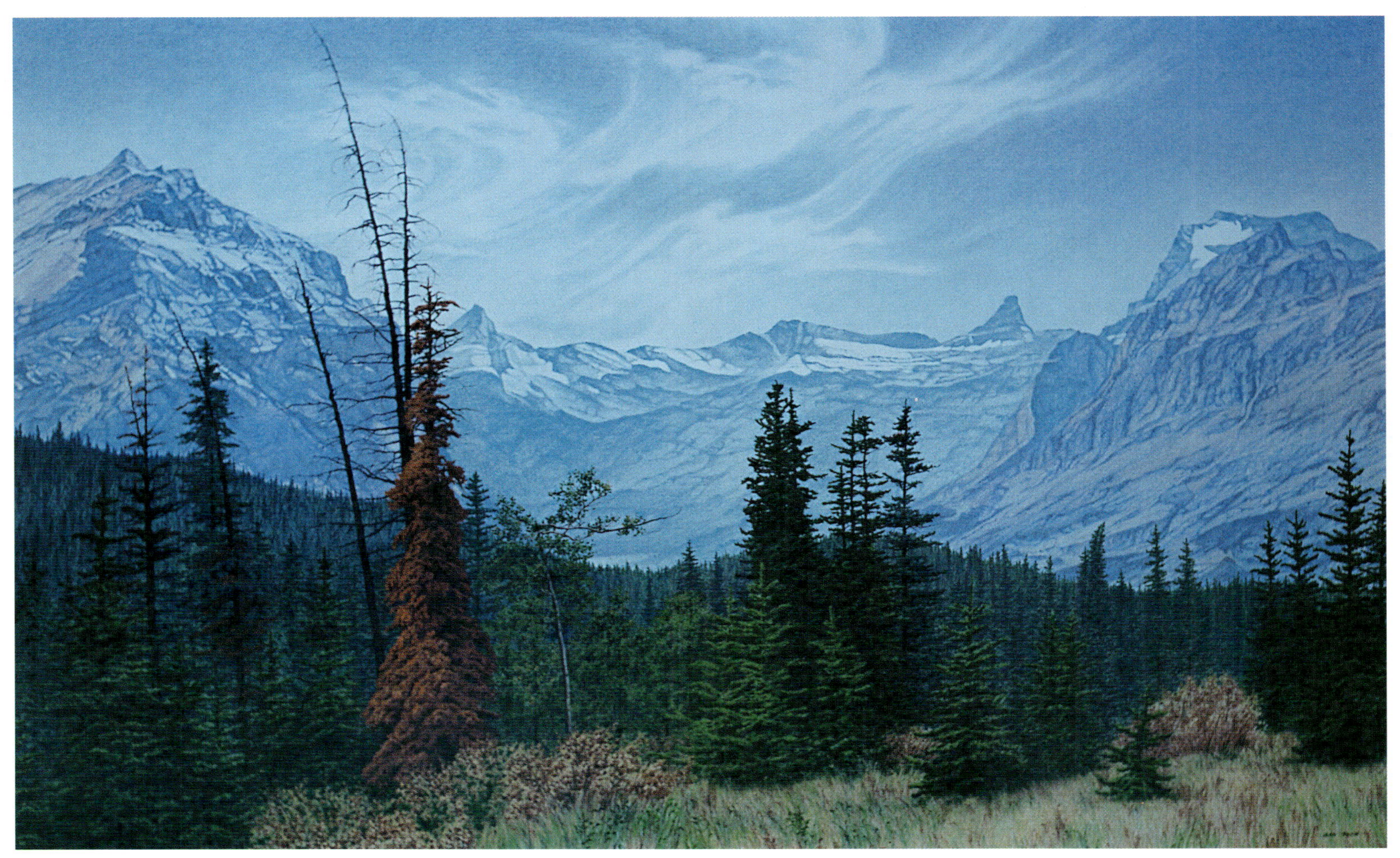

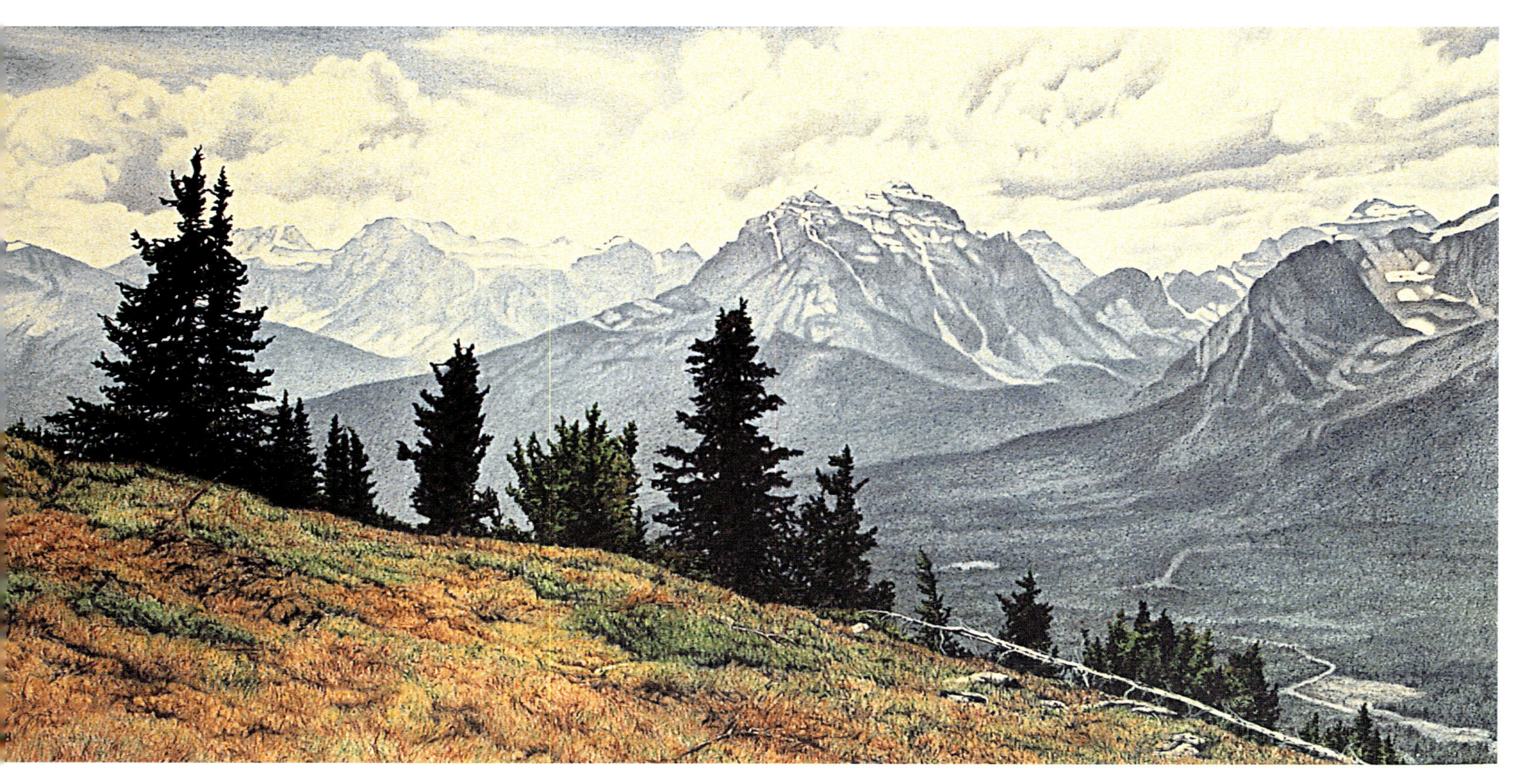

Jean Pilch

Fade to Blue

10 ½" x 22"
140 lb. Arches hot
pressed watercolor paper

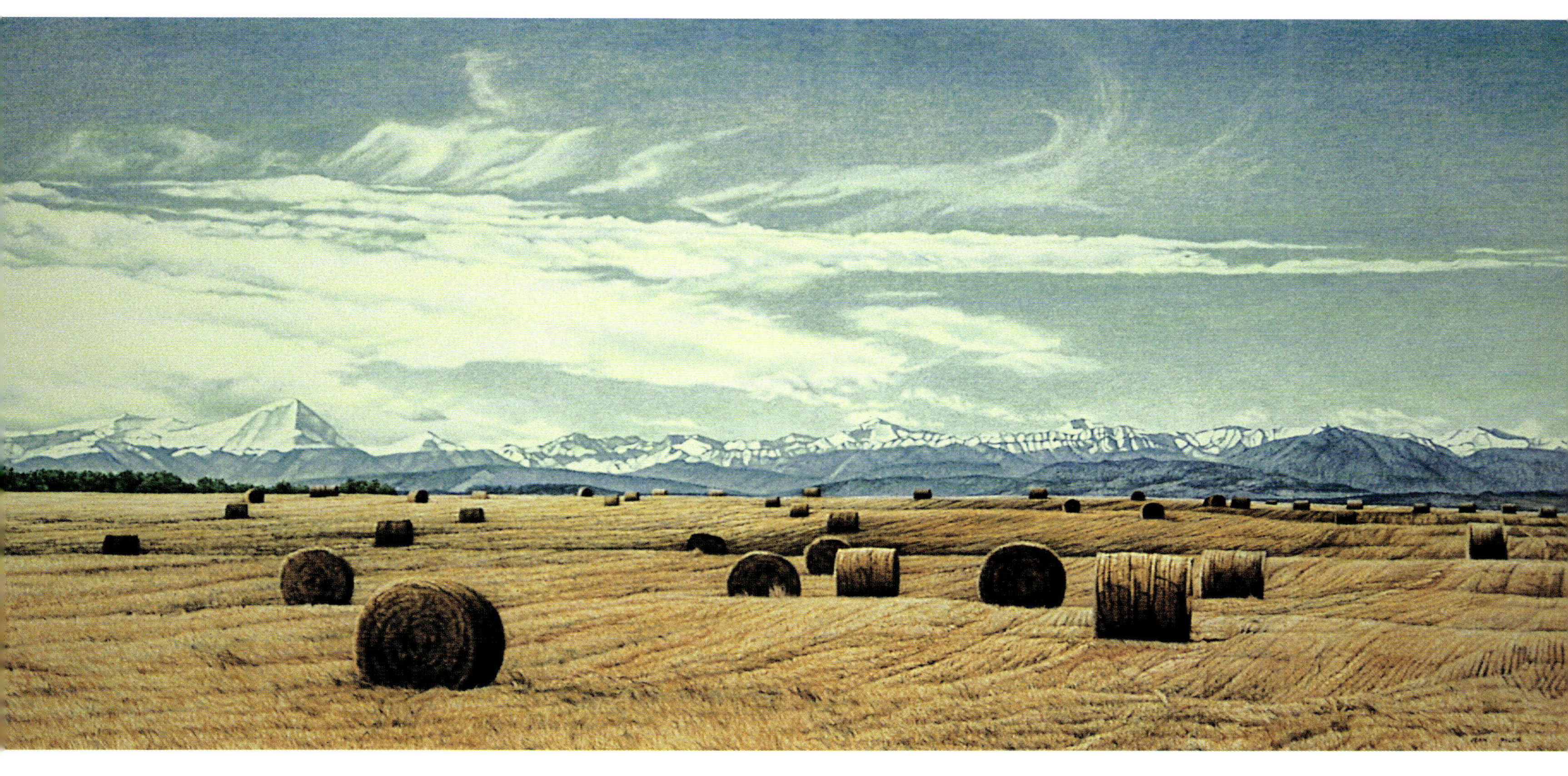

Jean Pilch

Harvest Gold

12" x 26"
140 lb. Arches hot
pressed watercolor paper

Geoffrey Jamieson

Painting outdoors is not for sissies. There are invariably many unwanted distractions (insects, for example), and also the constantly changing direction of light and shadows. This can be maddening, especially when complicated by the coming and going of small clouds.

The imminence of the storm dictated that the painting below be completed in the studio from photographs I took on location.

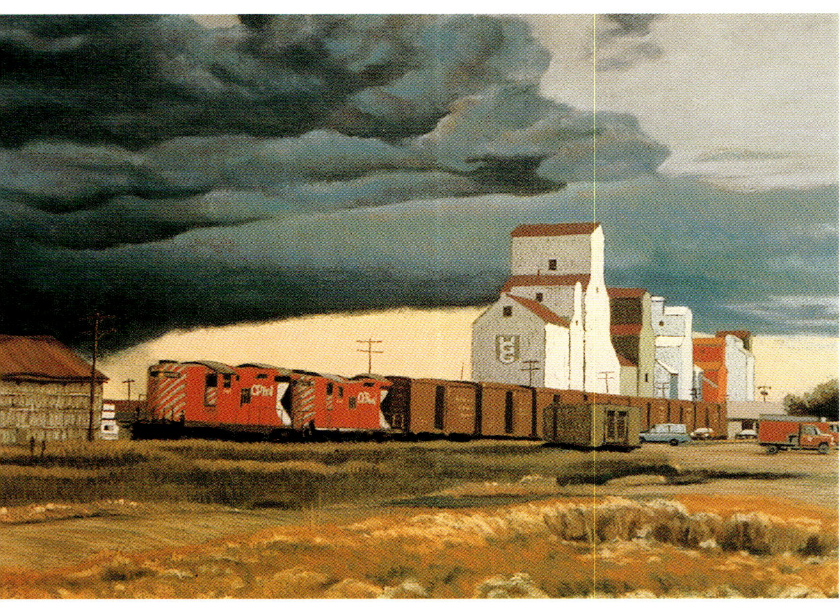

Prairie Express

18 ½" x 24"
Canson Mi-Teintes

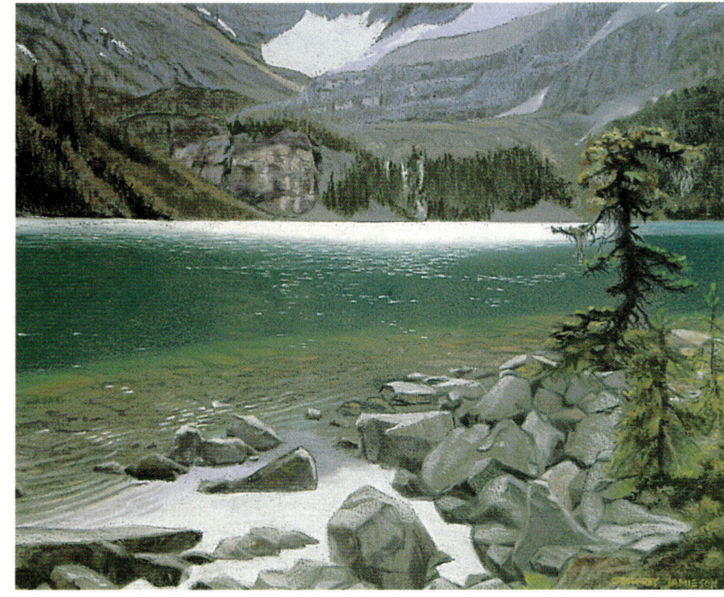

Late Afternoon, Lake O'Hara

12" x 15"
Canson Mi-Teintes (medium gray)

Pierre Petel

I worked in oil colors all my life, and even won many prizes. Then, about ten years ago, I got tired of the complications of oil paints--linseed oil, cleaning brushes, stretching canvases, using turpentine and its odors--and turned to pastels. I realized that I could draw and paint at the same time with so much ease--not facility. I started out painting directly from nature but later turned to photography for turning out details. I find that the details are better done from photographs.

Convent Girls in a Quebec Village

24" x 32"
Pastel paper

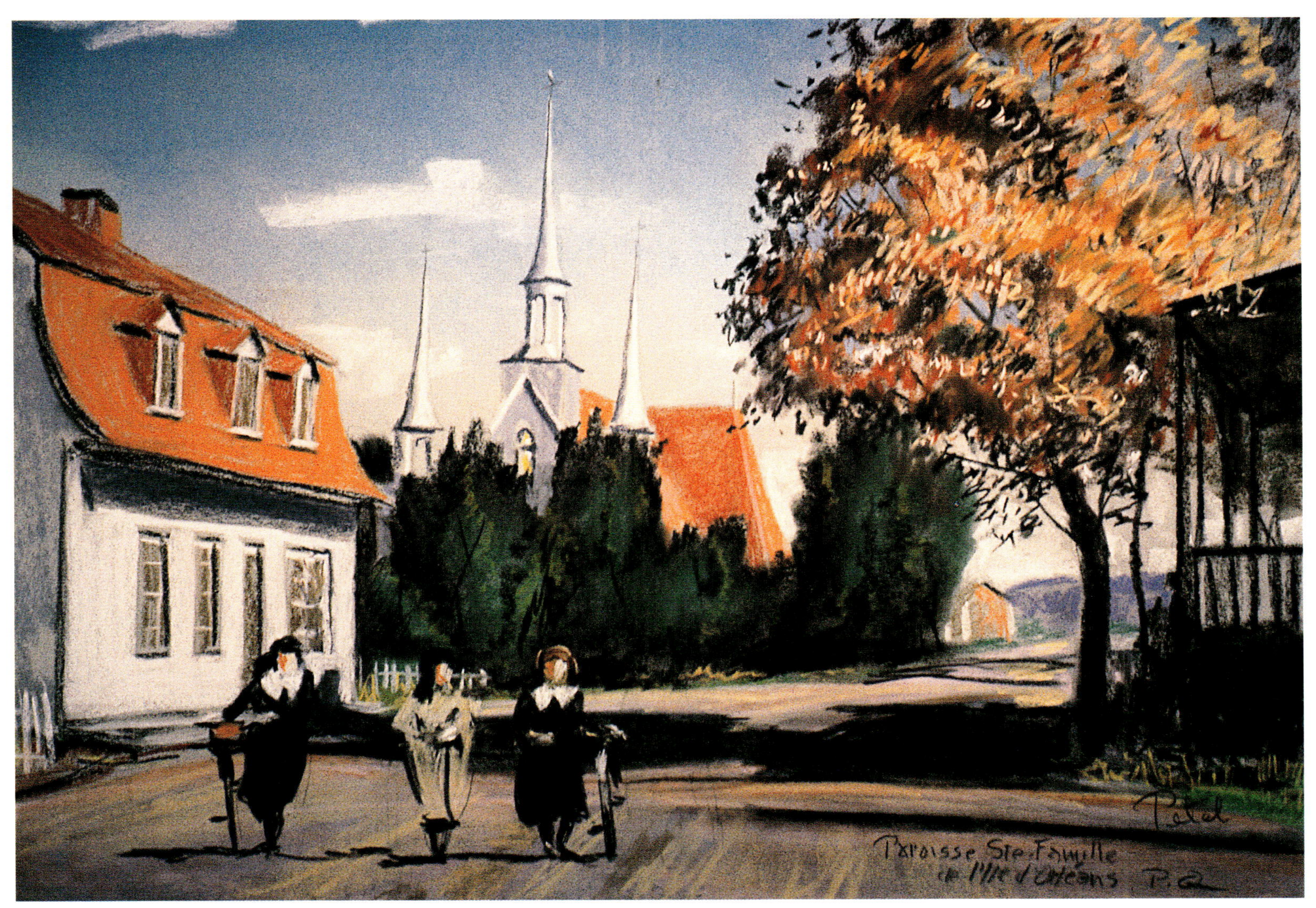

Robert Beaulieu

The procedure for painting all of my pastels is basically the same. I get out in the field a lot with my camera and do a load of photography. I know that out of every 100 pictures or so, only two or three will give me any inspiration for a painting. In fact, most of my paintings are composite creations that involve up to four or five different photographs. While I know many pastellists use fine sandpaper, I enjoy using Crescent illustration board No. 310, which I used for the paintings shown here. It's basically a 100% rag, cold pressed surface. While it's mostly intended for watercolor, it lends itself better to my pastel technique than rougher surfaces.

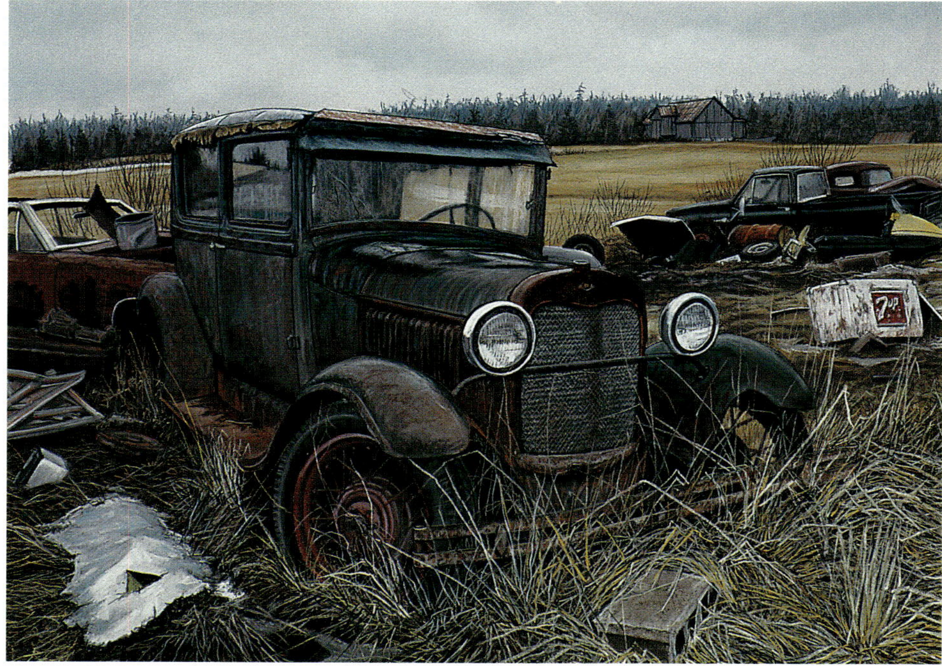

Bazou

22" x 32"
Crescent illustration board

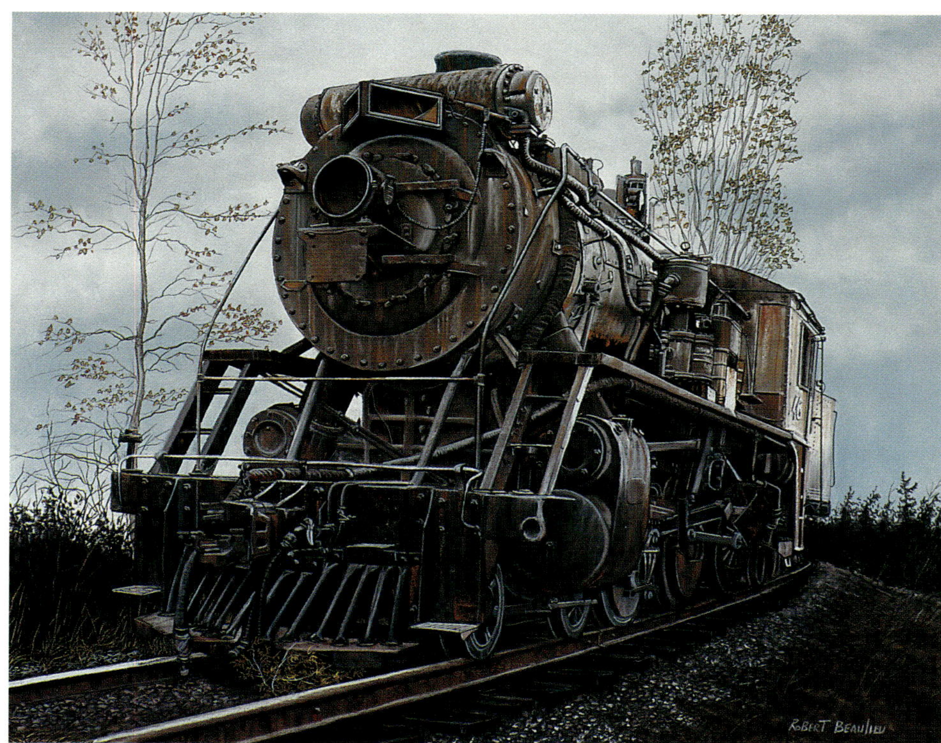

Silent Thunder

20" x 24"
Crescent illustration board

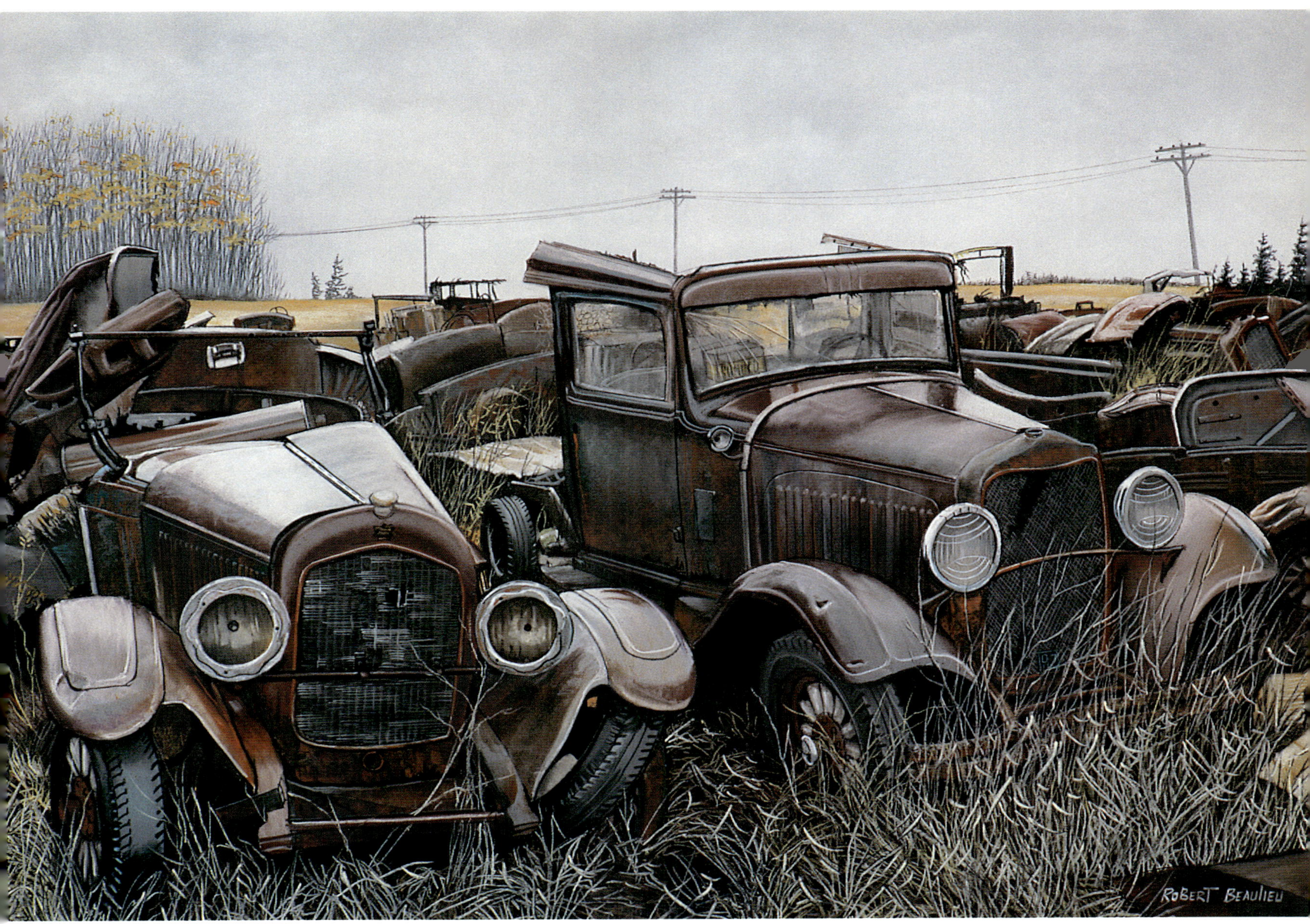

Old Friends

20" x 28"
Crescent illustration board

Rita MacKenzie

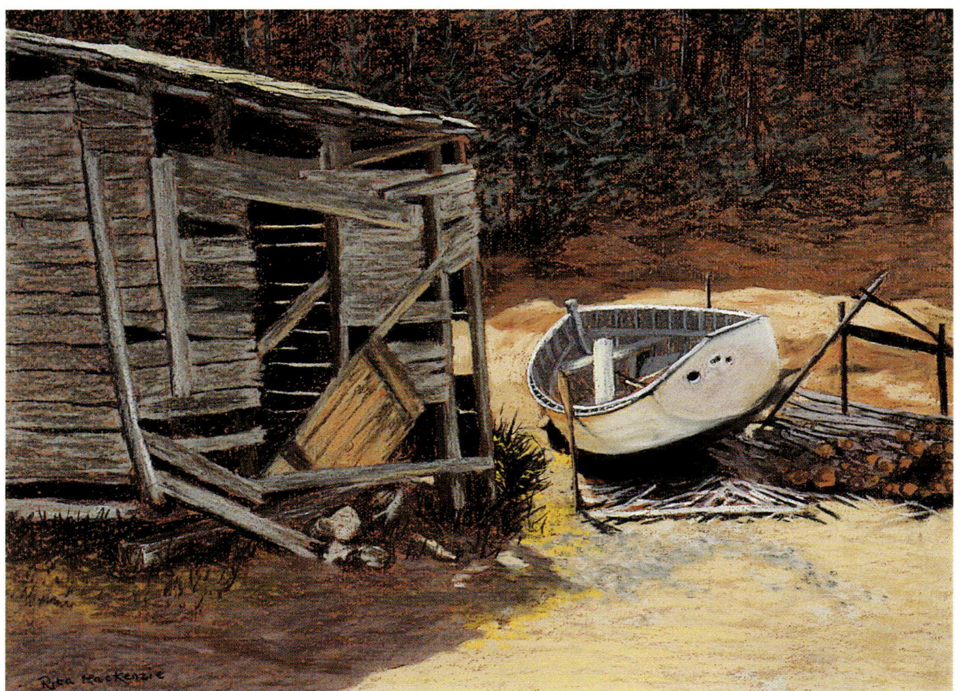

Derelicts

20" x 26"
Pastel paper

A deserted cove on Random Island, Newfoundland, on a Sunday morning. The air was still, the sun was hot. Everything glowed.

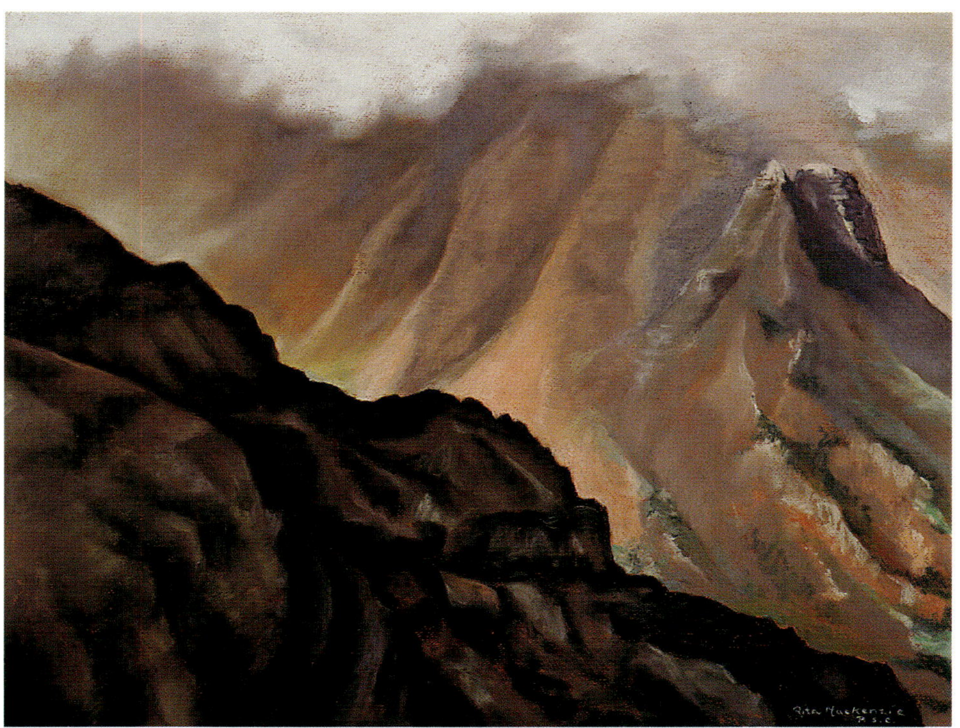

Volcanic Slopes

20" x 26"
Pastel paper

On the island of Kaui, Hawaii, after having painted four or five detailed studies of the canyon, I did this picture as a synthesis of my feelings about the horrendous volcanic origin of this part of Hawaii.

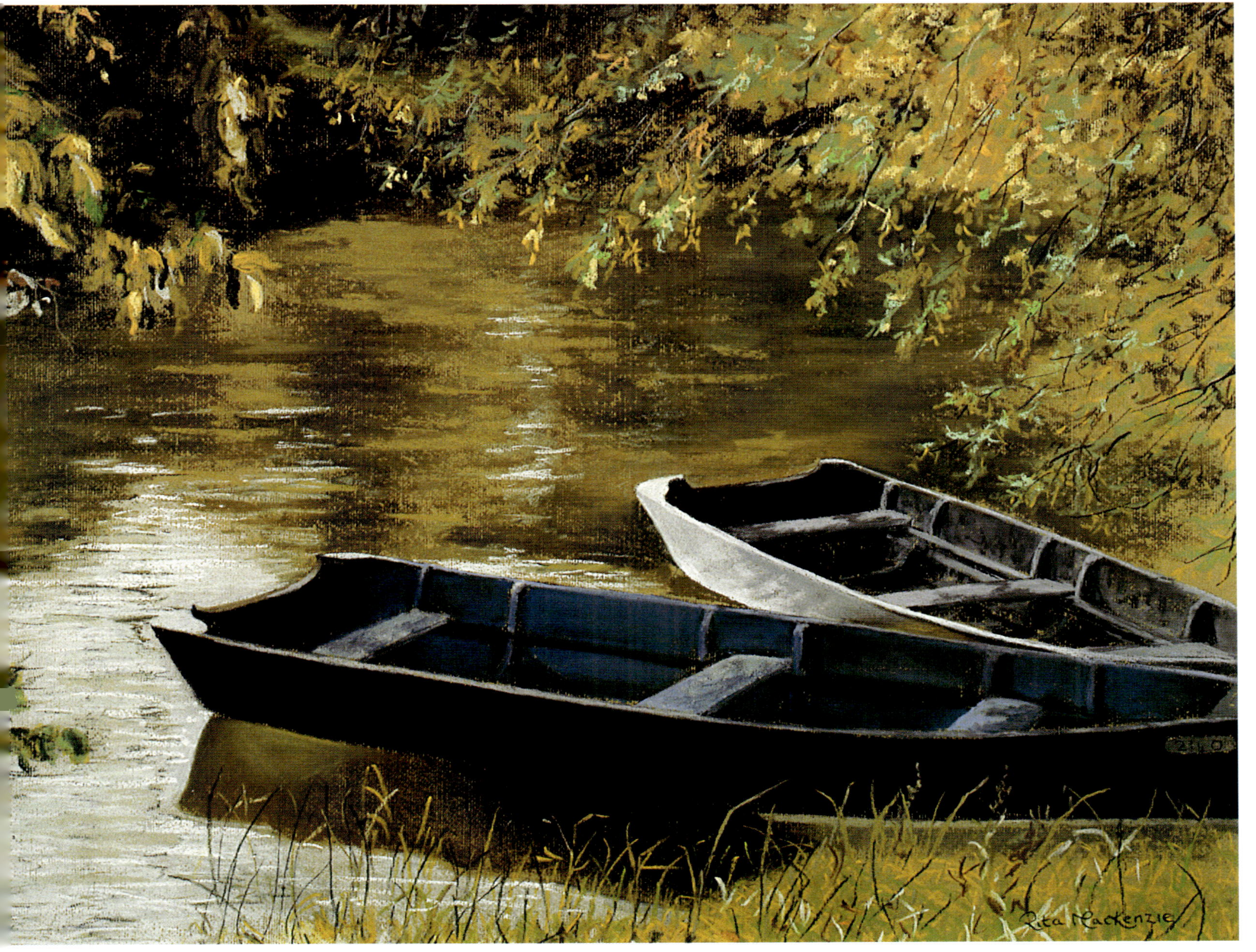

Invitation for a Summer Afternoon

20" x 26"
Pastel paper

Rita MacKenzie

Sunday Afternoon

20" x 26"
Pastel paper

At this cove in northern Newfoundland, with the fishing season not yet started, the locals find themselves getting interested in anything out of the ordinary.

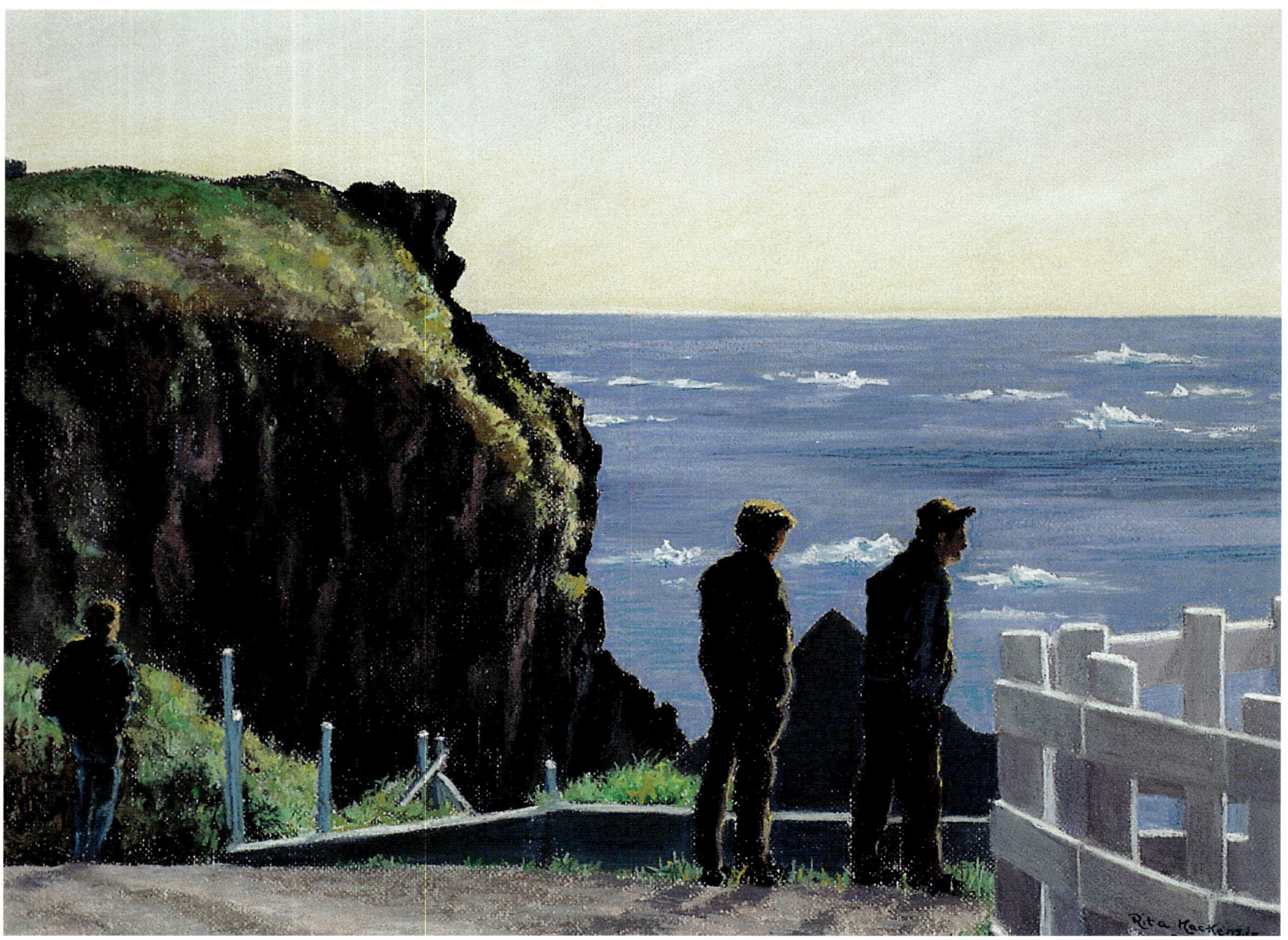

Alice Christenson

I work more or less directly with the colors that I need, building with layers when I'm after greater intensity or occasionally to create a blending of more than one color or shade.

Shuswap Country

16" x 22 "
Sabretooth paper

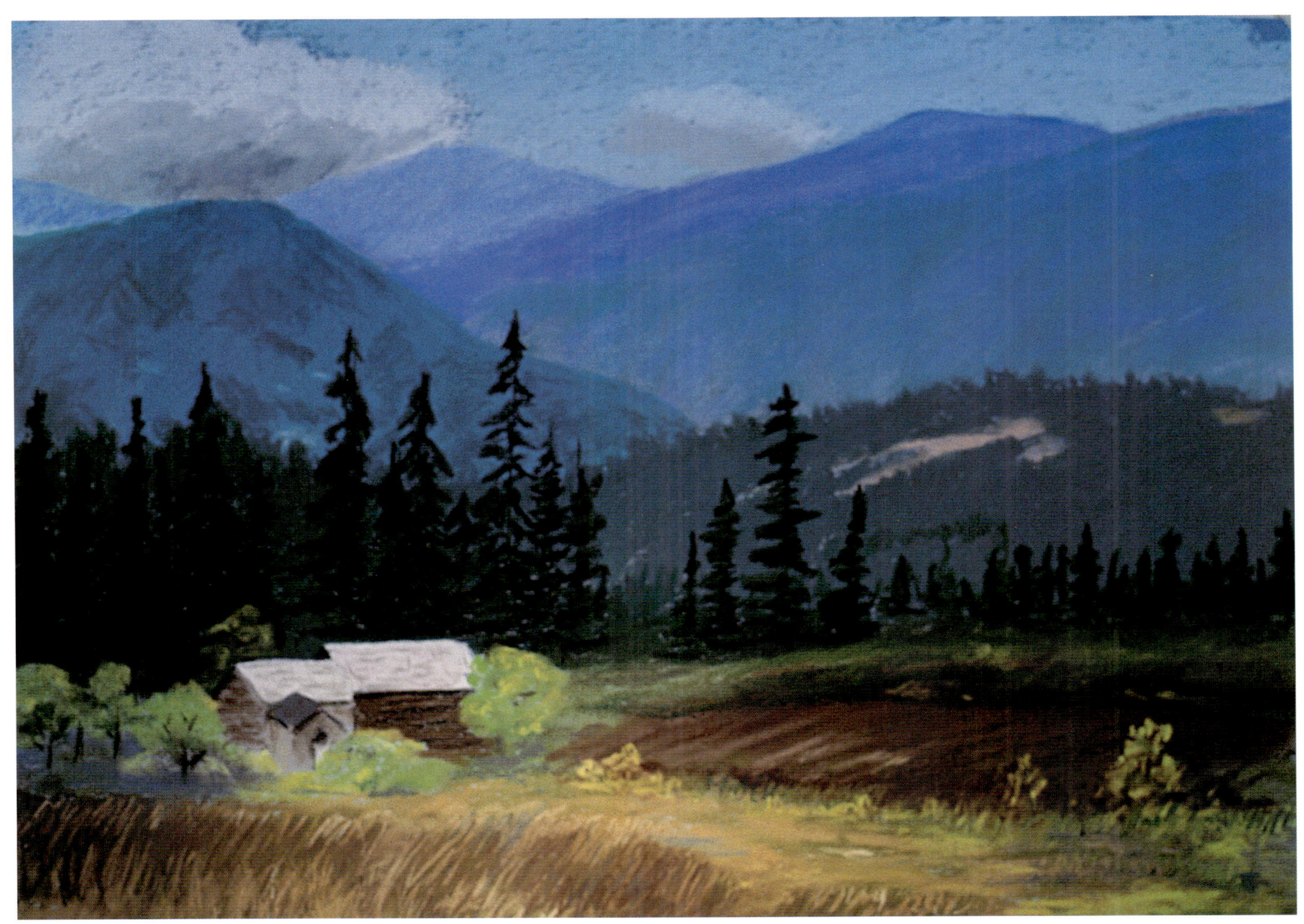

Audrey Pfannmuller

After using acrylics, watercolors and oils, I discovered pastels. Their forgiving nature, intense color, and pure pigment appeal to me. Extended with mixed media, pastel has a wide range of application at the discretion of the creative artist. The layering and direct mixture of the color on the painting surface creates the substance of color I need to interpret the layers of the land, transitions of the seasons, the drama and variations of the landscape

Summer Pond

23" × 37"
Arches 300 lb.
watercolor paper

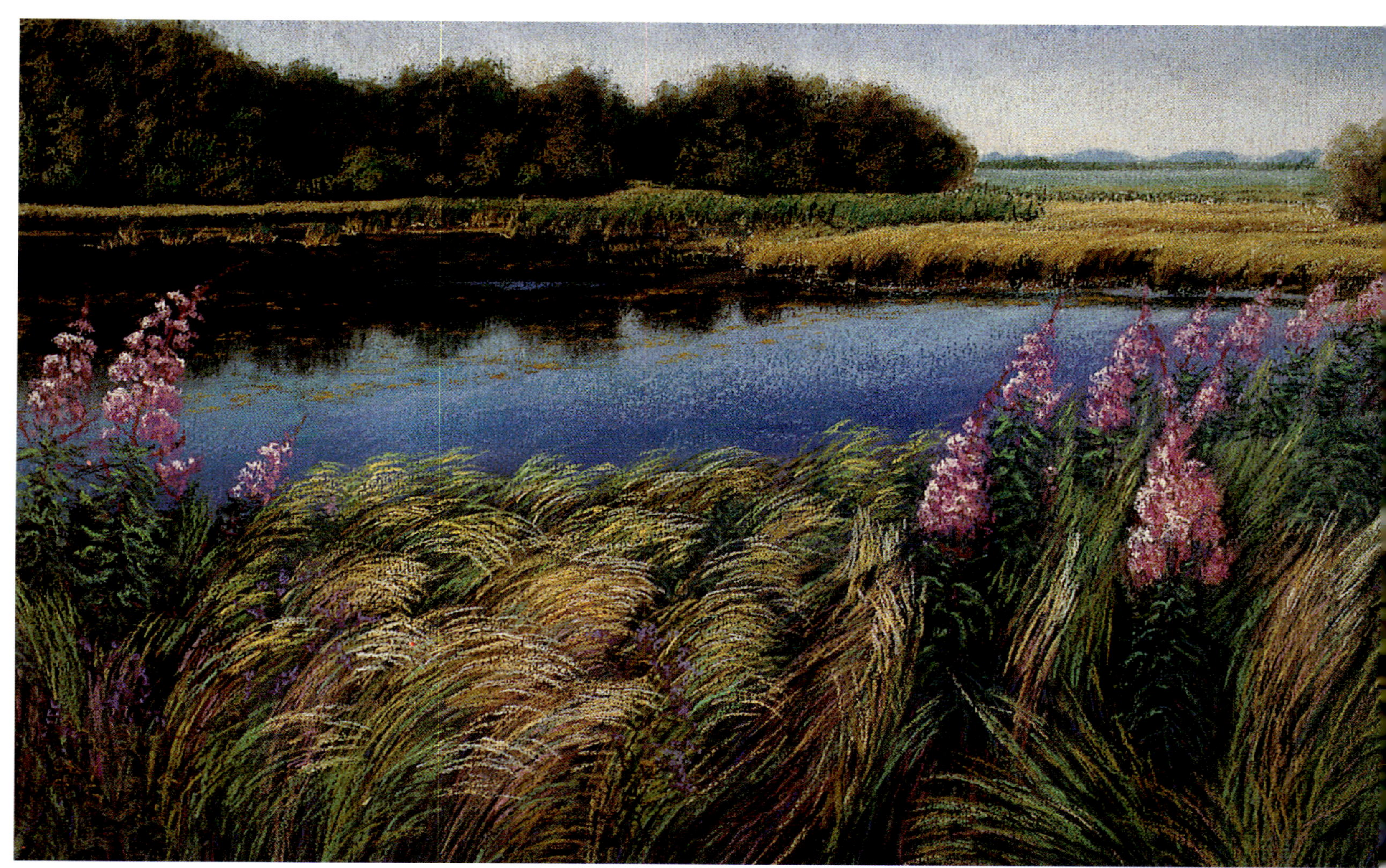

Red Willows Spring

20″ × 27″
Sabretooth by St. Armand,
a dark blue smooth sandpaper

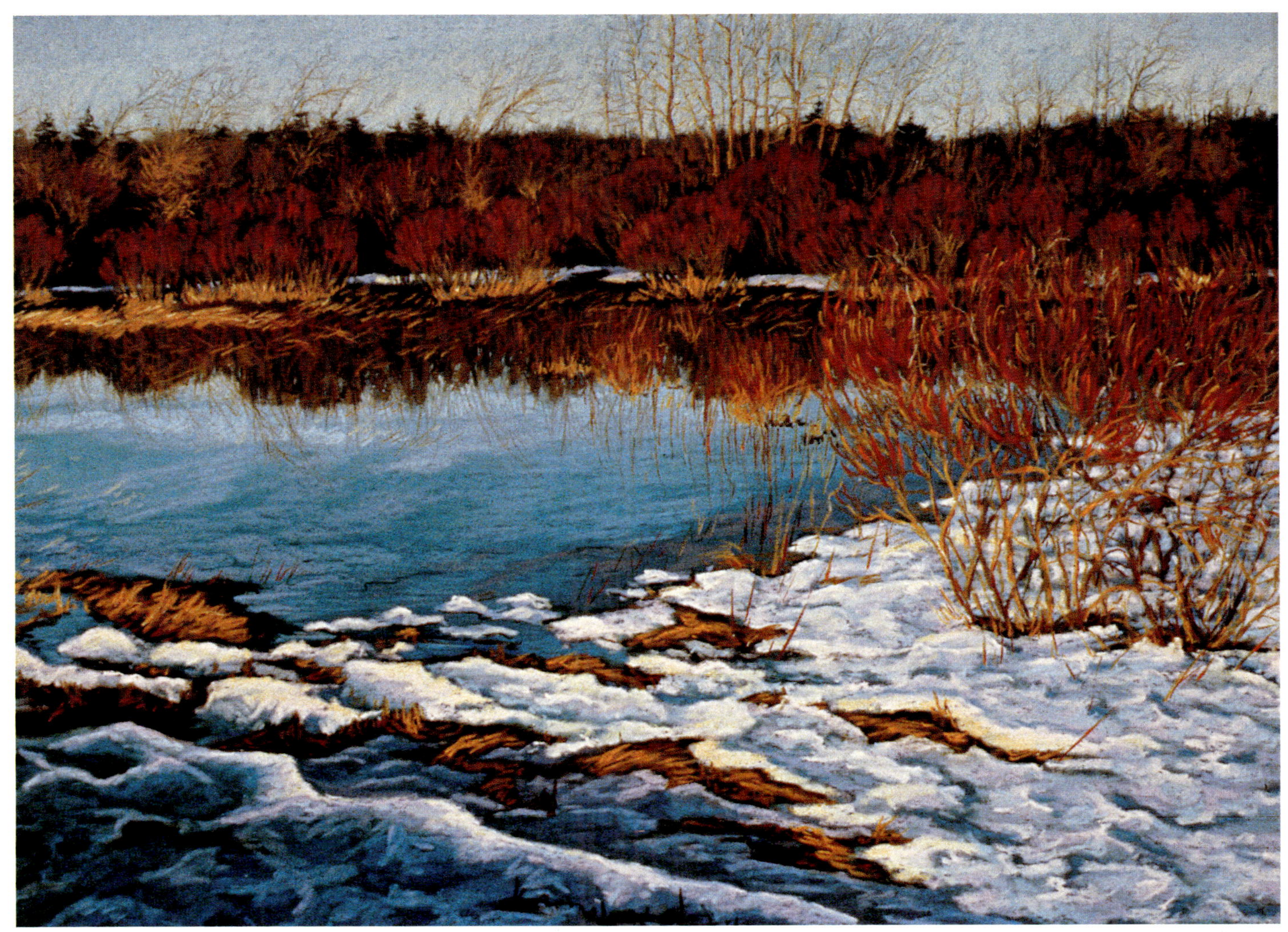

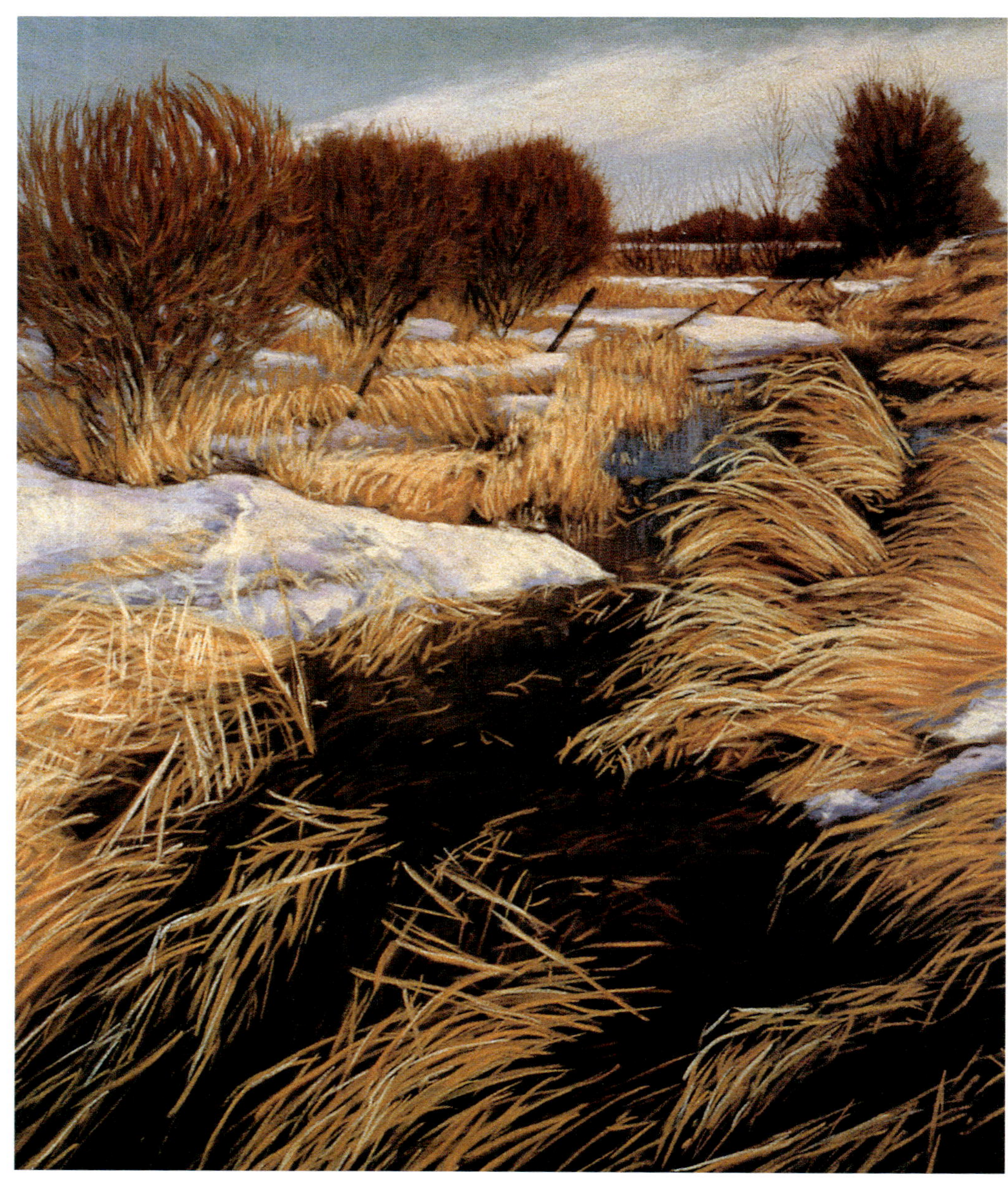

Audrey Pfannmuller

Roadside Runoff

19" × 23"
La Carte pastel board

Guylaine Jacques

Using sandpaper as my surface, I seek to give a greater depth to my palette thanks to the optical effects I can get with this particular material. At the same time, it reinforces the natural softness of pastel, which is my favorite medium. The result is a texture that is full of surprises in which the dominant cold colors reveal an often times symbolic atmosphere.

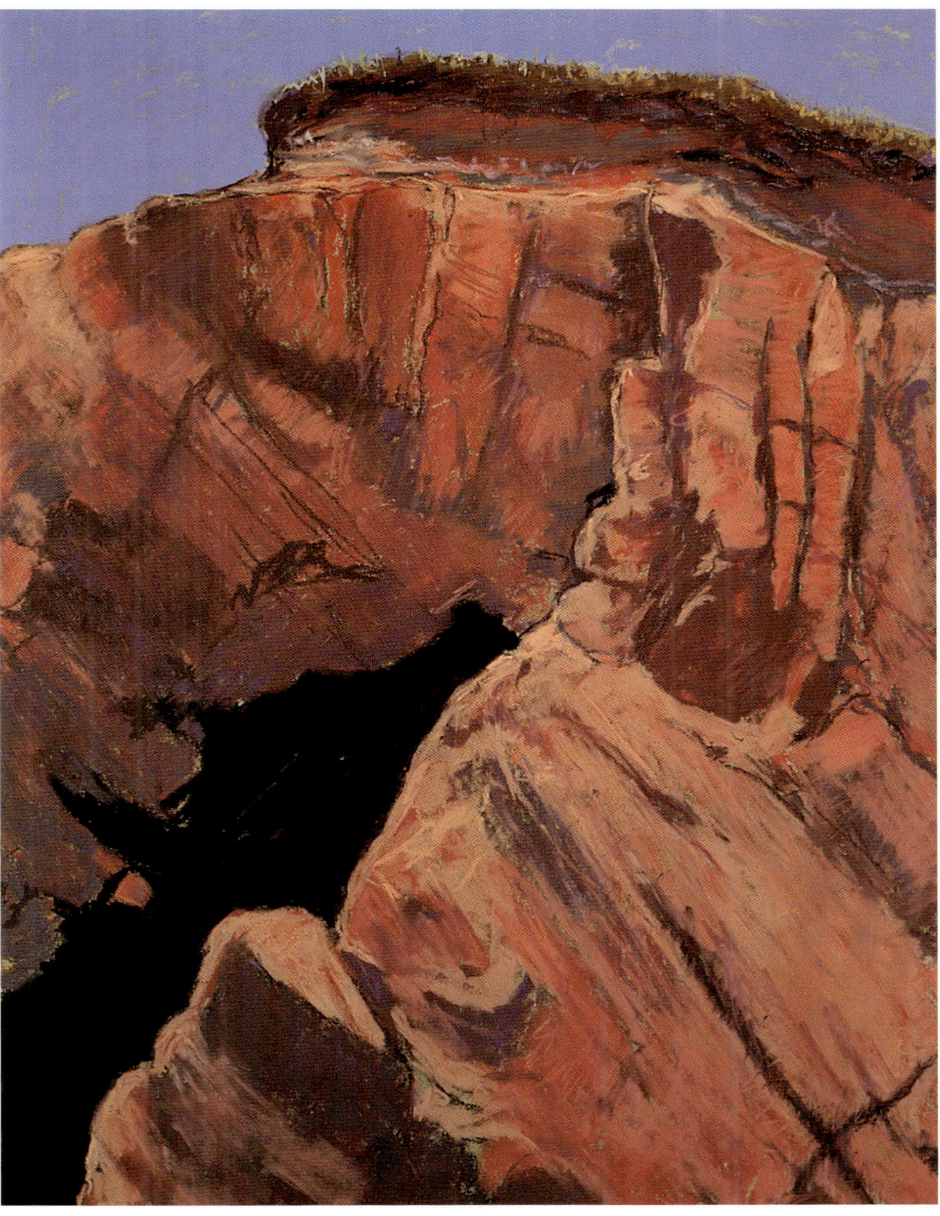

Graffiti de Sable

11 " x 15"
Sandpaper

Lucienne Zegray

As I stand and observe my subject, I take mental notes regarding composition and the mood which prevails. Although I have the whole gamut of colors of Canson Mi-Teintes at my disposal, I carefully select that color which will re-create the mood and atmosphere desired, and which will transmit the feeling I wish to communicate with my painting. Note that the paper always shows through the pastel and becomes an integral part of the painting, balancing its composition. I usually paint on the smoother, less textured side of the paper – some would dare say the "wrong" side – because it gives my painting the softer, gentler feeling I am searching for, the feeling that is more conducive to my personality.

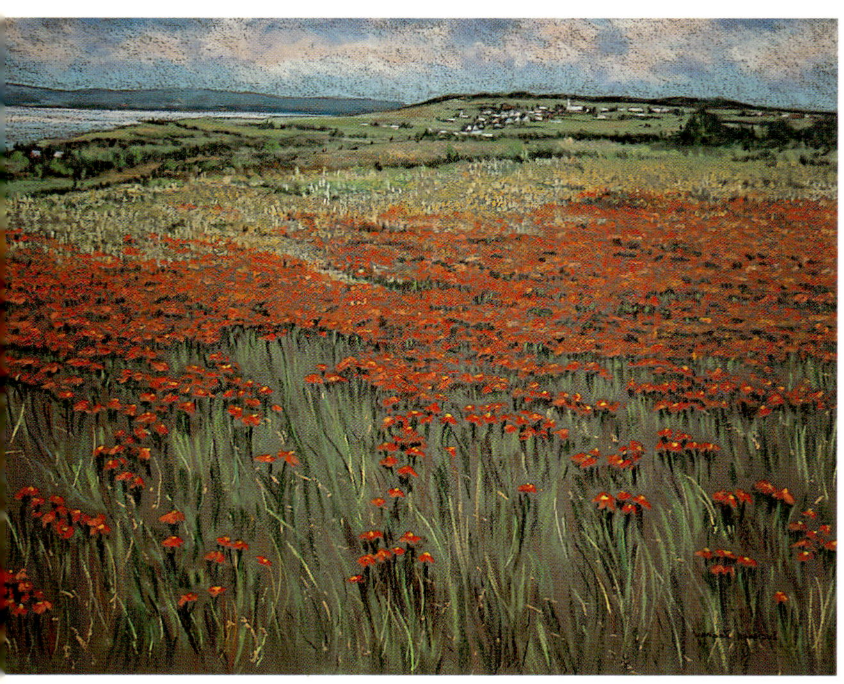

Wild Flowers

20" x 25"
Canson Mi-Teintes

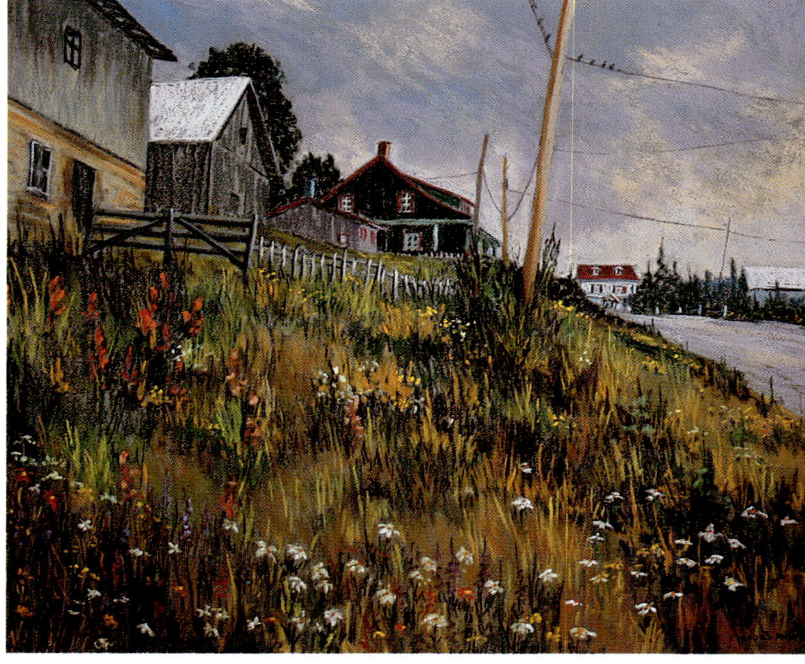

Roadside Flowers

20" x 25"
Canson Mi-Teintes

Christiane Plante

For some period of time, I had busied myself with portraits, fascinated by the changing expressions in human beings. Sometimes harsh, sometimes soft and kind. This was trying for me and that's why I changed my artistic direction to painting the landscape of my native Abitibi, a remote region of northern Quebec. I prefer to paint this beautiful region in either the early morning or late afternoon when the effect of light is most striking and shows the contrasts of the subject matter..

October's Day

18" x 24"
Sanded paper

Little Path

15" x 26"
Sanded paper

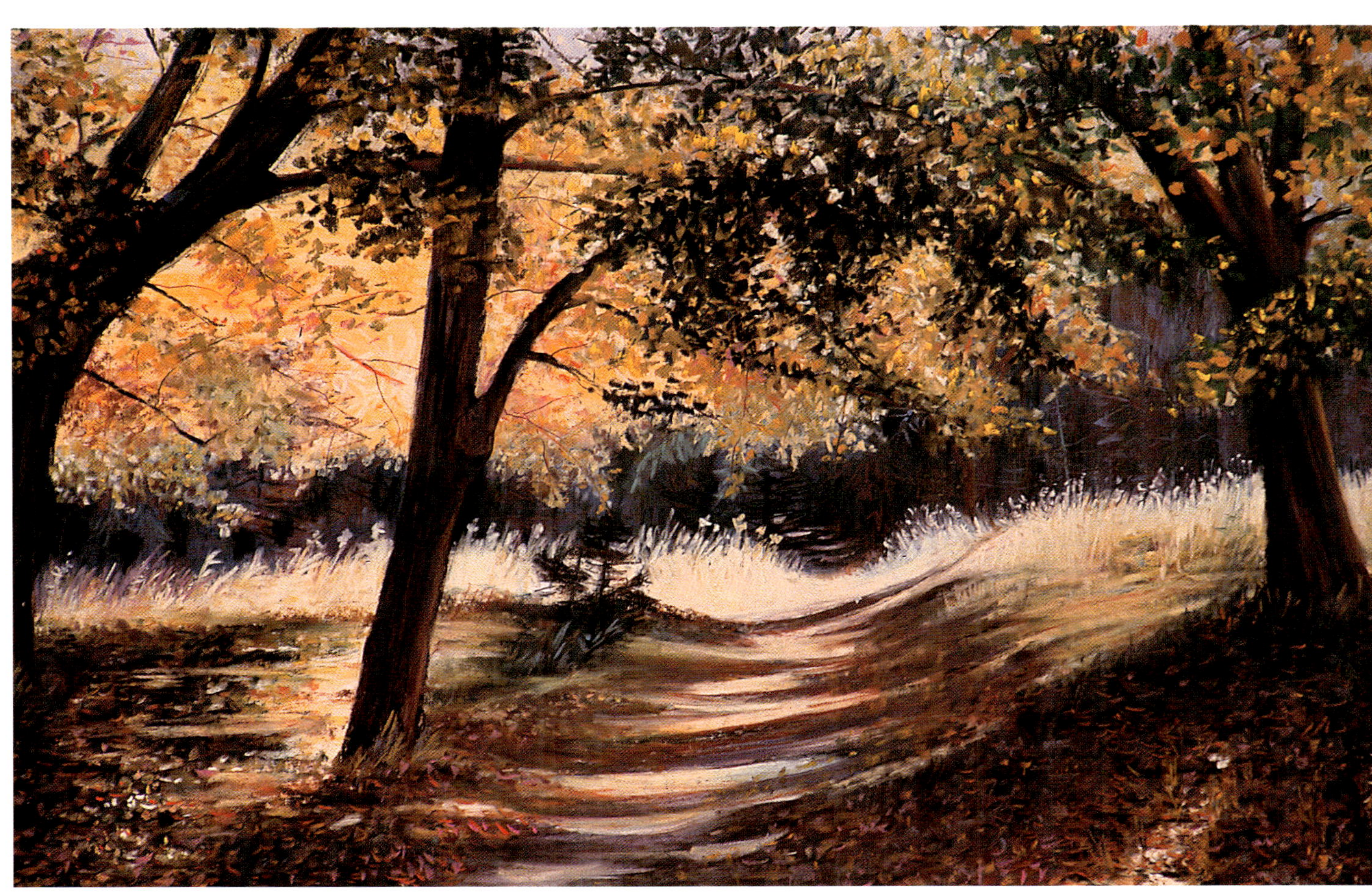

David Whitzman

I use short strokes in a broken color technique and do very little rubbing. I like working on rough sanded surfaces on which I can build up textures. If you look at my work, you will see that I am a colorist first and foremost. You will also notice some calligraphy and other means of pastel application. I have no great aims in art. No axe to grind. No world ailments to cure. I paint to please myself and to bring pleasure to others.

Sackville River in Winter

16" x 20"
Sanded paper

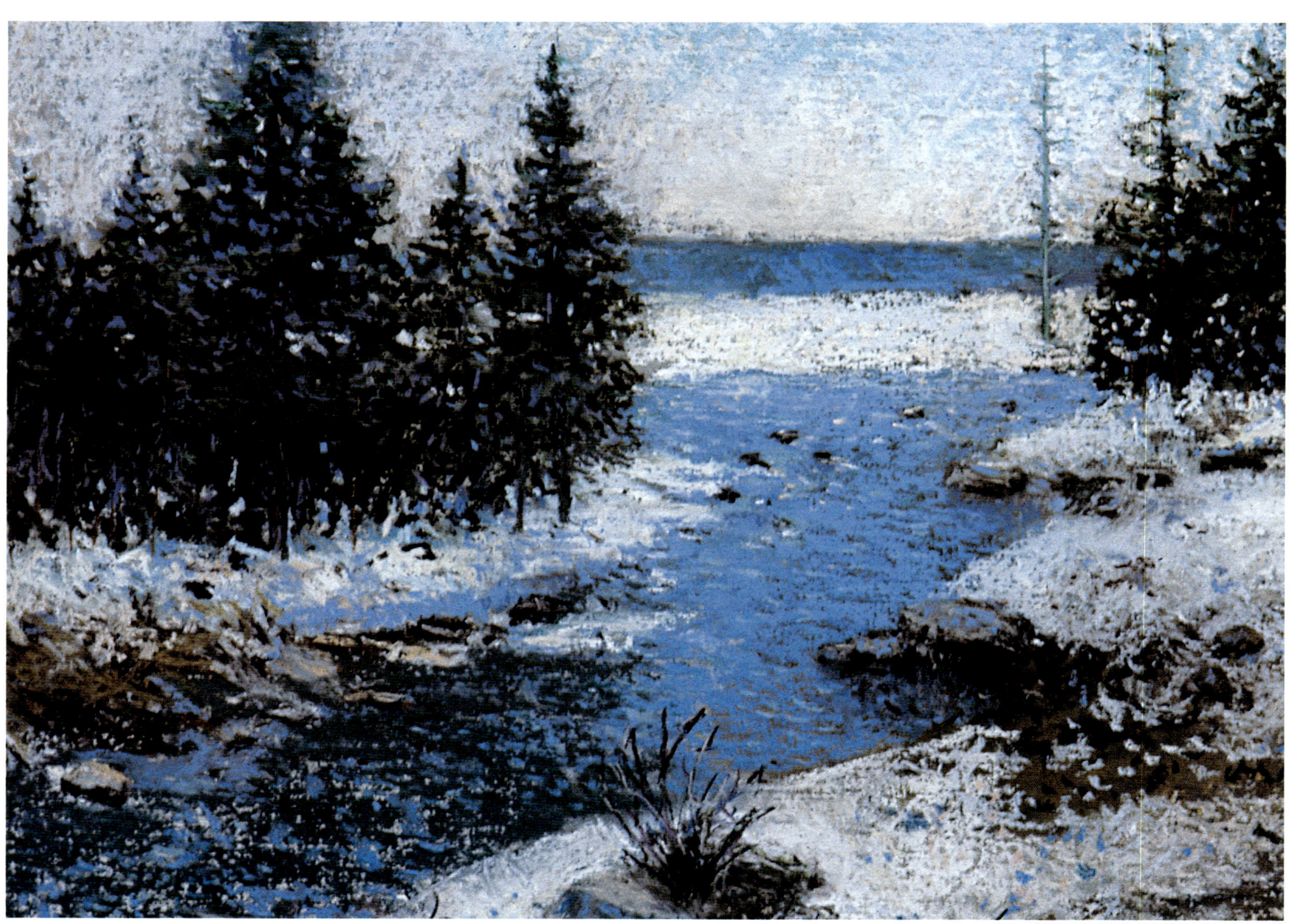

Dried-up River Bed

16 ½" x 23"
Sanded paper

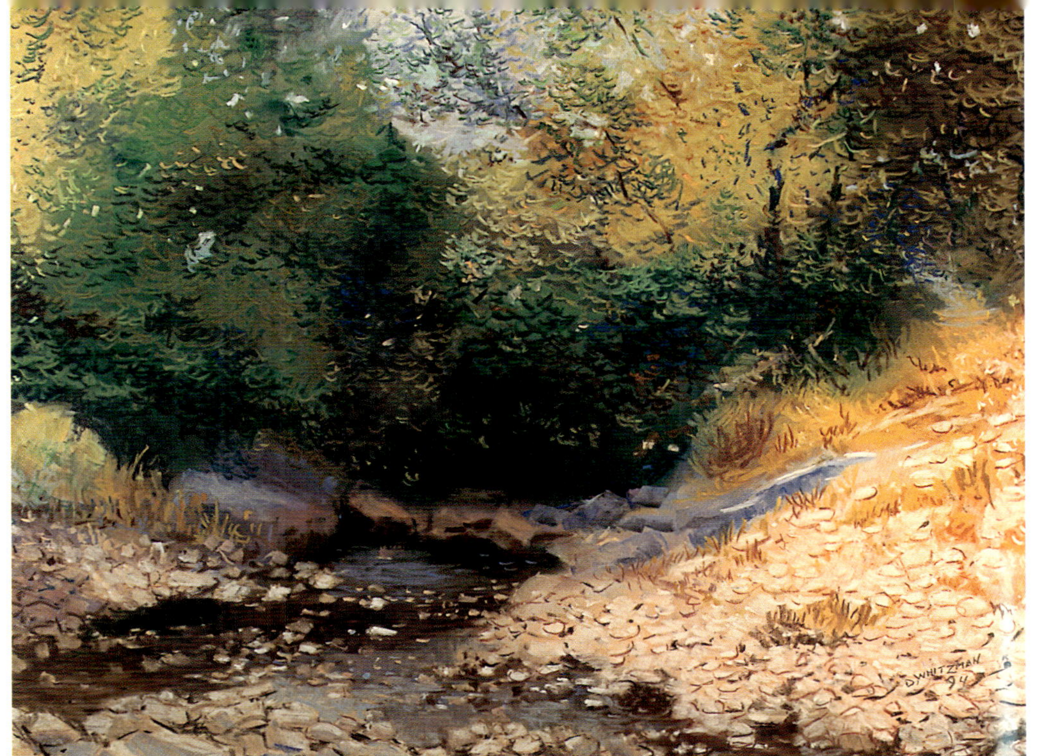

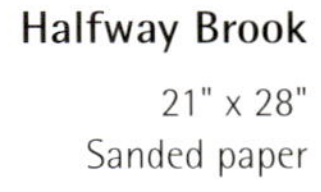

Halfway Brook

21" x 28"
Sanded paper

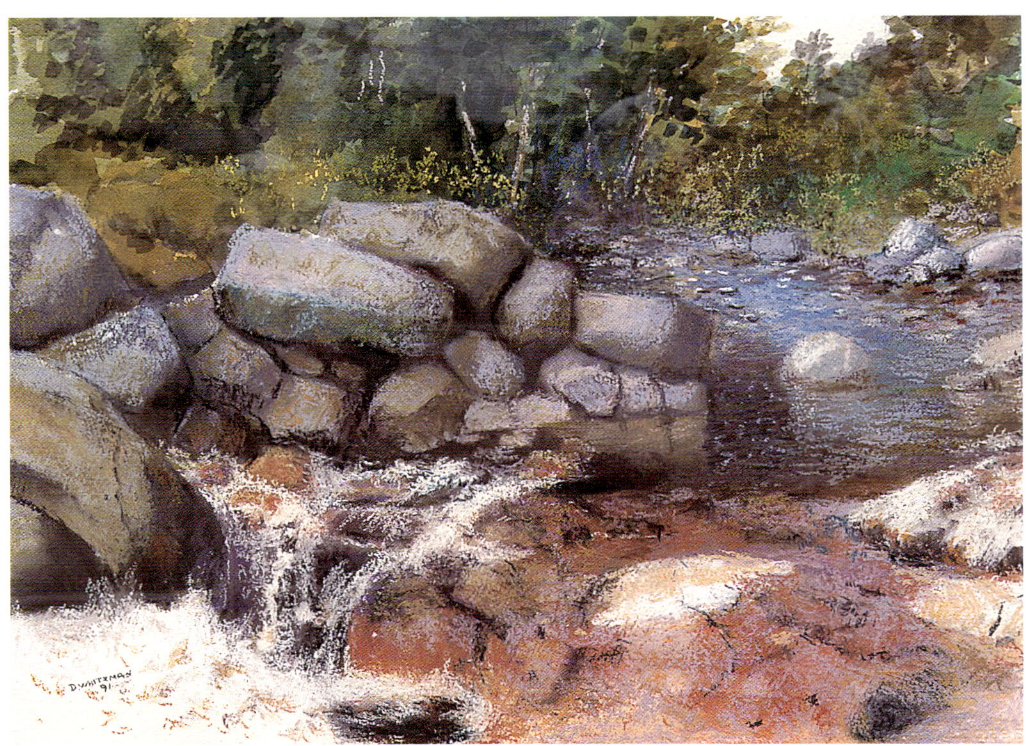

Barbara Elmslie

This was a sentimental piece of work; the subject was my parents' country veranda and the chairs had been made by my father. Working on something so personal was fun and the contrast between the white shapes and the background patterns proved to be a challenge. I painted this picture on a green-colored Canson pastel paper.

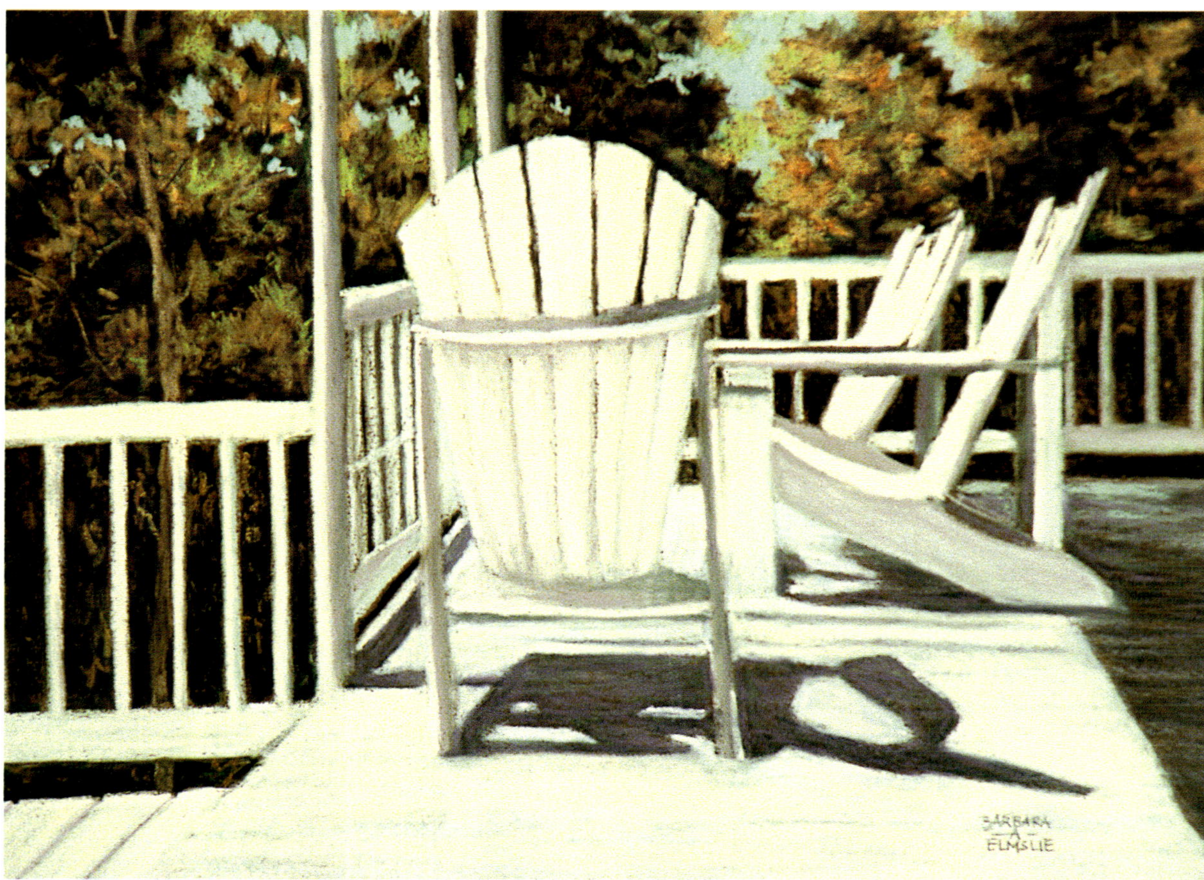

Country Porch
16" x 20"
Canson Mi-Teintes

Douglas Manning

The application of pastels varies according to the painting. Sometimes I render the background first, if it is dark, then lightly spray with fixative in order that the color does not go into the main subject. Apart from backgrounds, I do not use any fixative on completed paintings as it destroys the colors and sends whites to a grayish tone.

The Enchanted Forest

Distinction Plaque
21" x 29"
Canson Mi-Teintes

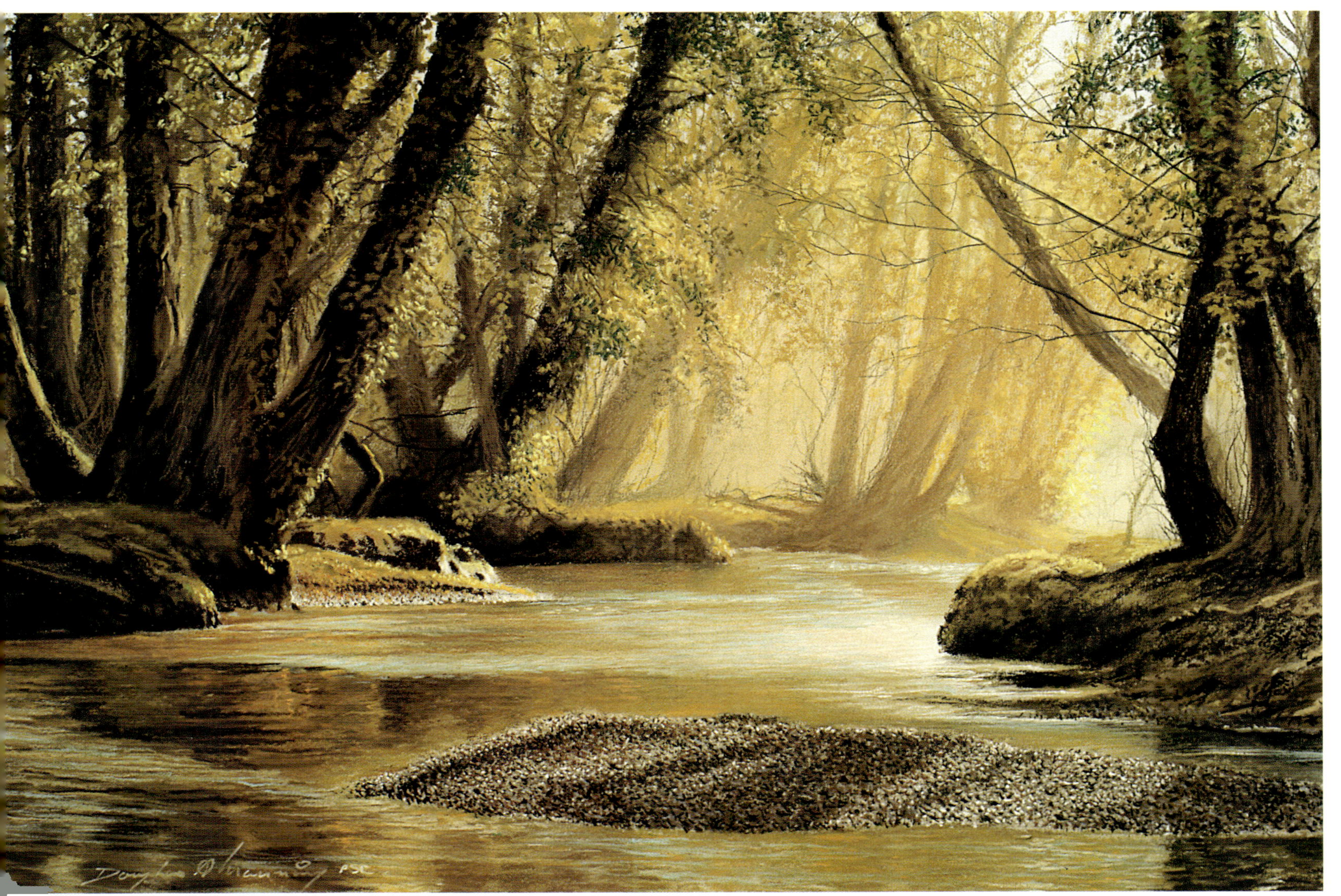

Horace Champagne

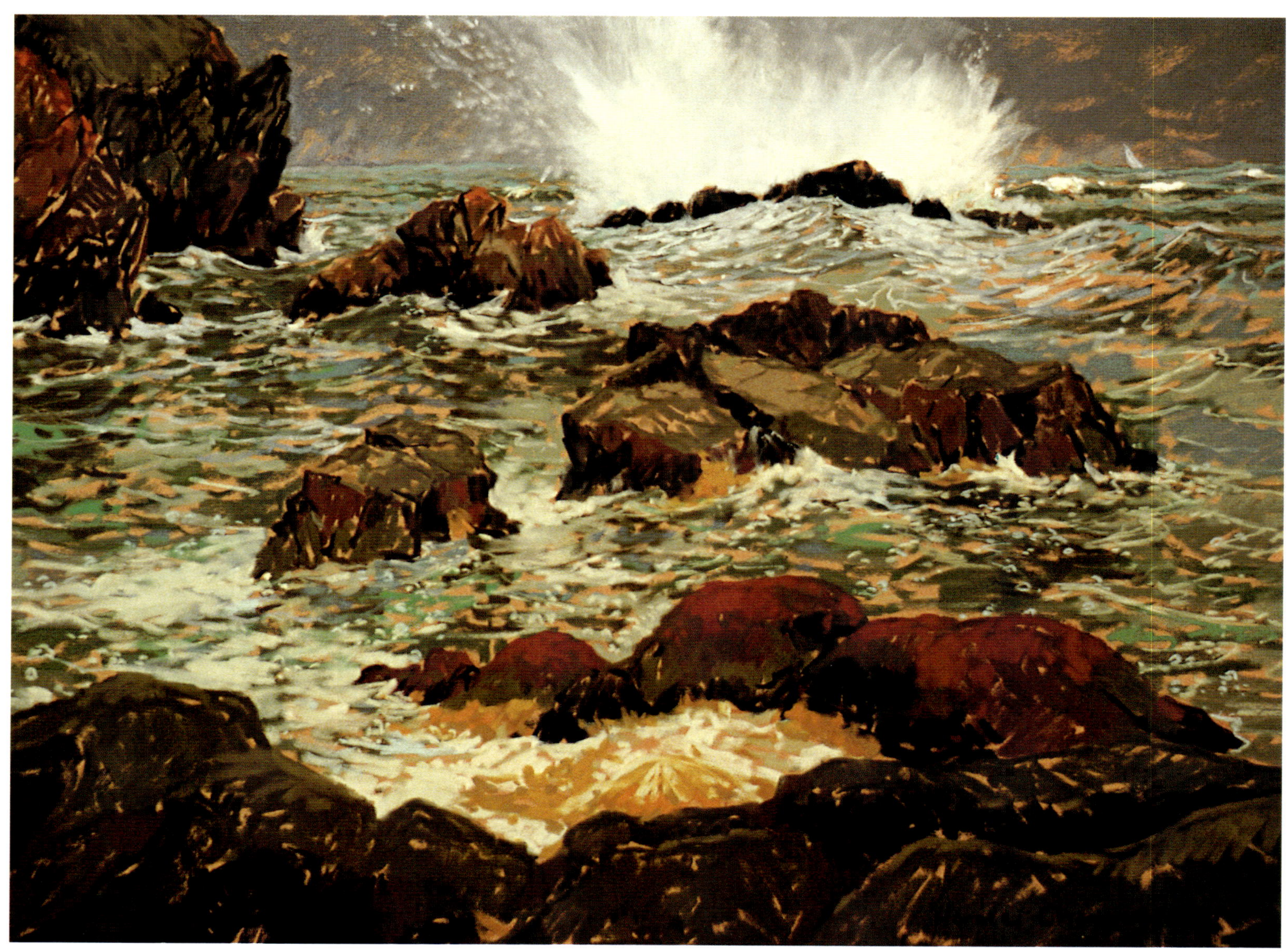

Crashing Surf

18" x 24"
Toned pastel paper

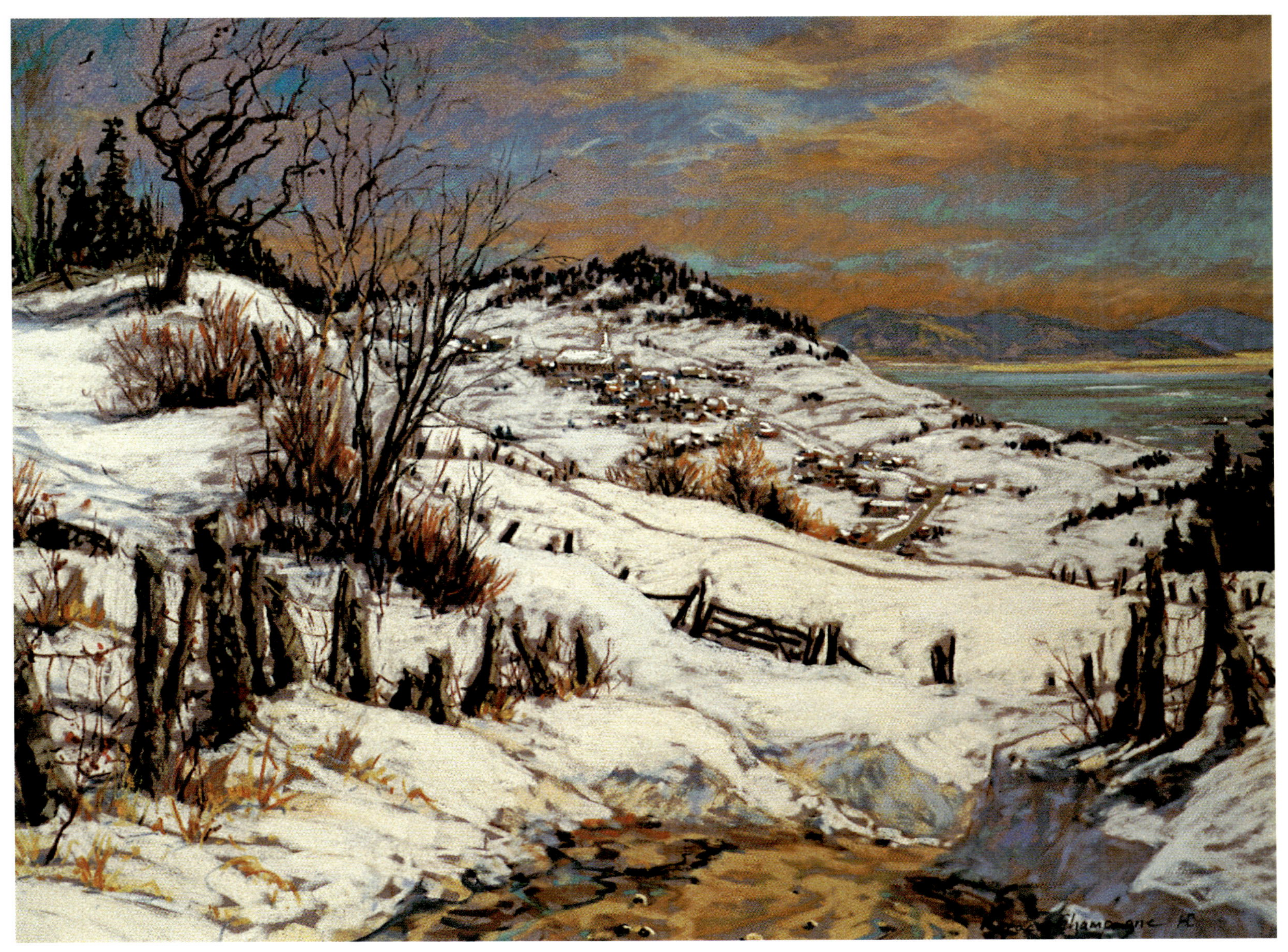

August Snow

18" x 24"
Toned pastel paper

Horace Champagne

Les Eboulements, Quebec

18" x 24"
Toned pastel paper

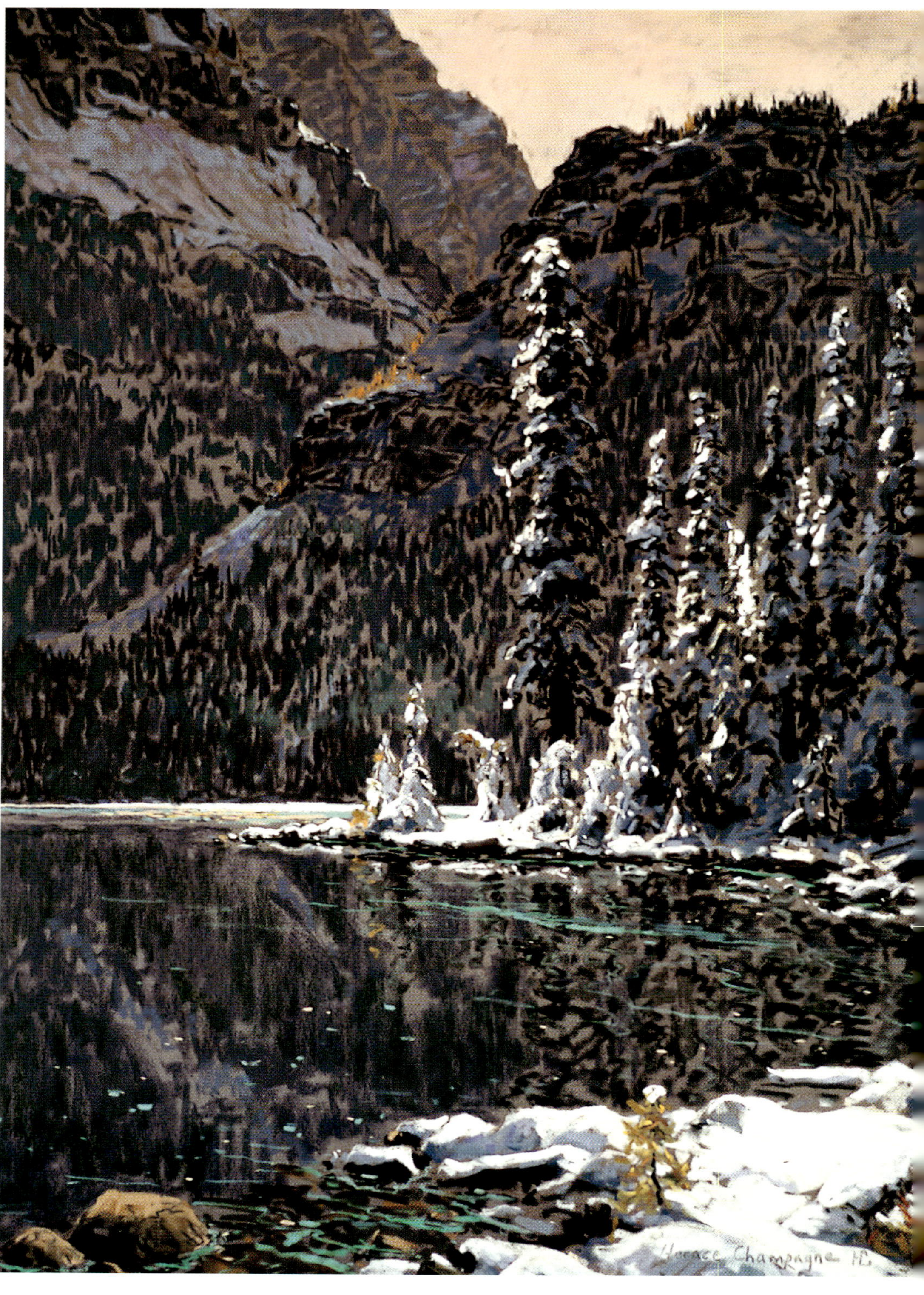

Dan Gray

All of my work is done with soft pastels on Canson Mi-Teintes paper. I paint directly from life with only minor adjustments that I make in my studio before framing. I first try to find my composition and mark my direction of light. In doing these, I run my fingers over the piece first as I visualize without doing any painting in the major shapes, light to dark. Then, I look while painting for the unique thing about where I have chosen, including people, clouds, birds, etc., as they wander in and out of my painting. The wind, sounds, light, people one encounters while working become the palette I draw from for inspiration.

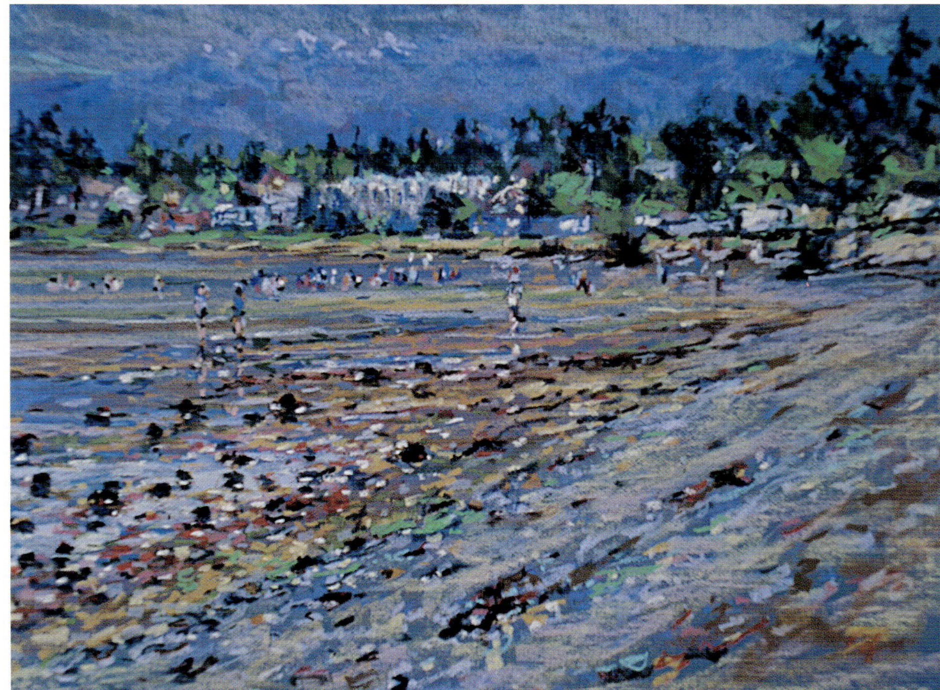

Parksville Beach
18" x 24"
Canson Mi-Teintes

Low Tide Eaglecrest
18" x 24"
Canson Mi-Teintes

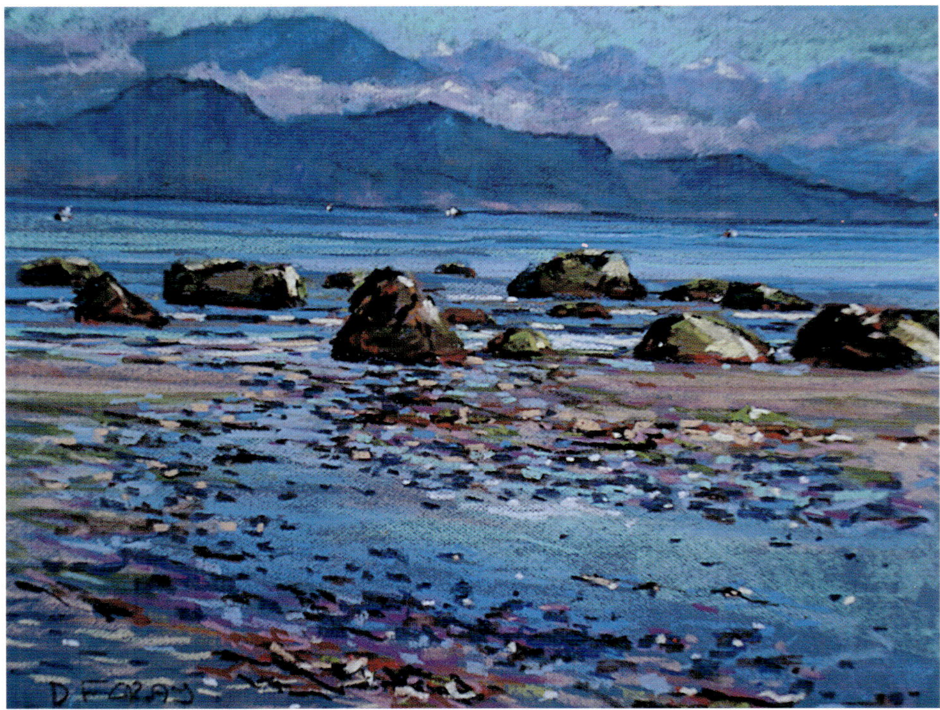

Andrew McDermott

I am passionate about this pastel medium because of its flexibility. It allows me to create subtle variations of mood, light and color. My philosophy about my work: "A painting does not begin when you put down your first stroke; it begins with the stroke beside it."

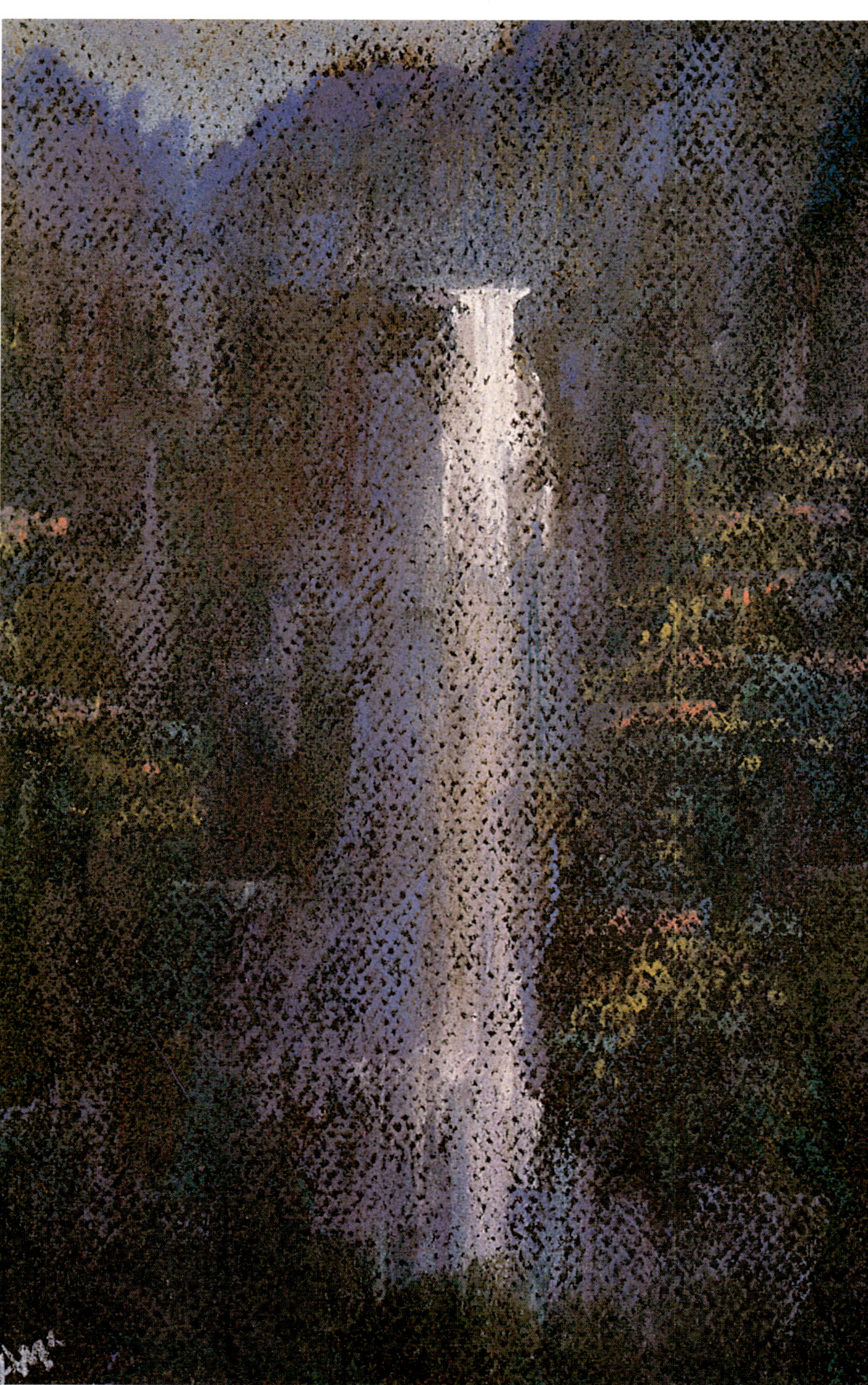

Waterfall

8" × 11½"
Neutral colored
pastel paper

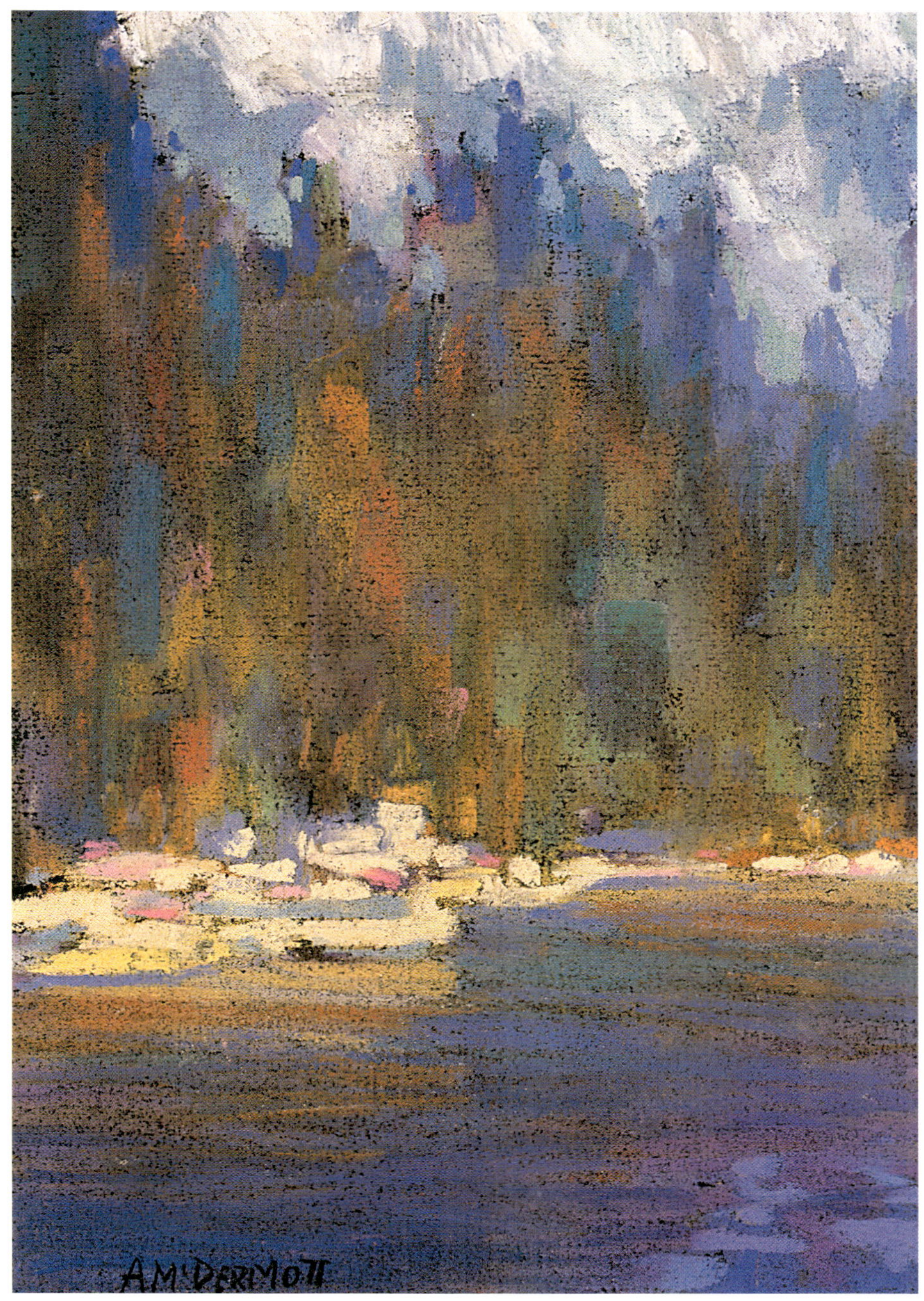

Island Trees

5" × 7"
Neutral colored
pastel paper

Andrew McDermott

Scotland

14" × 21"
Neutral colored
pastel paper

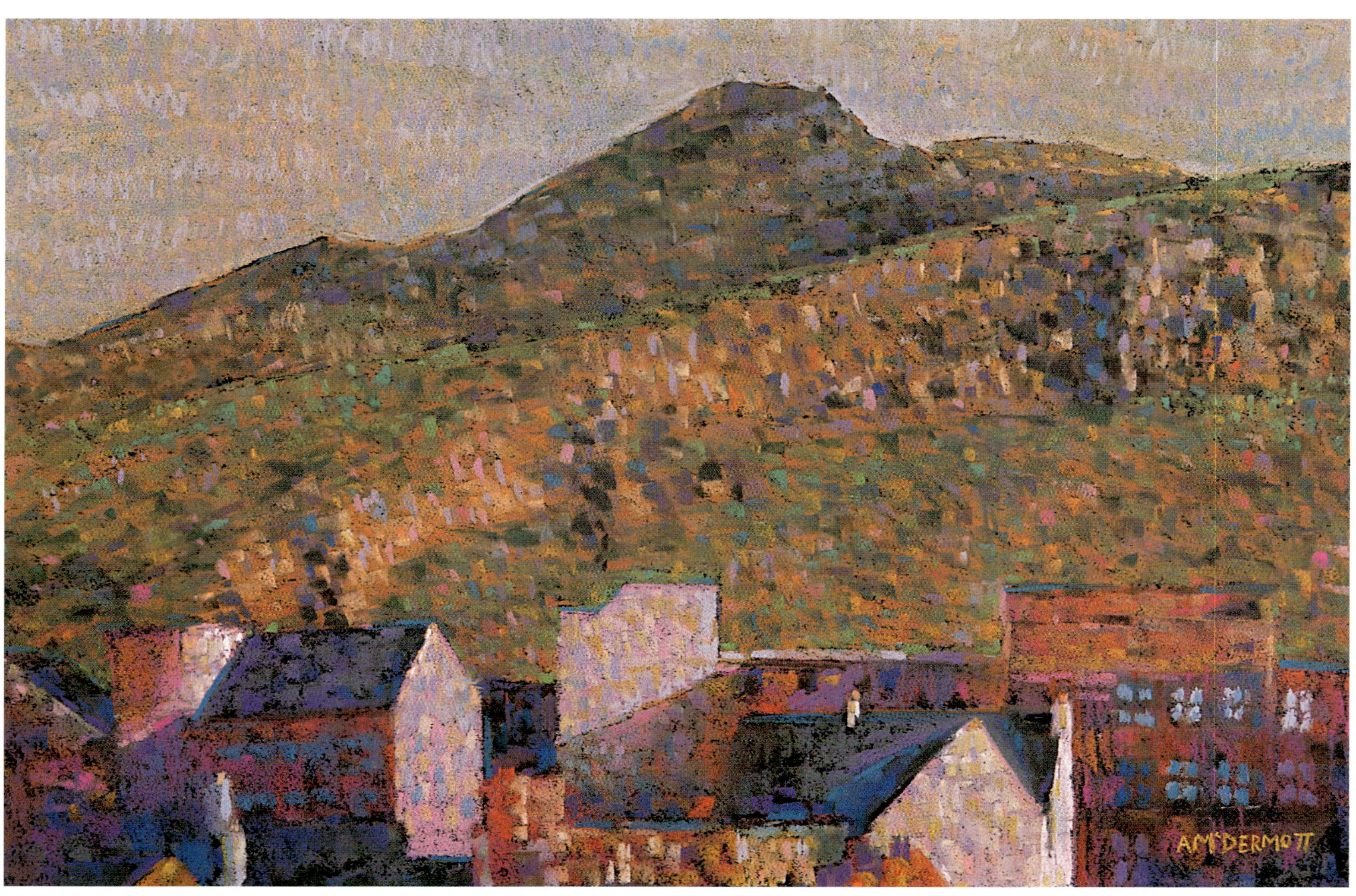

Lorna Dockstader

When painting, I prefer to ignore the local color of a subject in order to create a more emotional response. Van Gogh has influenced my work through his use of complementary contrasts. My preferred pastel support is La Carte Pastel board. The pastels adhere very well to it. Being able to build strong value contrasts with intense color is important to my end result. Hard pastels are first applied in broad strokes to fill in most of the large shapes, then followed by glazing layers of color on top, adding more detail with softer pastels as I continue. Pastels are never blended with a finger or stump; they are applied directly and left alone. And I seldom use a fixative spray. All of these precautions help to keep the colors fresh and lively.

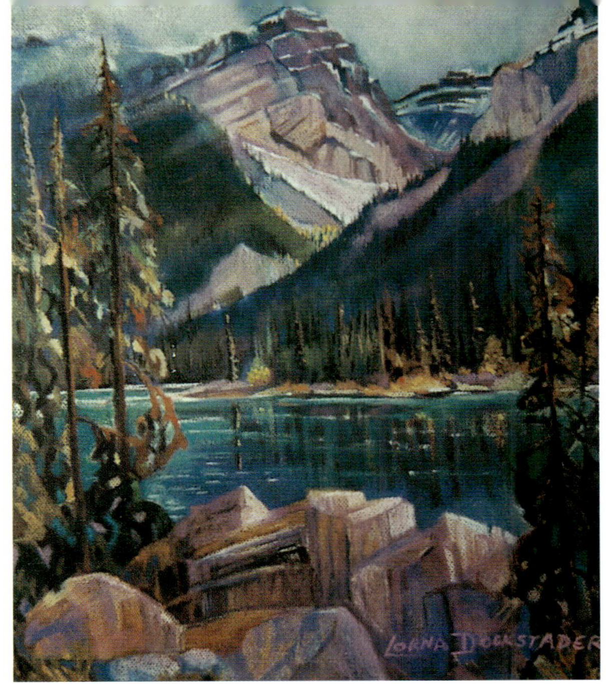

Mountain Lake

19" x 25"
La Carte pastel board

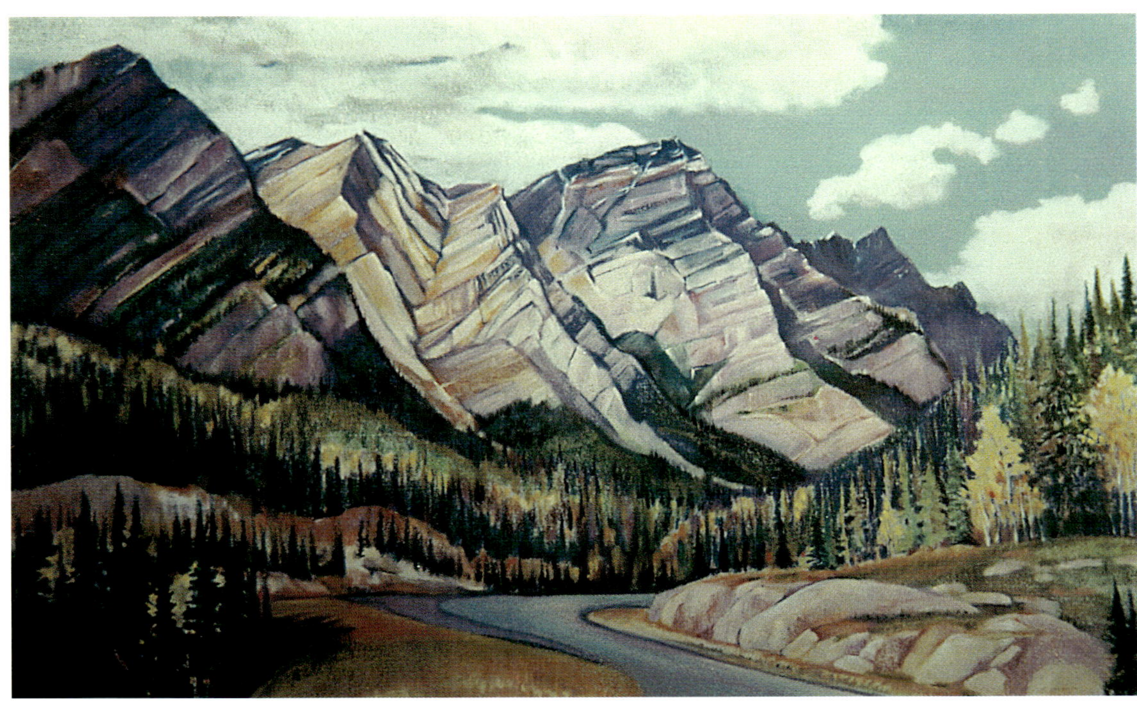

Leaving Kanaskis Country

19" x 25"
La Carte pastel board

Bert Huizinga

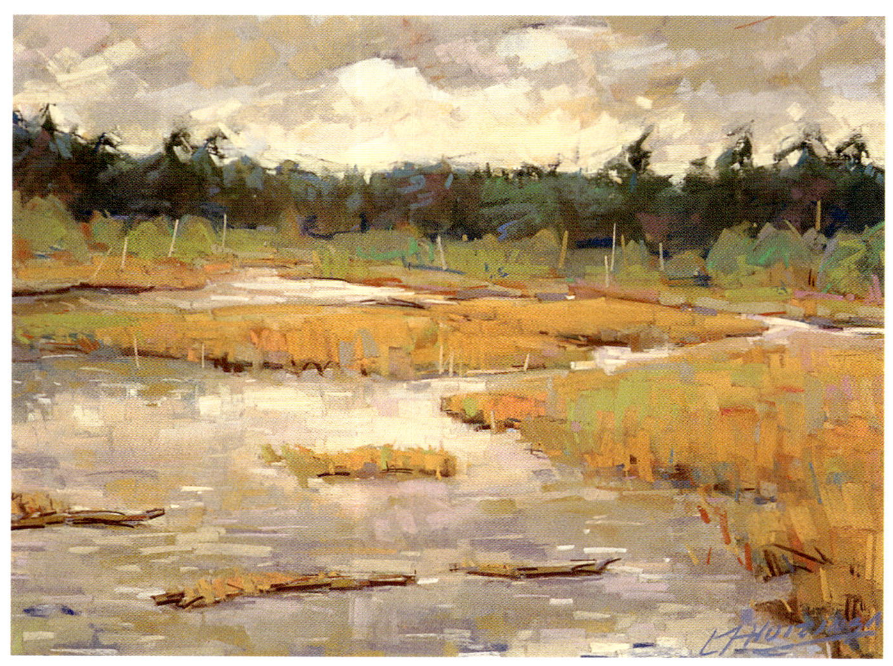

Northern Swamp

18" x 24"
Light Cream Stone Hedge paper

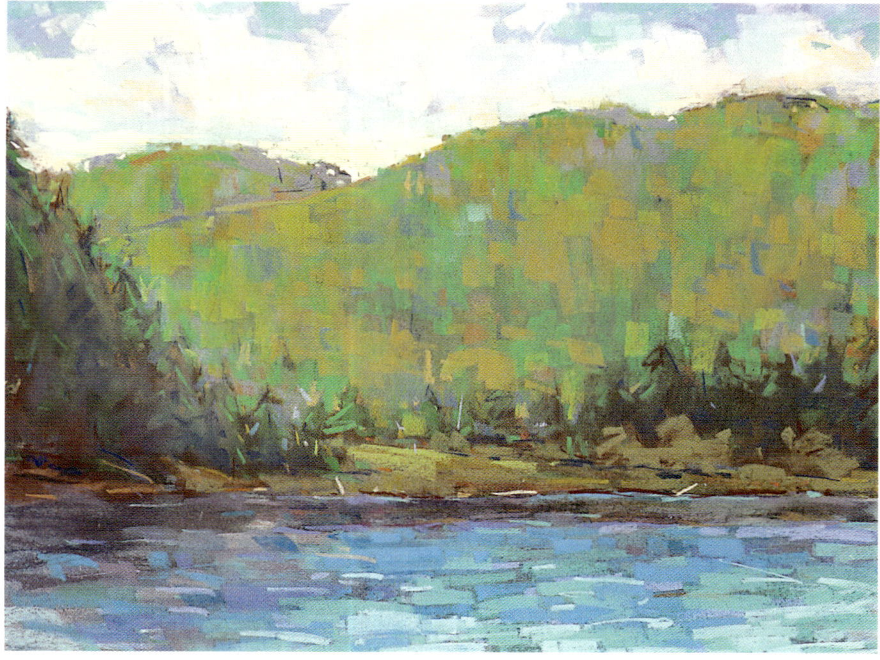

Emerald Hills

18" x 24"
White Stone Hedge paper

Purple Loosestrife #5

17" x 24"
White Stone Hedge paper

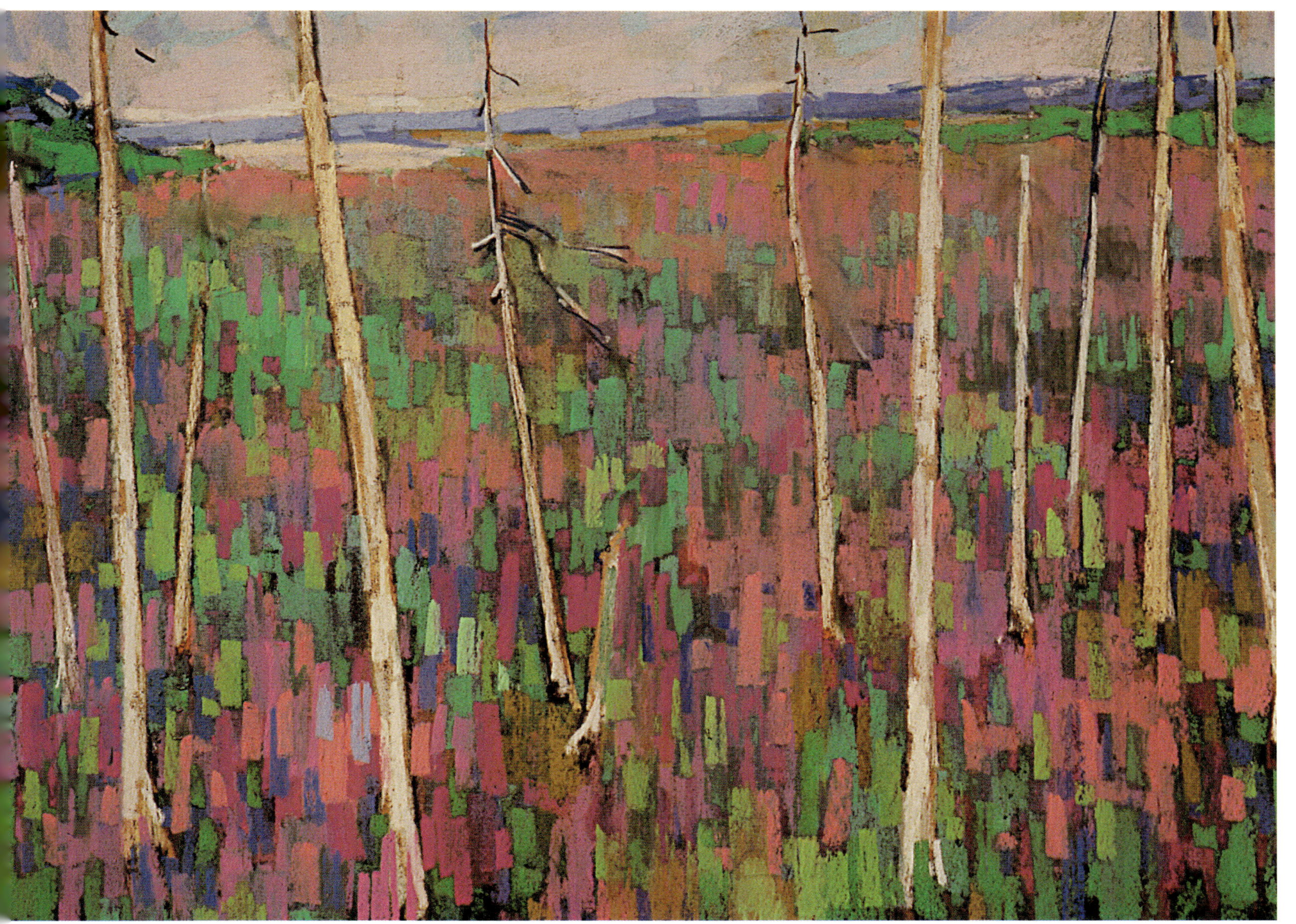

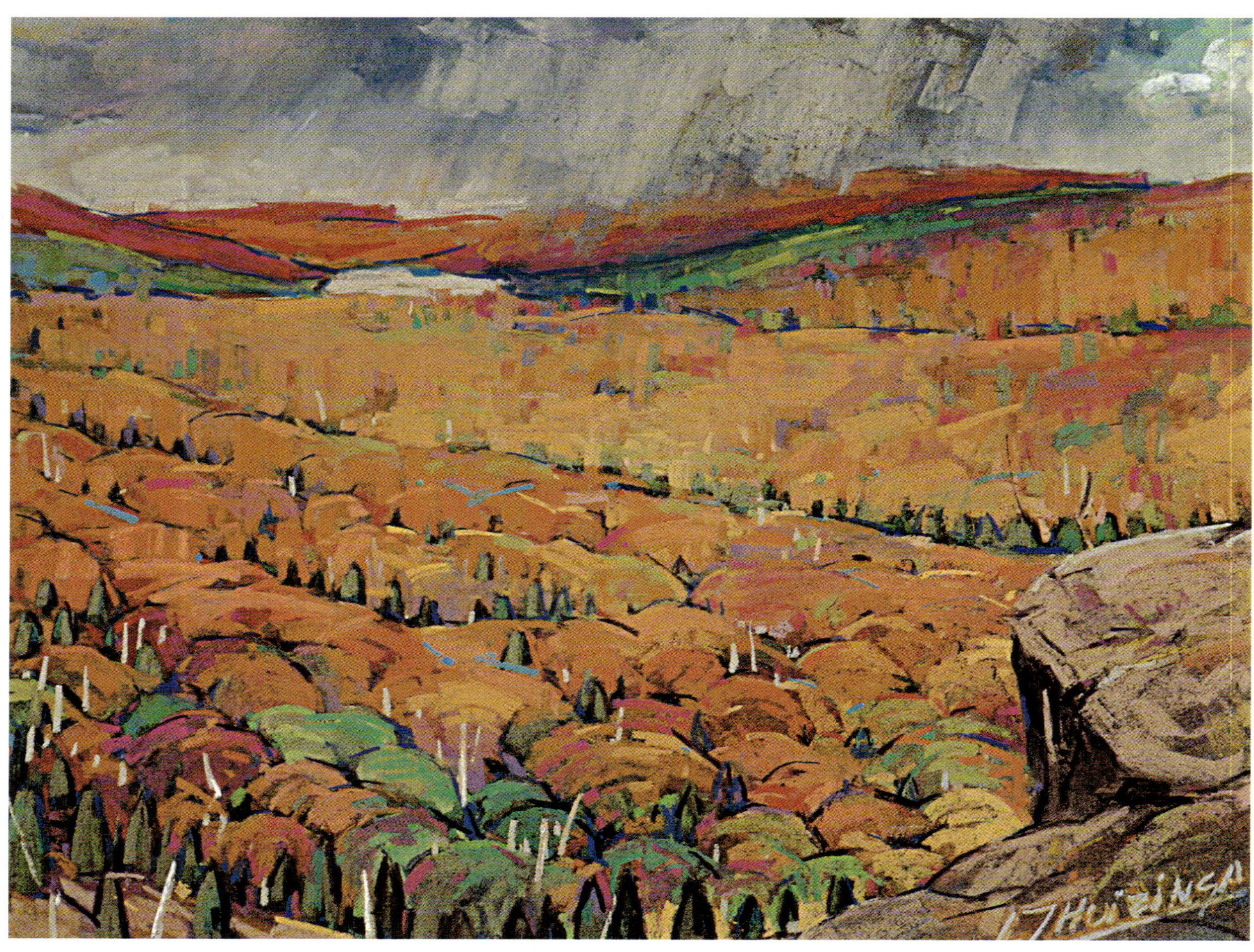

Bert Huizinga

Fall Showers

18" x 24"
Light Cream Stone Hedge paper

David Whitzman

Summer Time

16" x 20"
Sanded paper

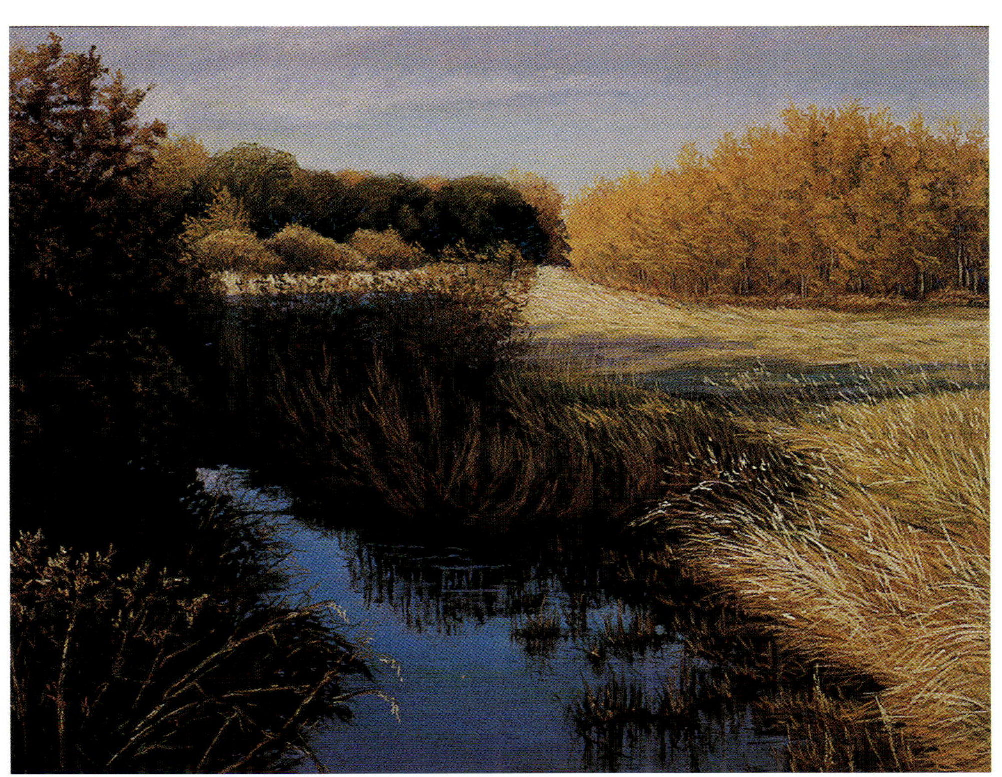

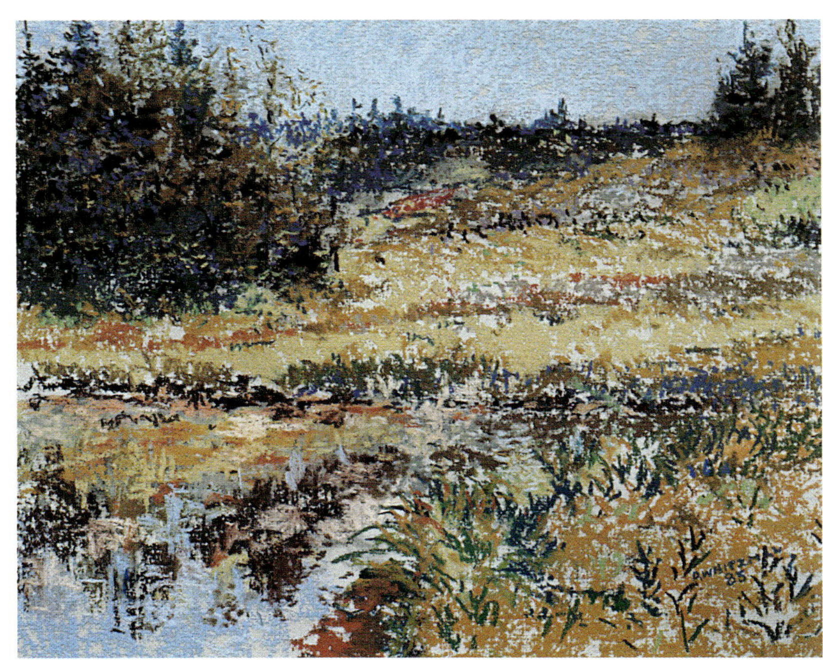

Audrey Pfannmuller

Braim Meadow

30" x 38"
Pumice coated board

Mireille Collet

The sky has five layers of pastel, from dark gray to intense blue. This is possible because the Sennelier sandpaper surface has a very good tooth and grabs the pastel well.

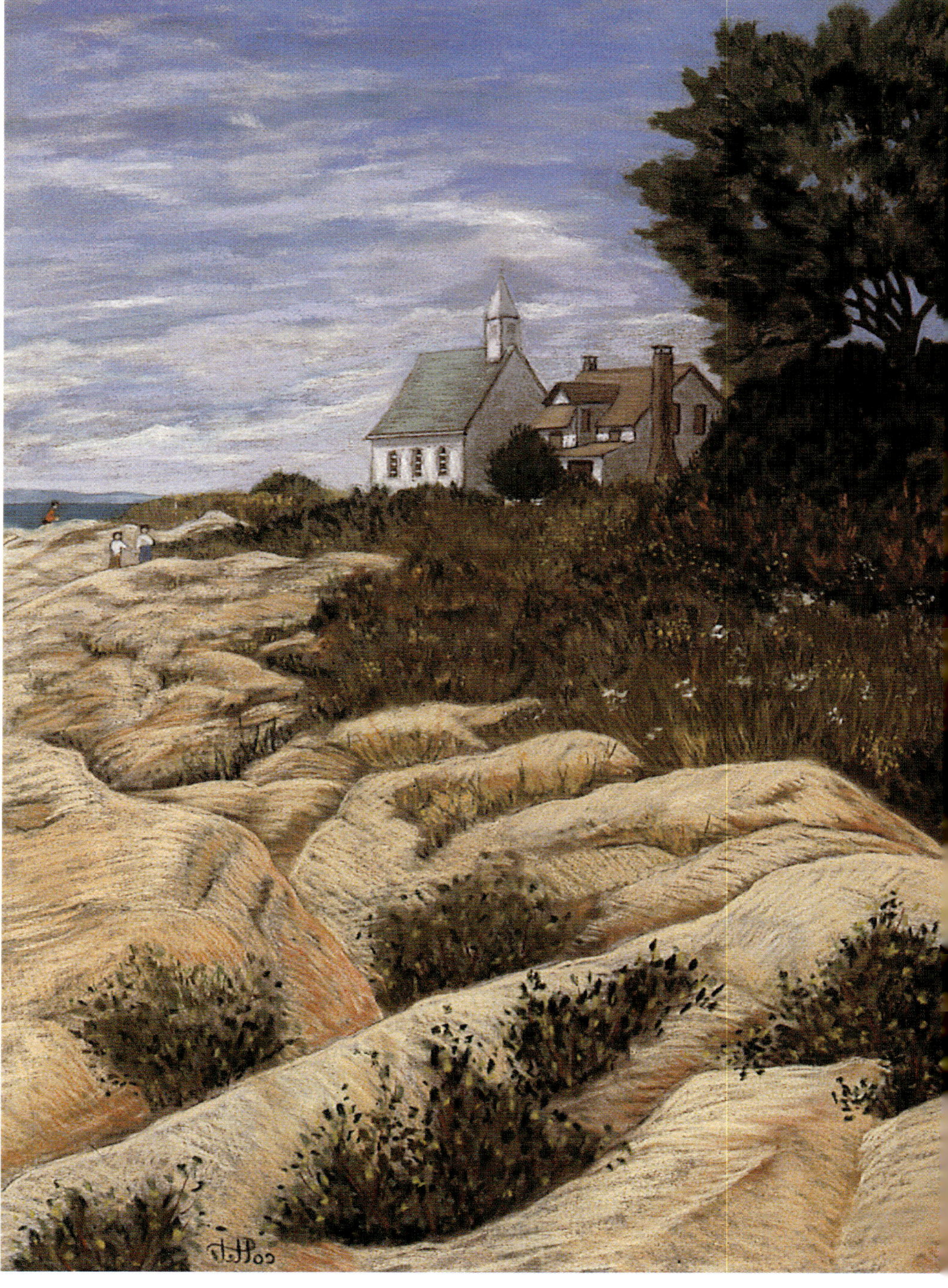

Port au Persil
19" x 25"
Beige Sennelier sandpaper

Joyce Dessert

High Water on the Blaeberry

19" x 25"
Canson Mi-Teintes

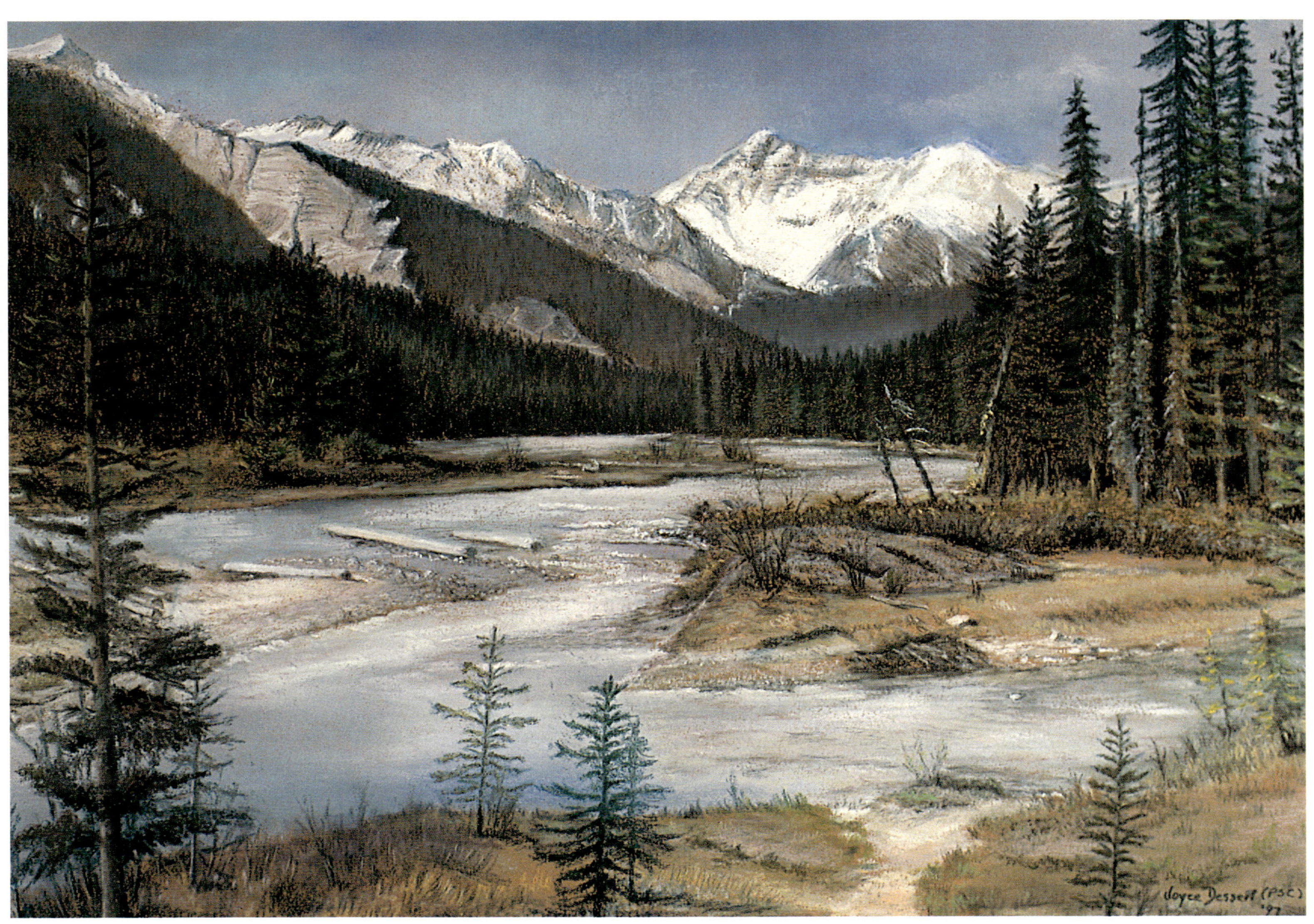

John Brezinskis

My interest in pastel painting was aroused by looking at Degas's pastels. I have been painting watercolor landscapes for a long time, and I was fascinated, for one, by the fact that with pastels one can add sunny highlights over a dark background. I also like the more forgiving nature and the versatility of pastel application, offering the artist the choice of strong, individual strokes on smooth, fused areas with hazy contours.

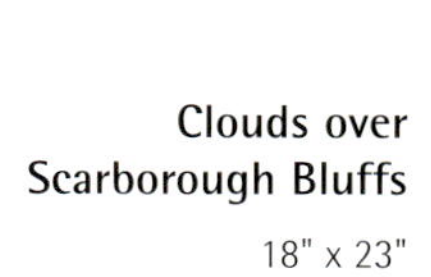

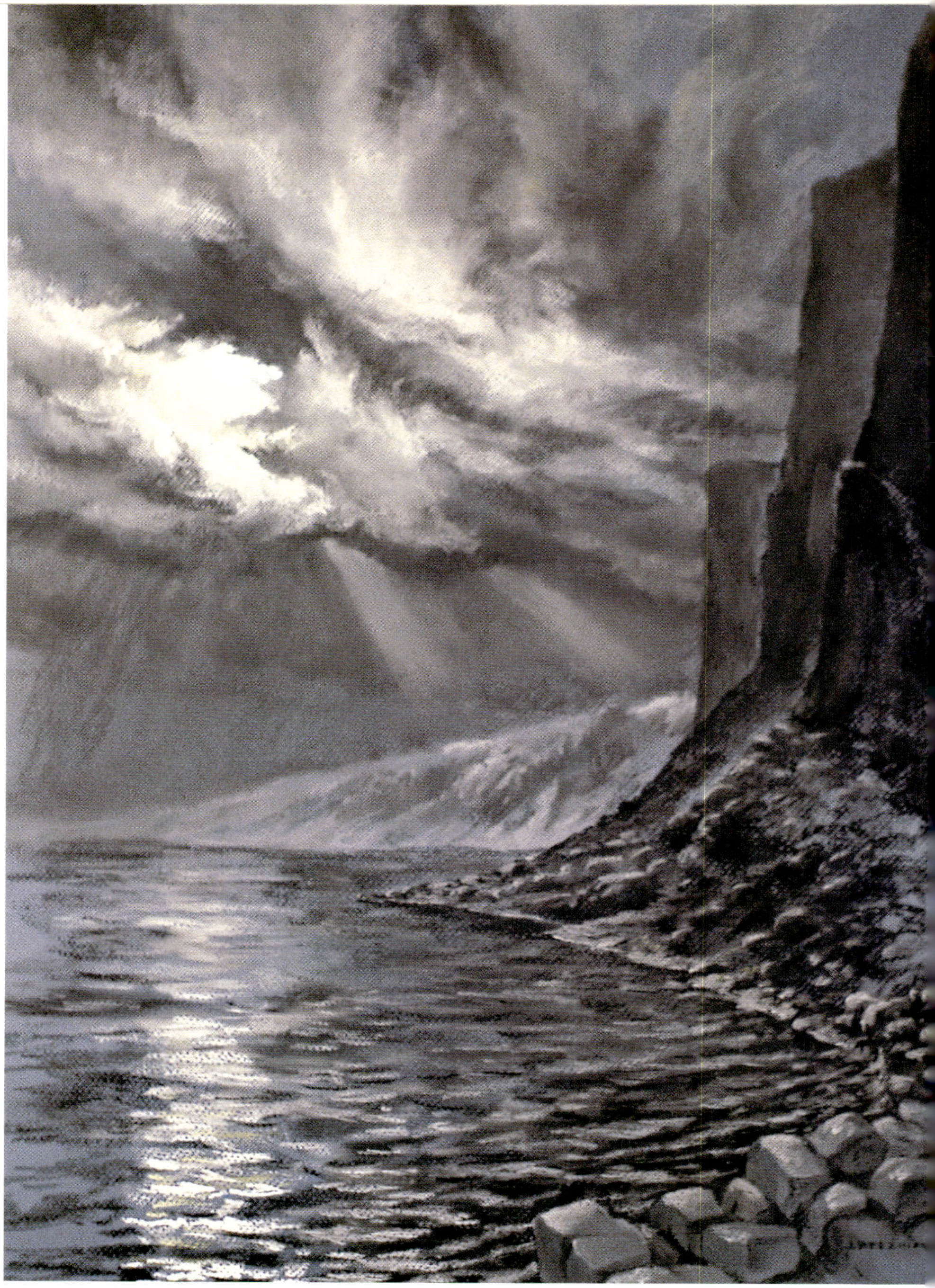

Clouds over Scarborough Bluffs

18" x 23"
Canson Mi-Teintes paper

Morning Mist

12" x 18"
Canson Mi-Teintes paper

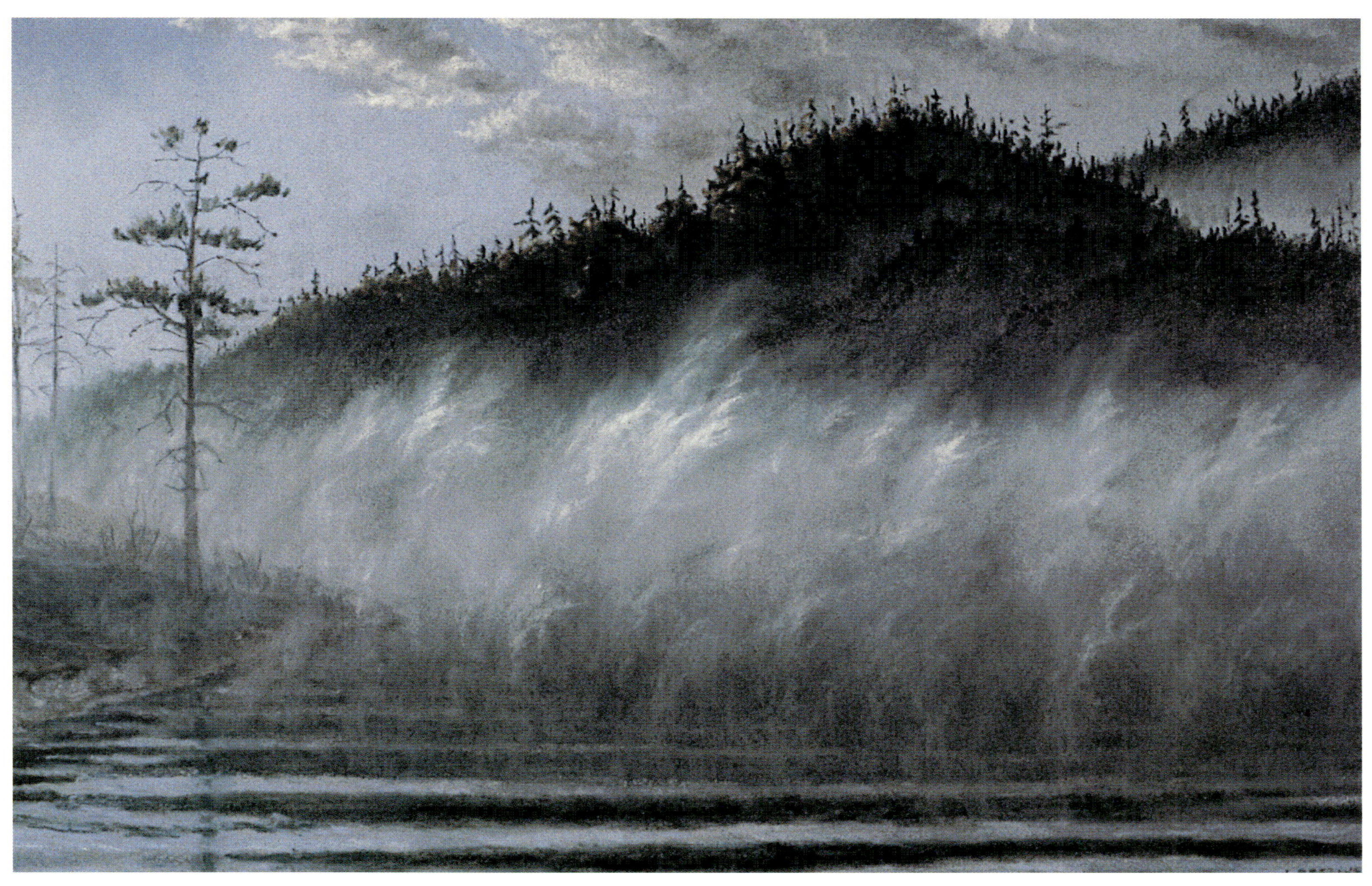

John Brezinskis

Bullrushes

17" x 23"
Canson Mi-Teintes paper

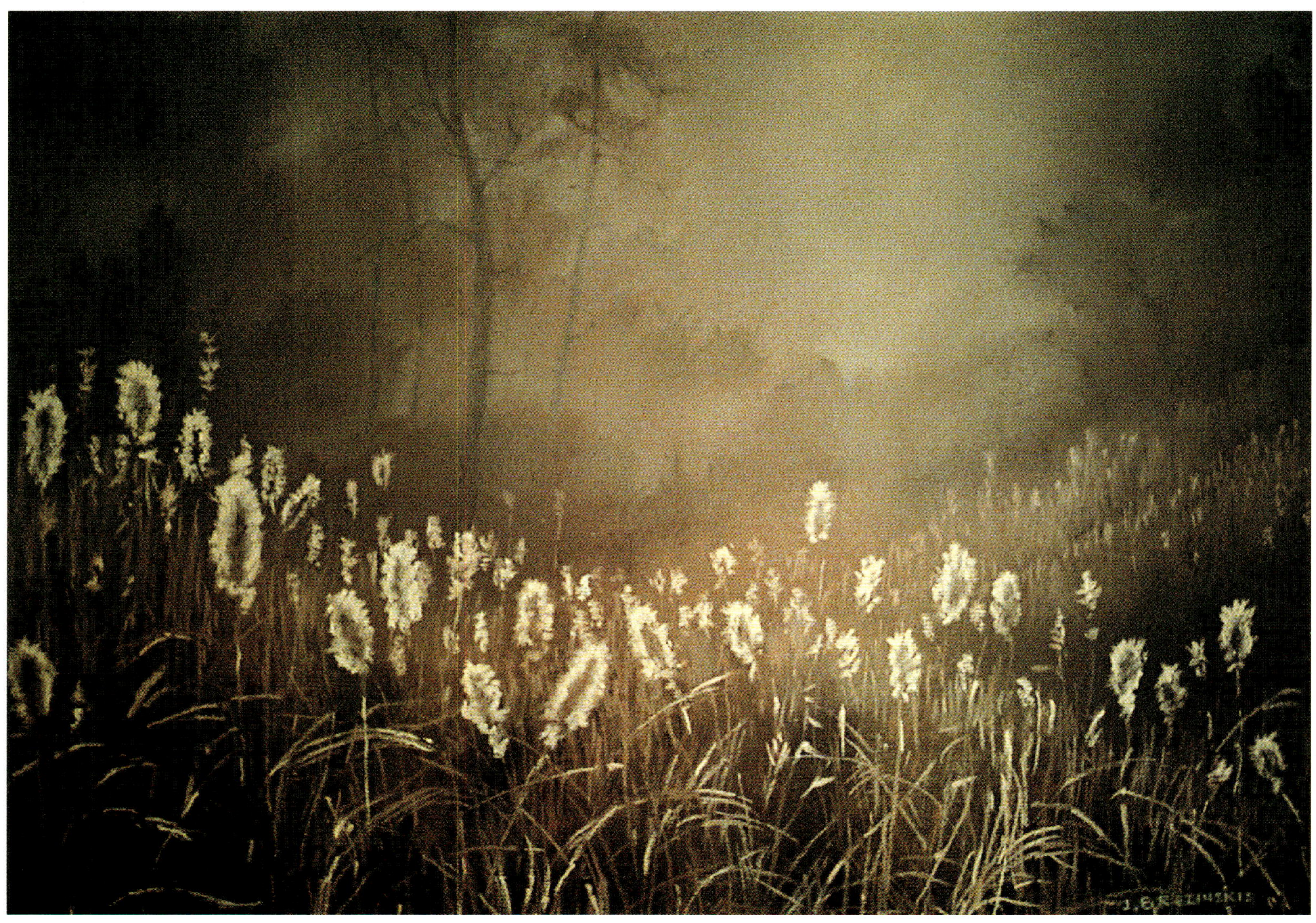

Gilles Mailloux

Of all the elements in a good painting, one stands out in my mind — ambiance. I cover my paper all over first with two or three colors, then I blend these colors together. I do a lot of blending mainly because of my favorite subject in a landscape being the mist in nature. My paintings must be from my imagination only. Creating a scene, therefore, from the beginning to the end is a fantastic feeling.

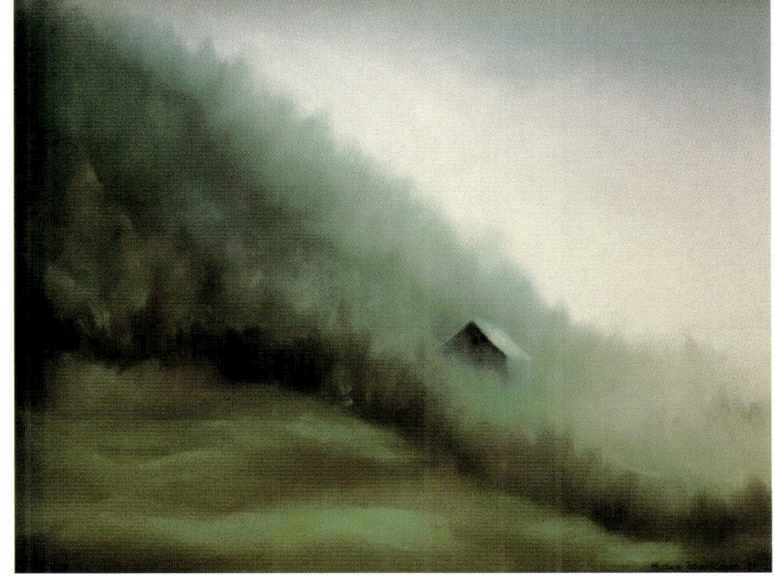

Le Refuge

14" x 18"
Canson Mi-Teintes

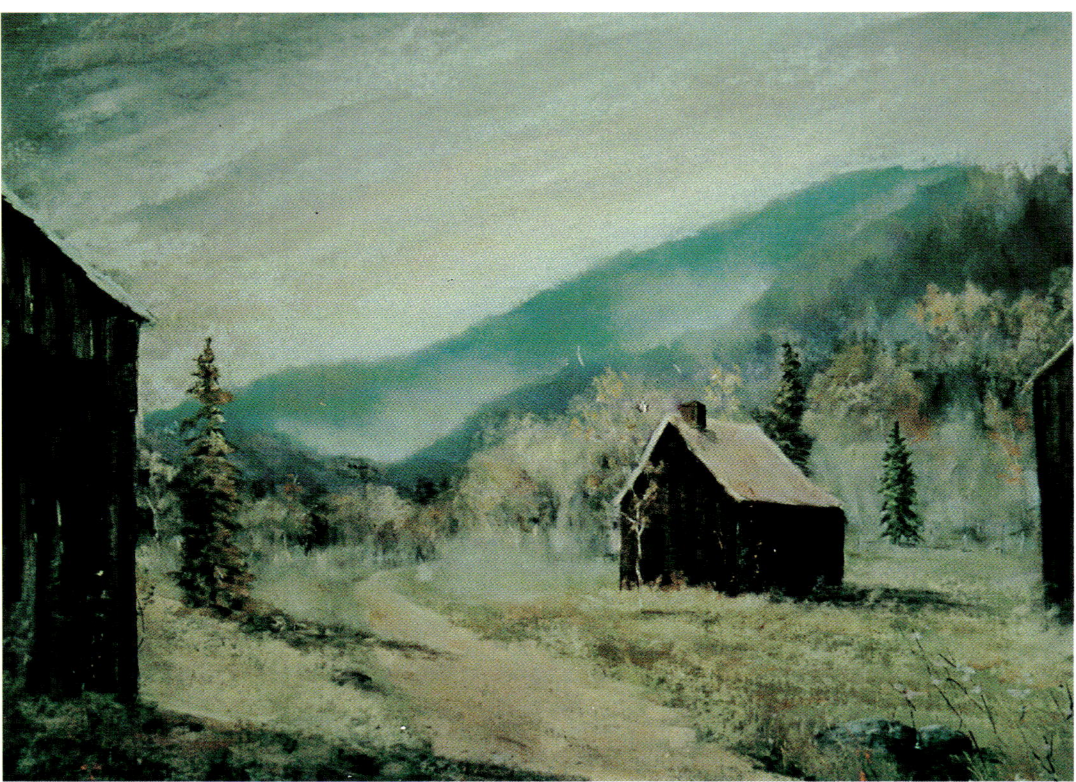

Le Petite Ferme

14" x 18"
Canson Mi-Teintes

Dick Griffin

No matter how small someone's piece of country is it's just what he needs.

Cache Lake Cabin

18" x 26"
Pastel paper

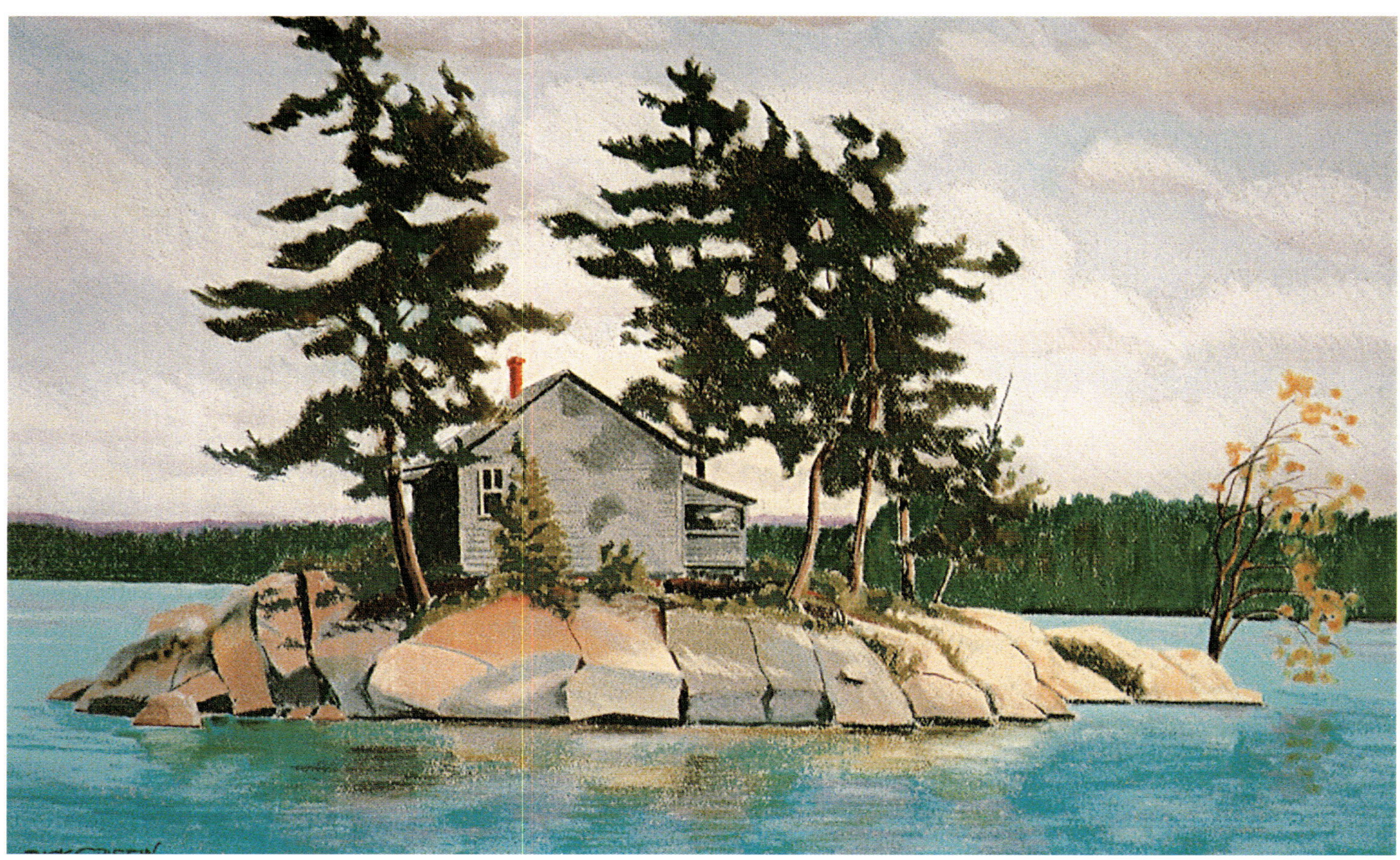

Eileen Armstrong

I love painting and have been working in pastels for many years. My goal has been fairly consistent: to create painterly images, good strong contrasts and to continue challenging myself to improve my work. My application of pastels is very loose and light in the early stages. I consider it a form of scribbling.

Mountain Stream

22" x 28"
Sandpaper board

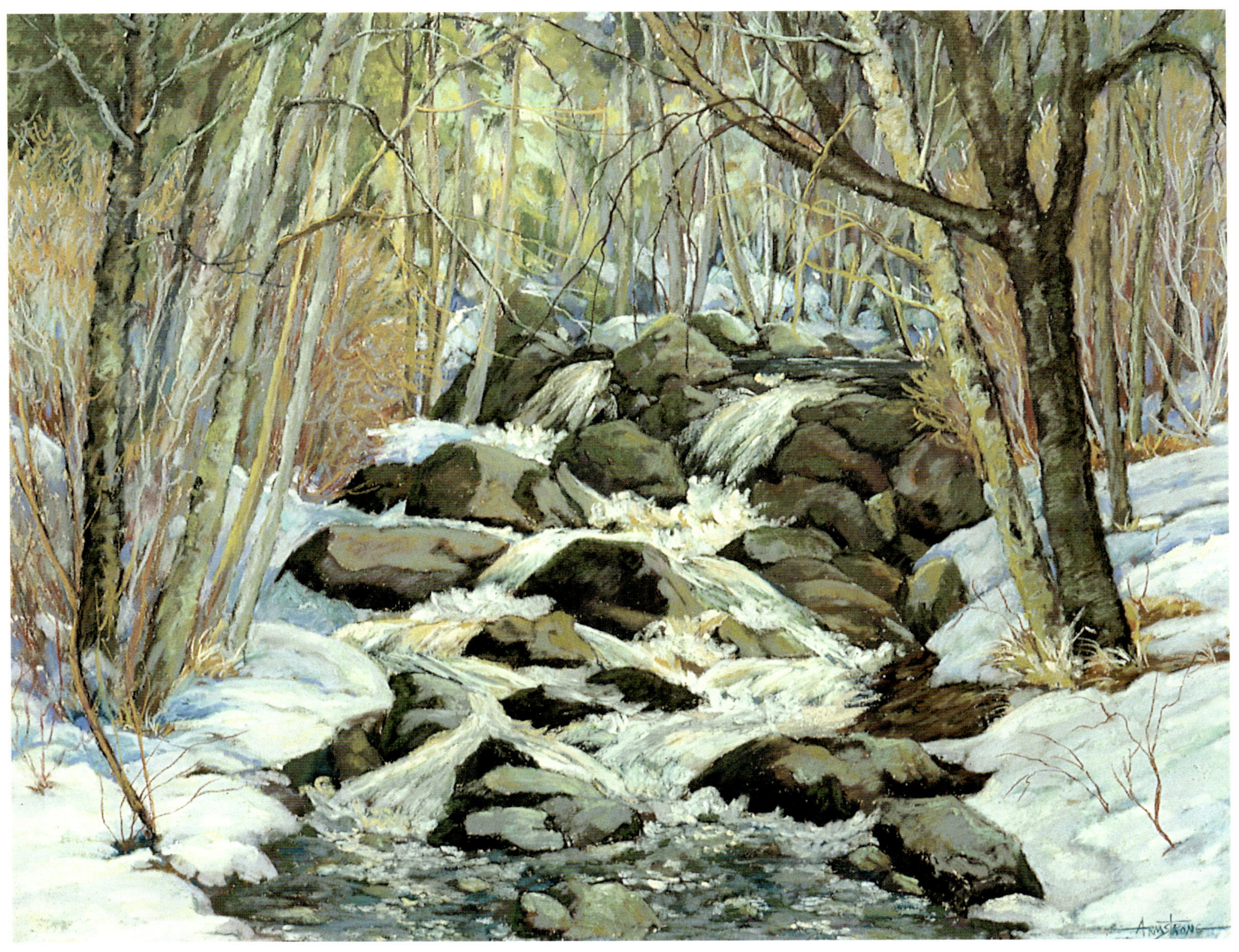

Lois McKercher

On the way back from our cottage, this light stopped me in my tracks. I took several snapshots and made copious notes of values and quality of light. Back in my studio, I painted this remarkable scene on a sheet of deep violet-blue paper.

Sundown on Stagecoach Road

14" x 21"
Canson Mi-Teintes (deep violet-blue)

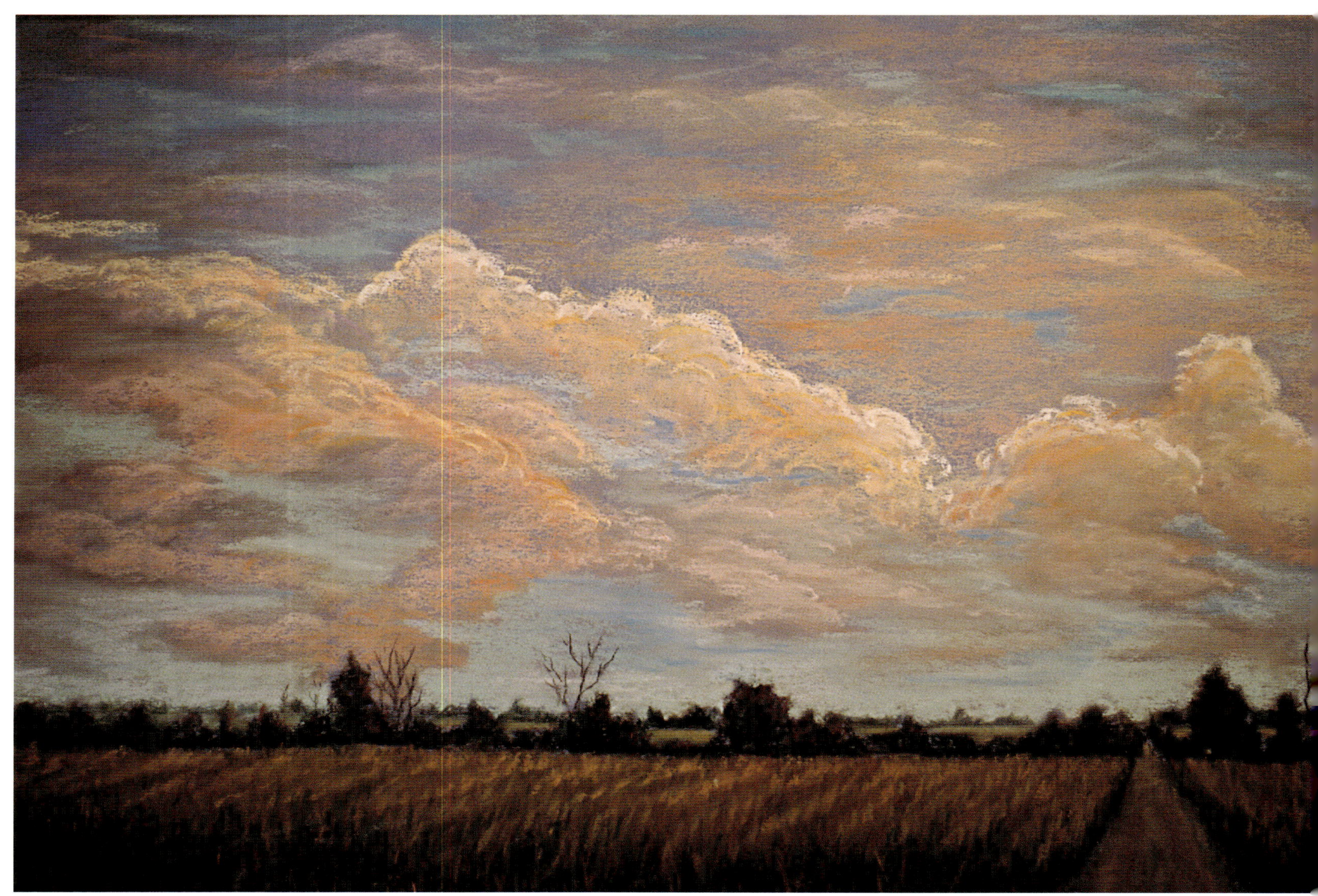

Albertina Steinbock

I start my paintings with NuPastel or pastel pencils. After defining the basic shapes I apply crosshatching strokes of medium soft pastels and then enhance the painting at the end with finishing strokes of soft pastels. Most of my paintings are done on Canson Mi-Teintes paper, which is available in many colors. I prefer middle tones. I also use Arches 300 lb. watercolor paper that has been sealed with marble dust.

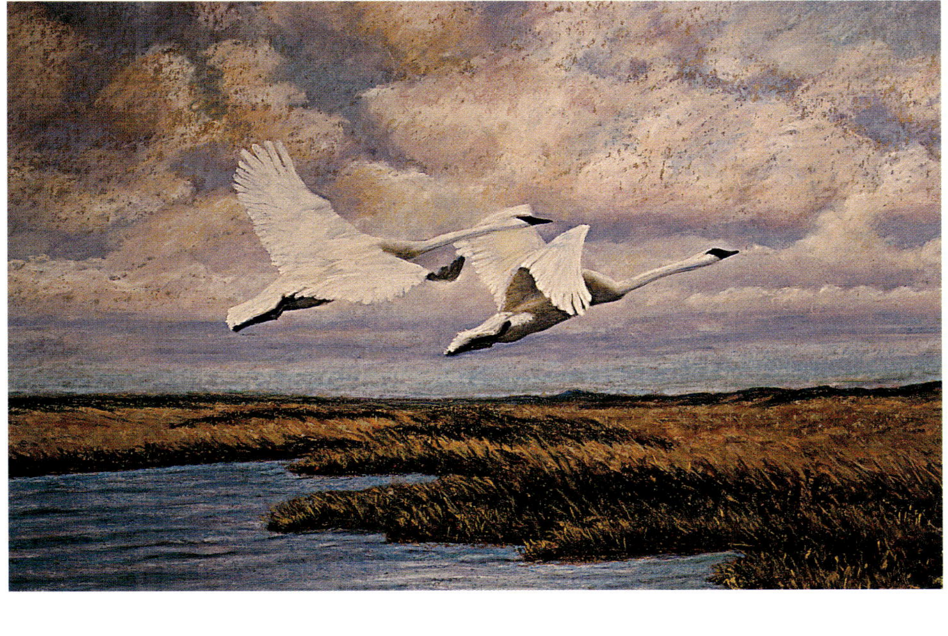

Trumpeter Swans Airborne

20" x 24"
Sanded paper

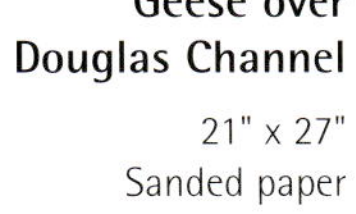

Geese over Douglas Channel

21" x 27"
Sanded paper

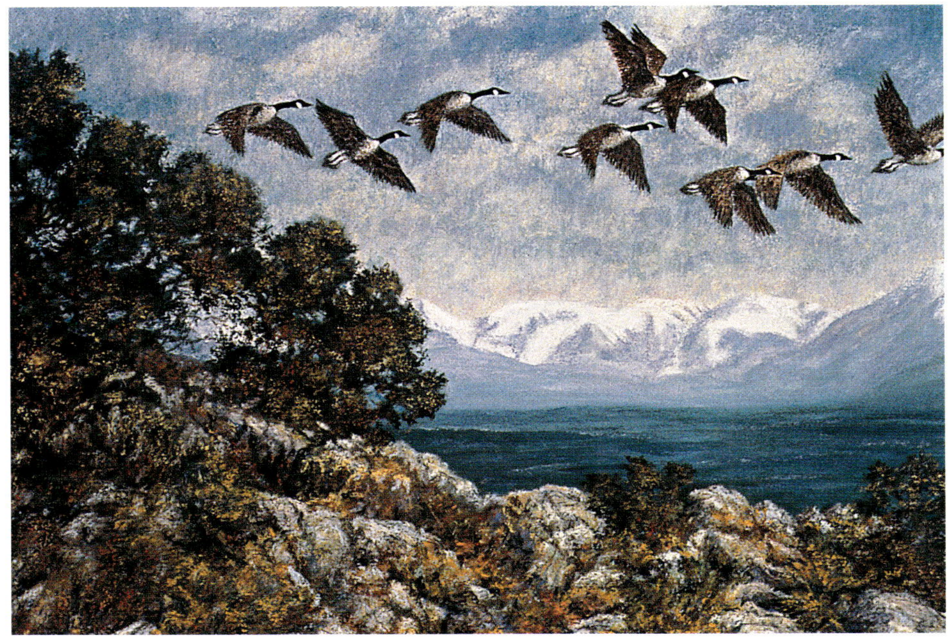

PORTRAITS

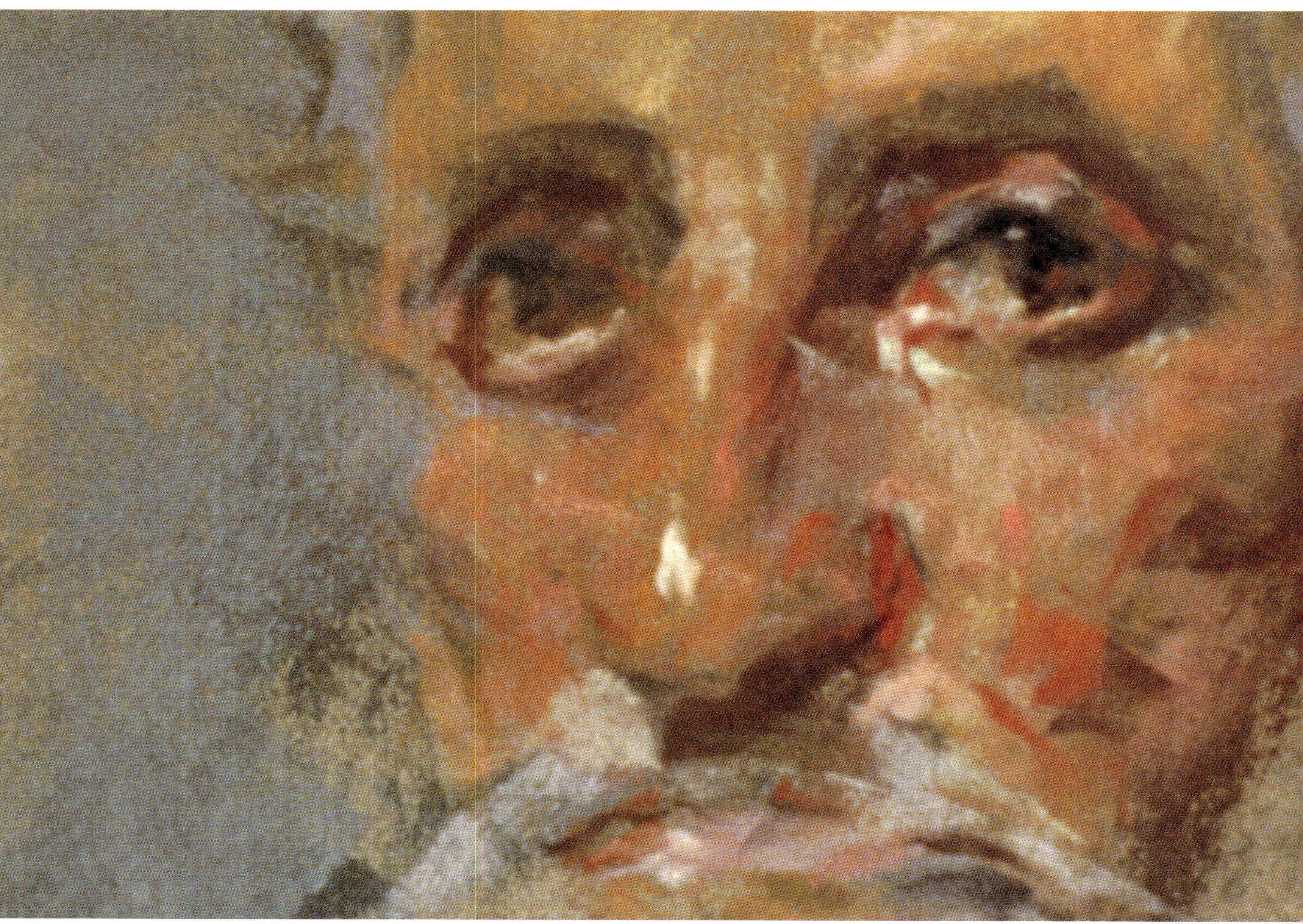

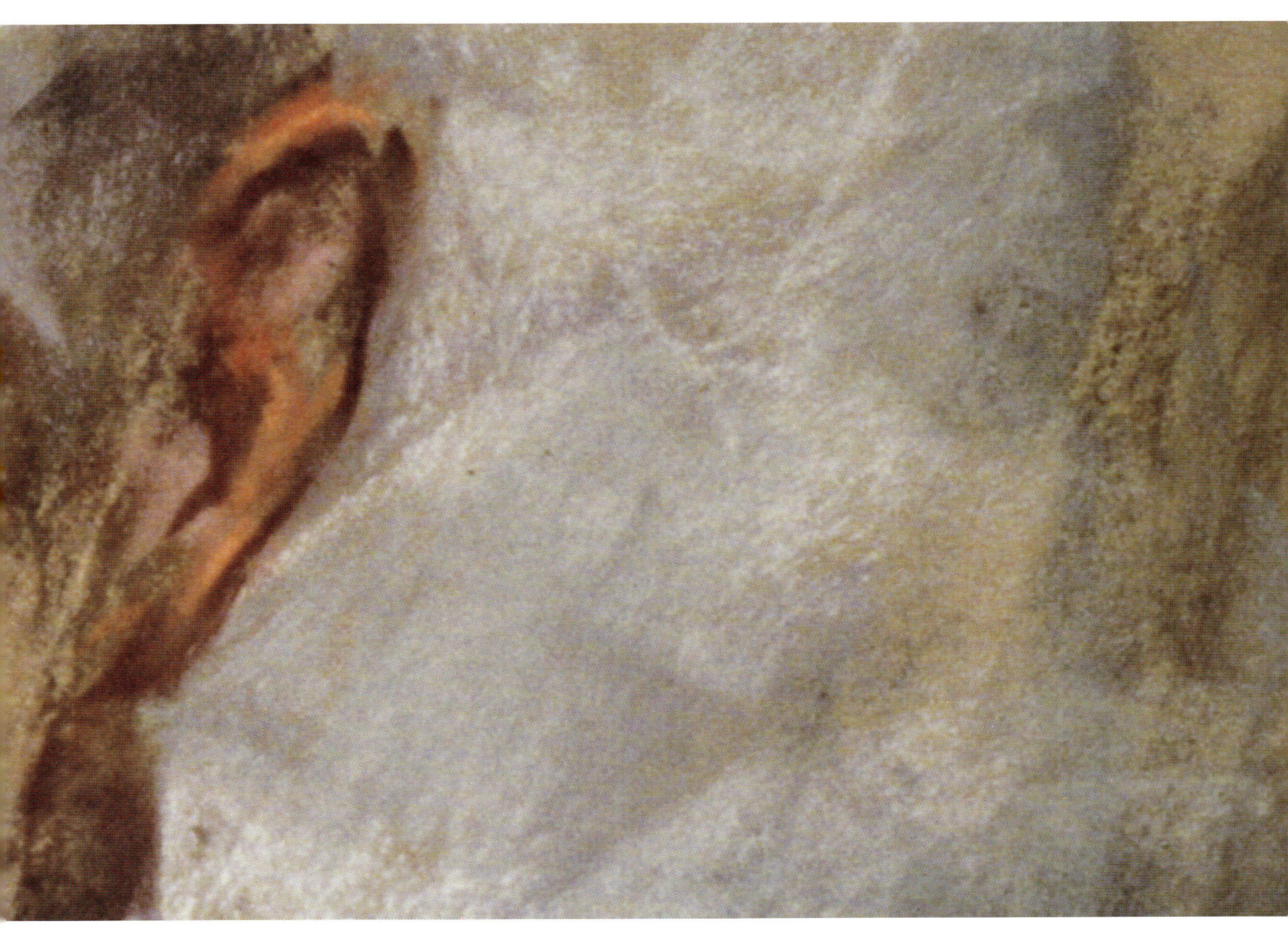

Dorothy Oxborough

I am an impressionist and most of my works are vignettes, which fascinate me in any medium. Since my paper shades are neutral colors, I can fade the subject out into the background. I also enjoy dark papers upon which I apply pastel only to where the light hits the subject and enough background to allow the viewers' eyes to complete the picture. My papers are velour for animals (and the only one I spray), Canson rough side and Sennelier La Carte. This is a beautiful paper with a seemingly endless bite. I sketch out the subject lightly with a neutral Conte, indicating the different planes of the face and where the light and shadows hit and fall. I work in the midtones, the highlights, the undertones, reflected lights. My highlights are last.

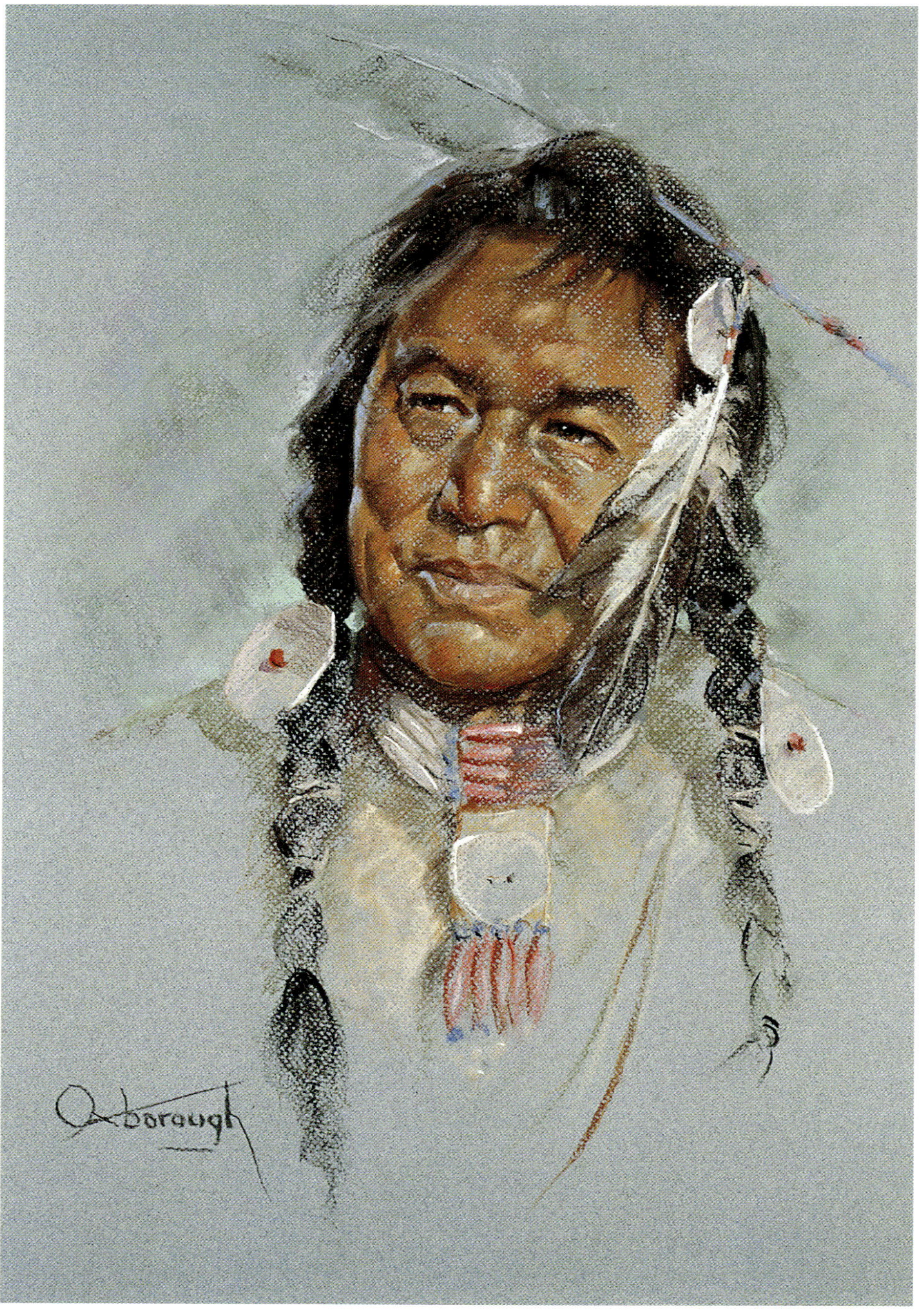

Walter
19" x 26"
Canson Mi-Teintes

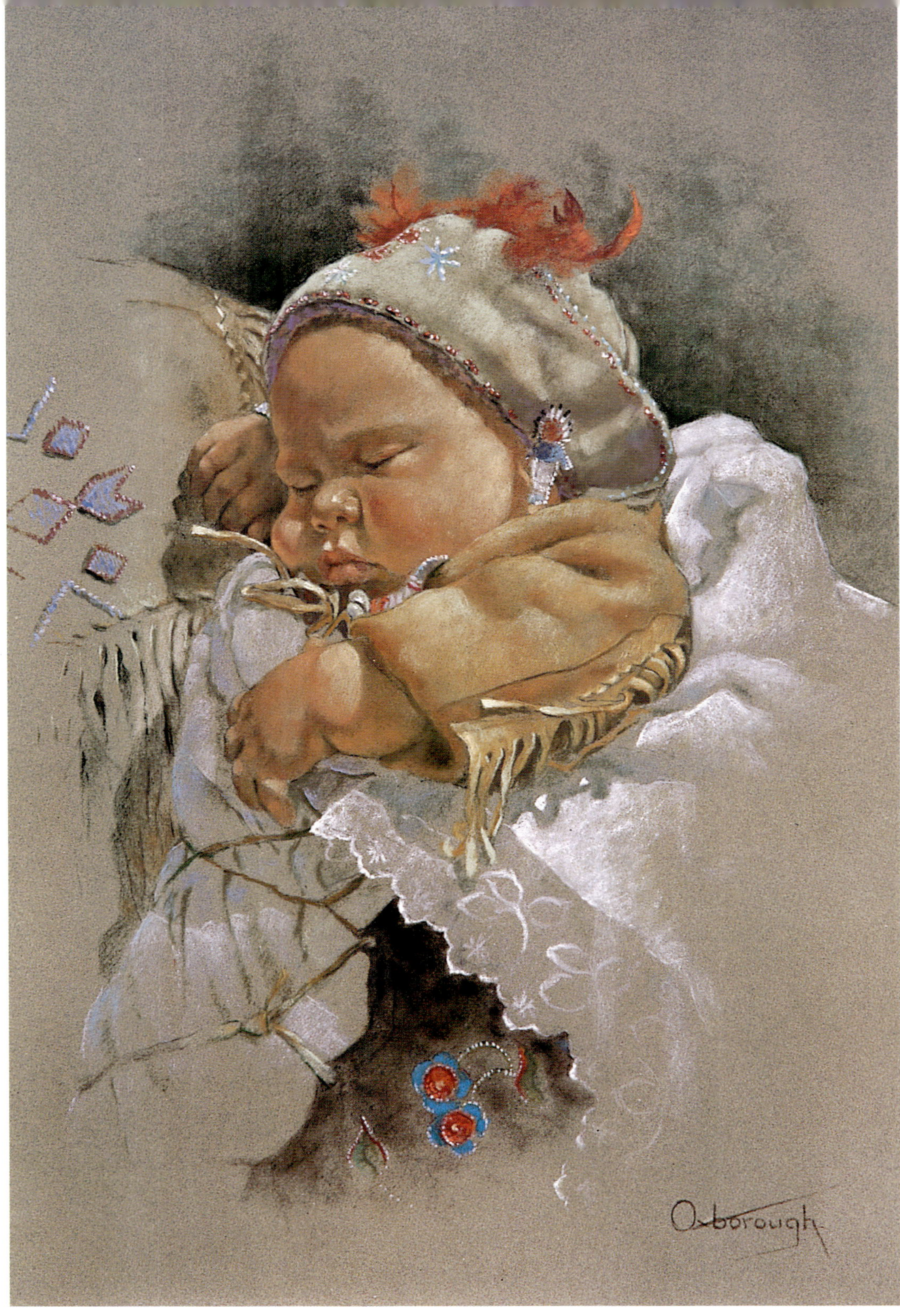

Buckskin and Lace

19" x 26"
Canson Mi-Teintes

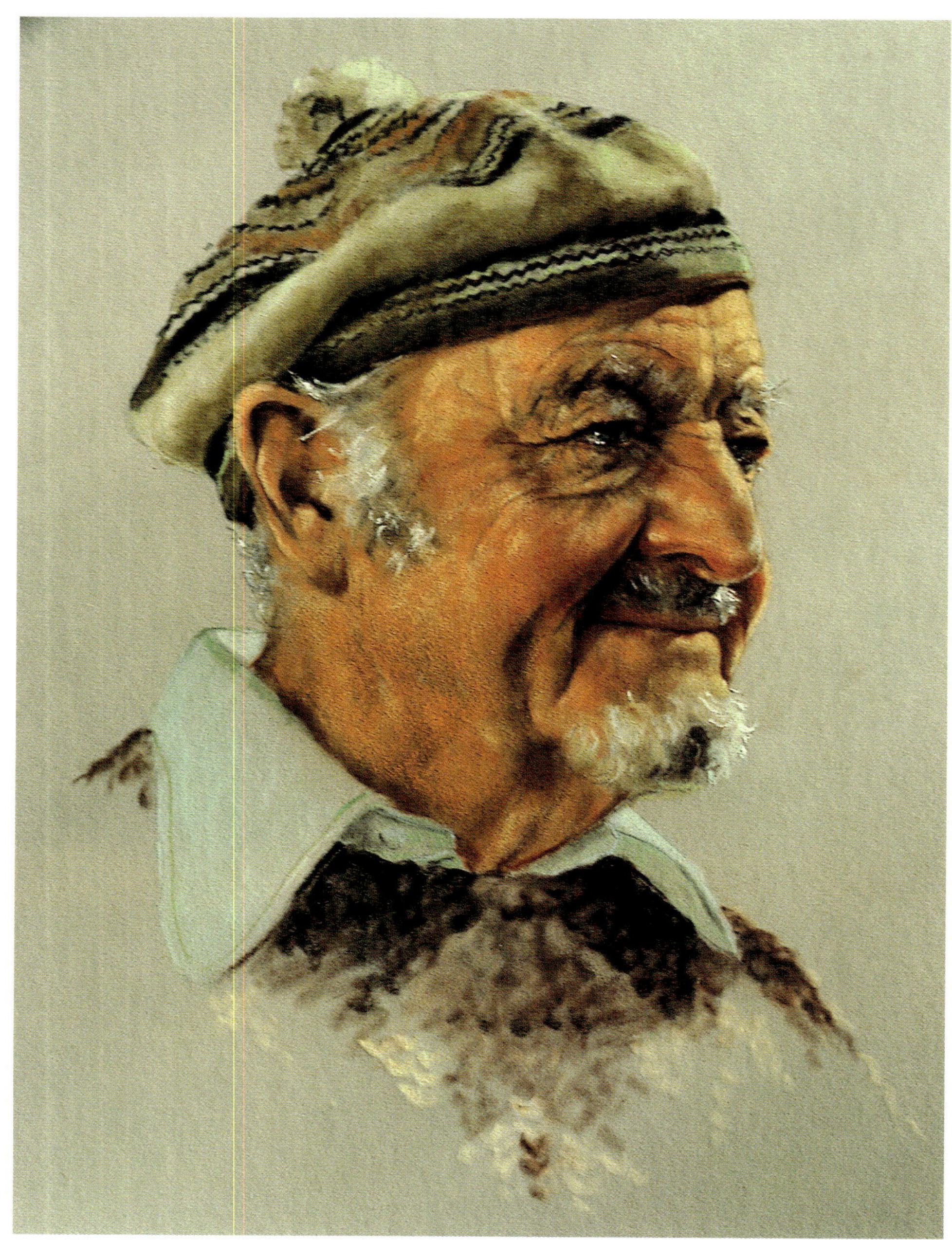

Dorothy Oxborough

Ned

19" x 26"
Canson Mi-Teintes

Mireille Collet

The background is worked first so that it is easier to get a good idea of how the subject matter is progressing. Strokes of pastel are applied and then blended slightly with finger to create a smooth vibrant surface of uninterrupted color.

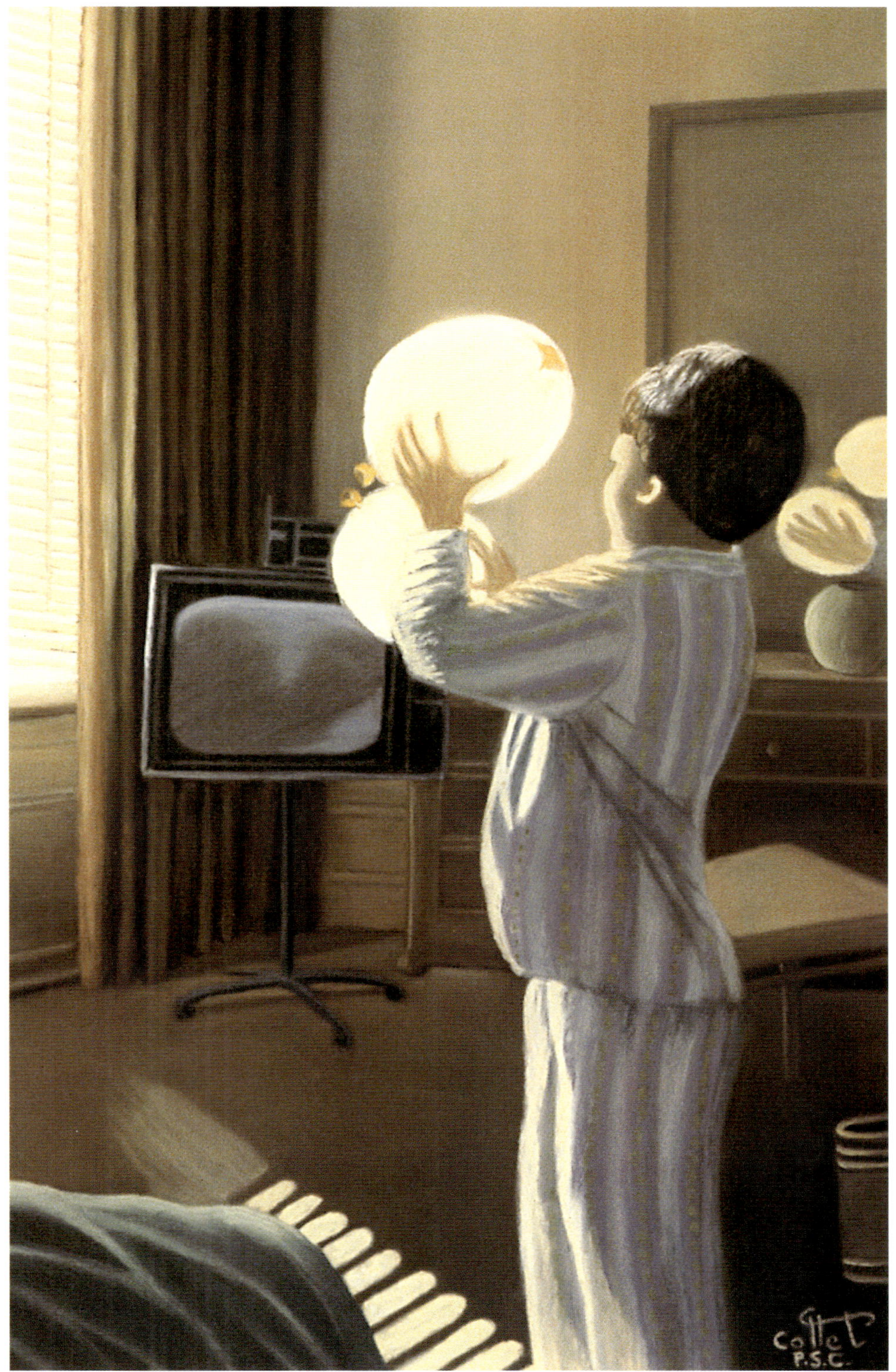

Christian

12" x 19"
Brown Sennelier sandpaper

Marilyn Ranco

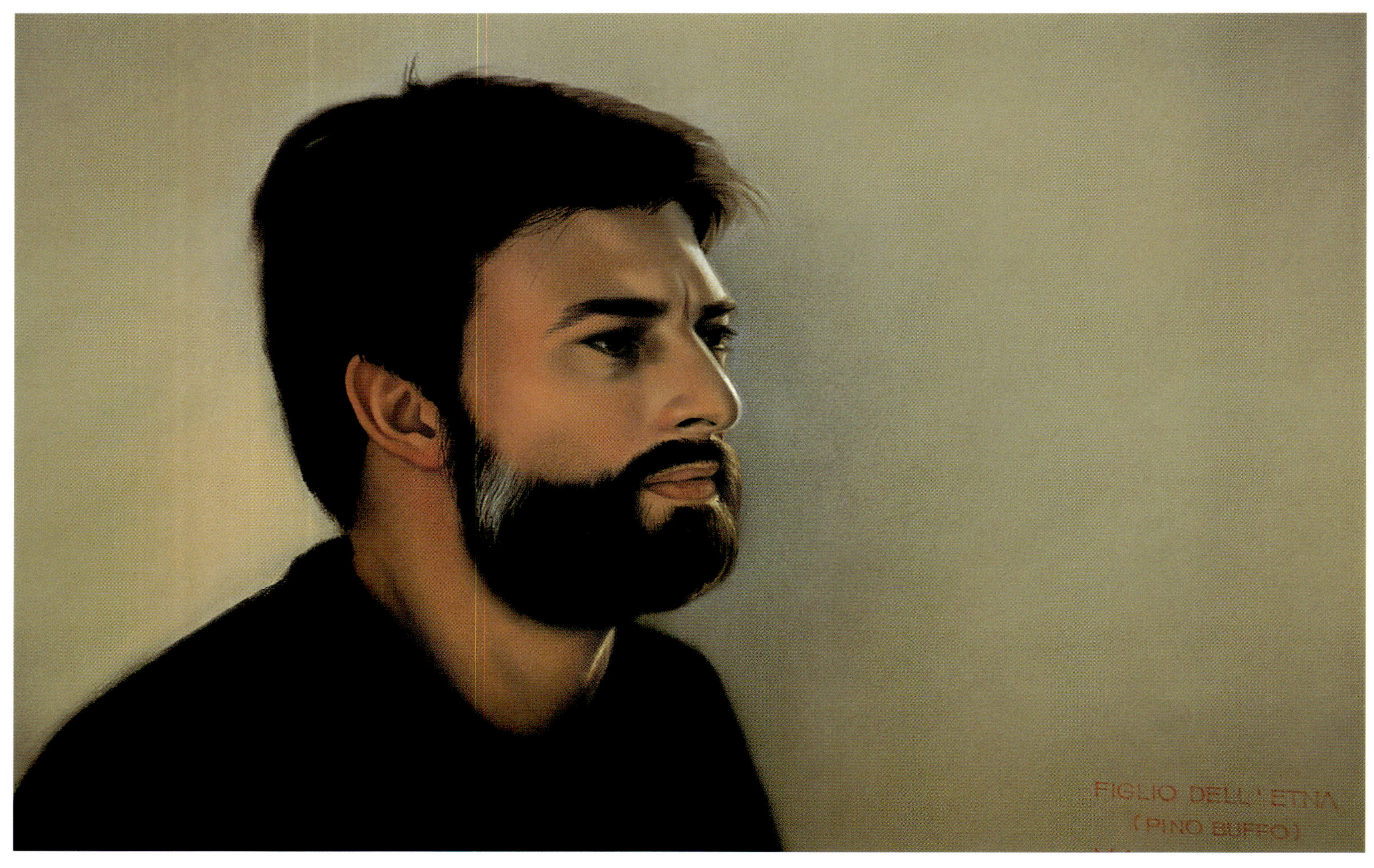

Figlio dell'Etna
(Son of Etna)

13"× 16 ¾"
Canson Mi-Teintes

Rene St. Jean

I use Rembrandt pastels exclusively. I like their texture; they are not as hard as others. I sometimes put color on a sheet of paper and apply it with my fingers to soften a cheek when I do a portrait or other parts of one. Although I also paint landscape, still life and abstract, I always come back to painting portraits.

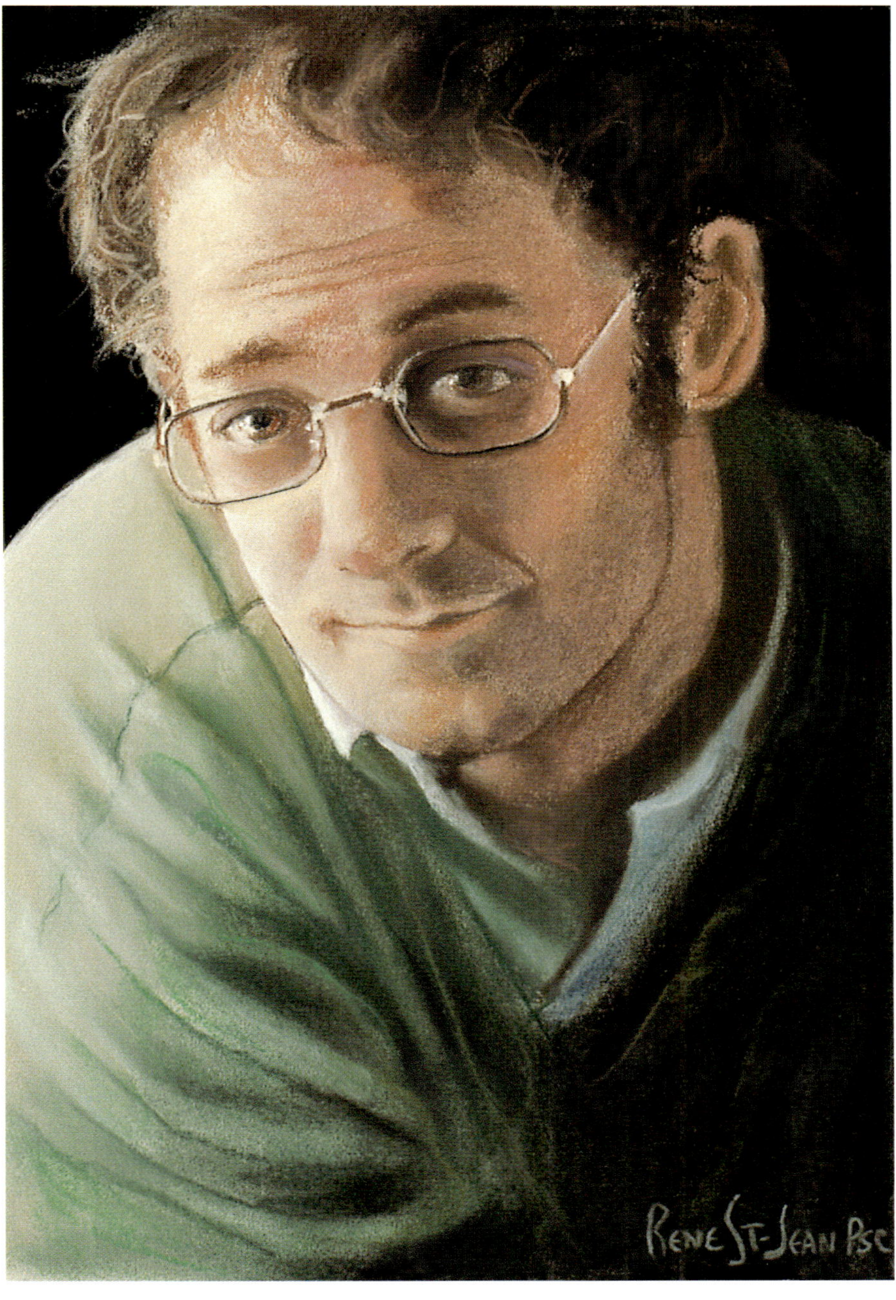

Vincent
14" x 20"
Pastel paper

Anita E. Kertzer

River Boat Gambler

19" x 25"
Pastel paper

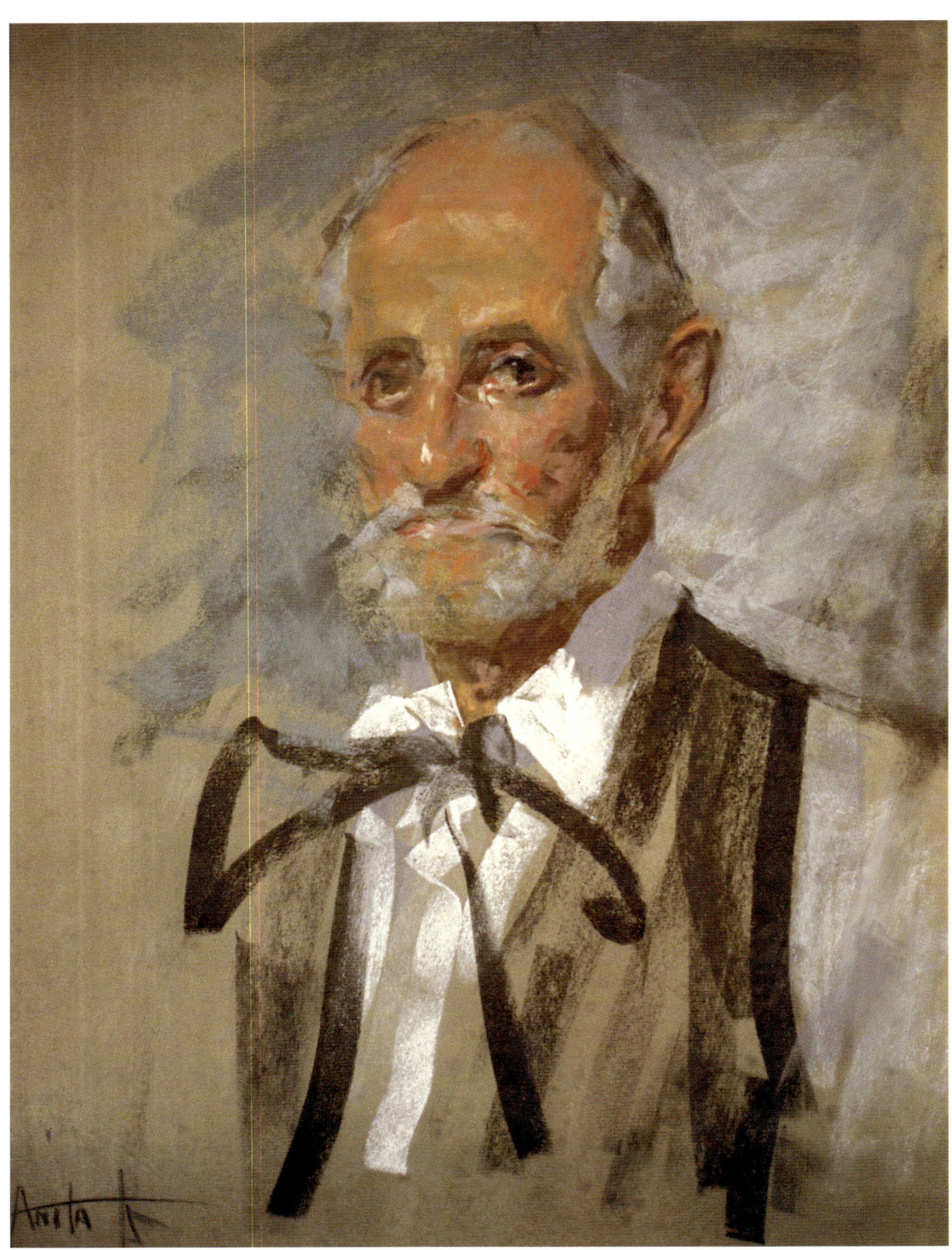

Warrior in Gray

19" x 25"
Pastel paper

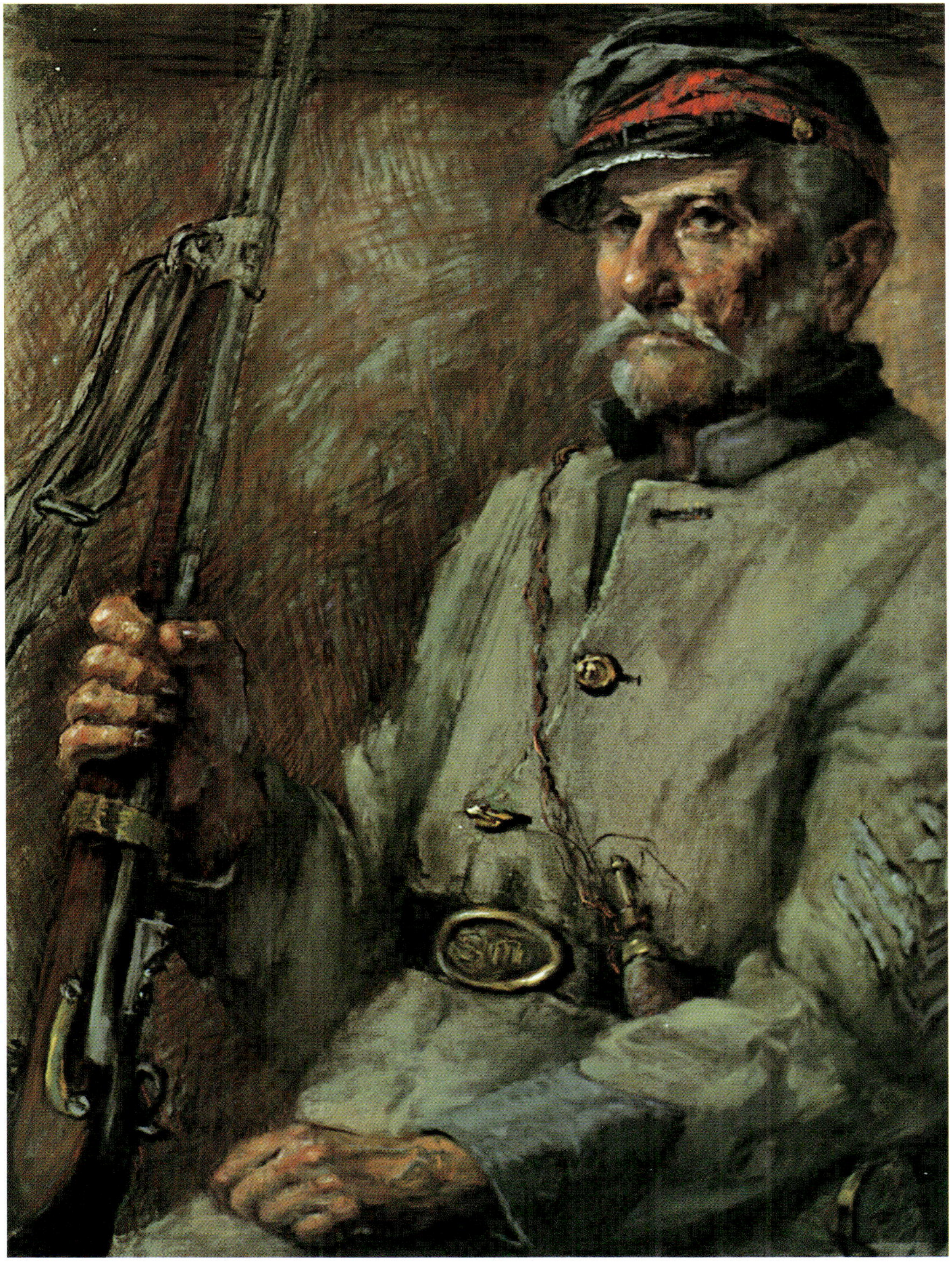

Pierre Petel

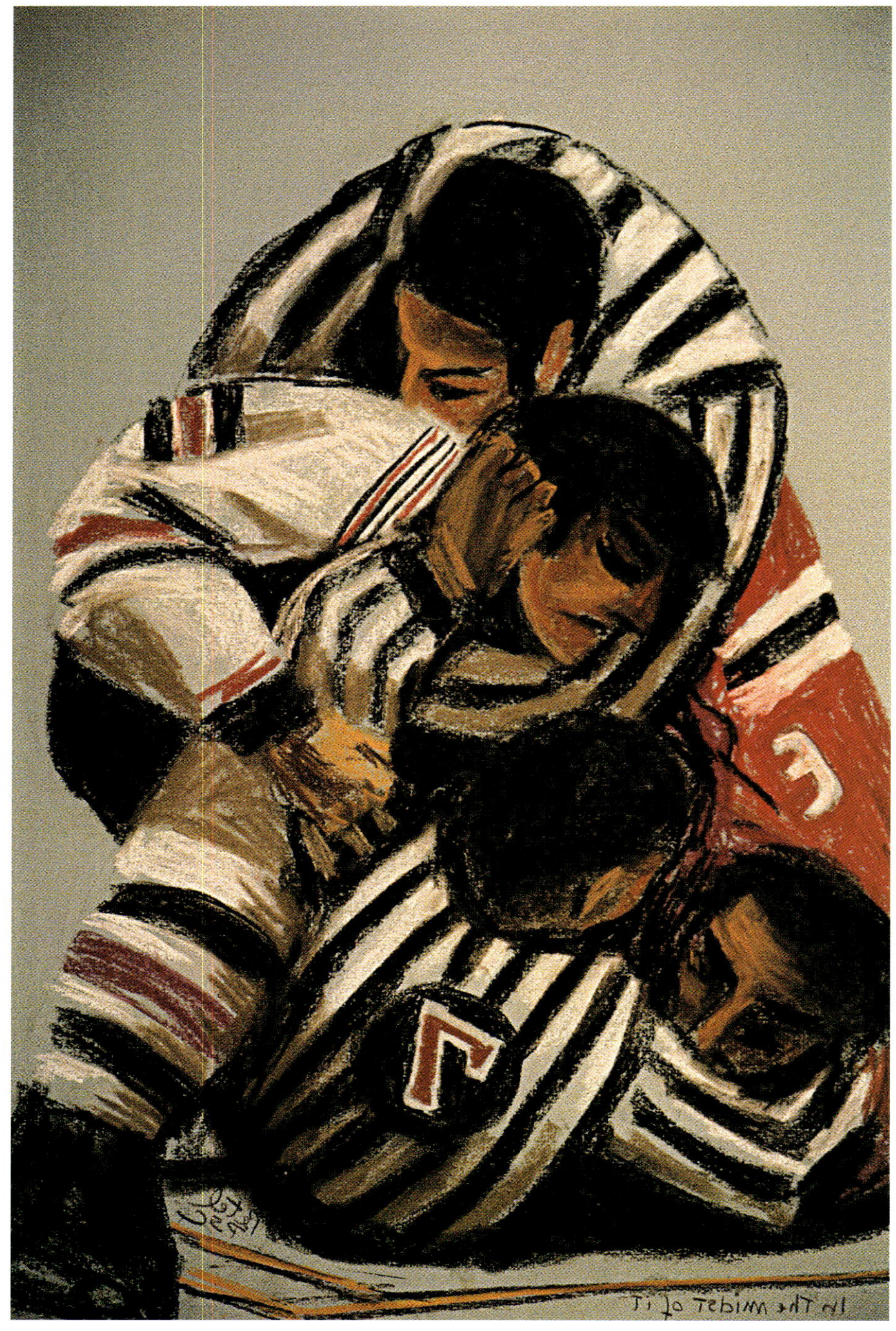

Hockey Pretzel
24" x 30"
Pastel paper

Barbara Elmslie

Shooting the Breeze

14" x 20"
Canson Mi-Teintes (burgundy)

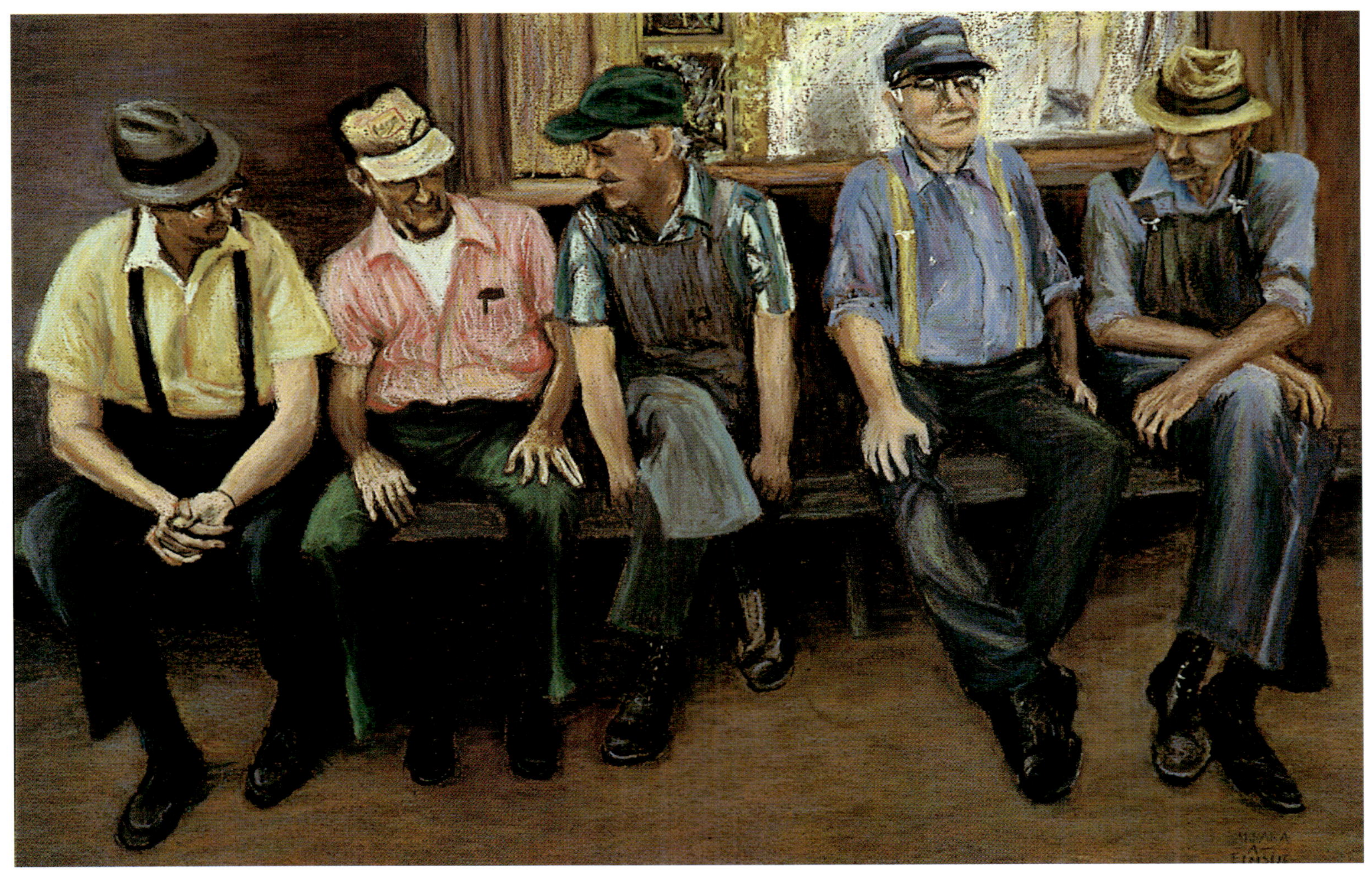

George Balcan

Taken from a sketch and photos of a woman making fritters in Brazil. Her costume tells us she's from the northern part of the country.

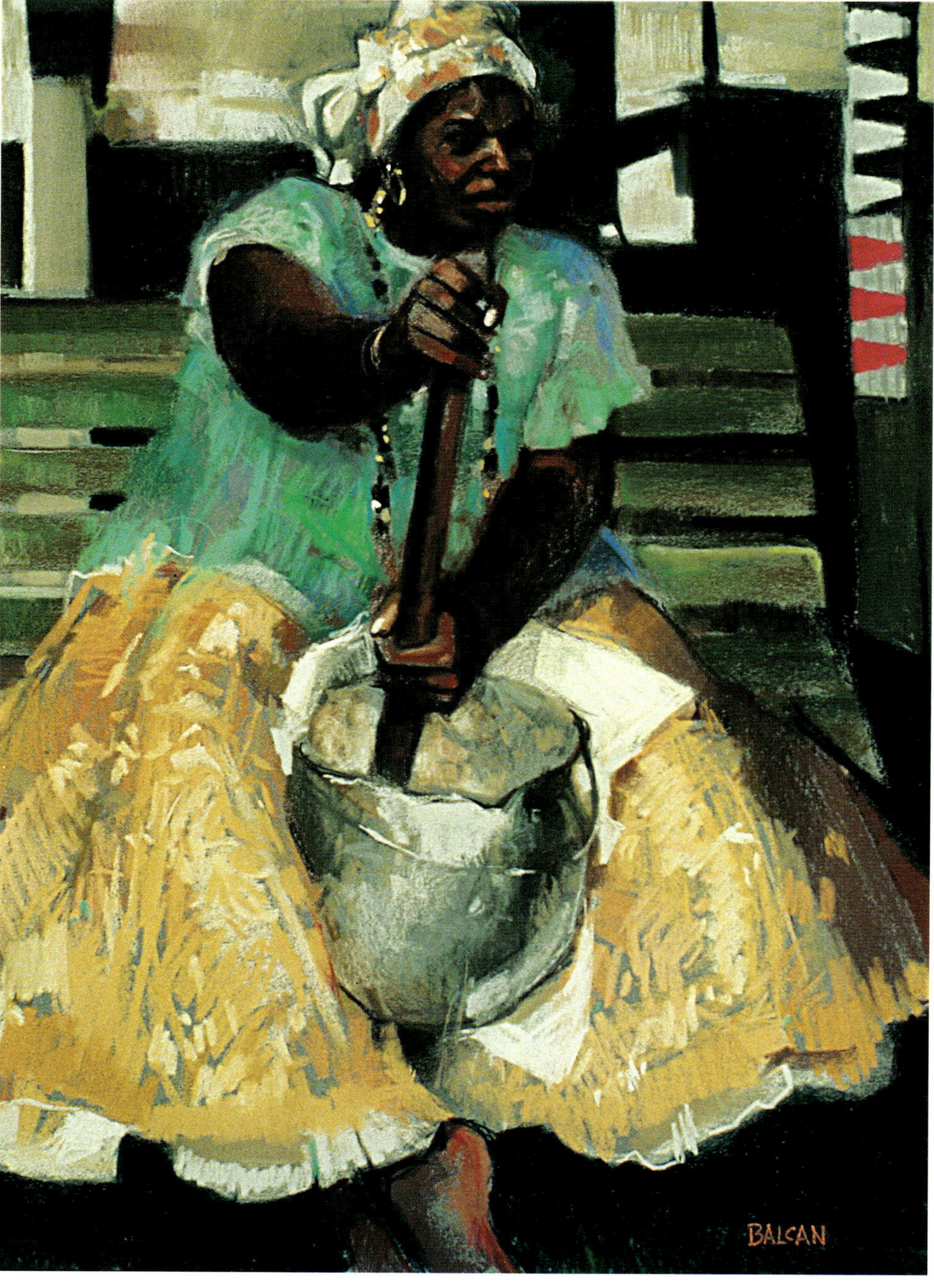

Sao Paulo Market

21" x 29"
Pastel paper

Eileen Armstrong

Angelita and Her Dolls

22" x 28"
Sandpaper board

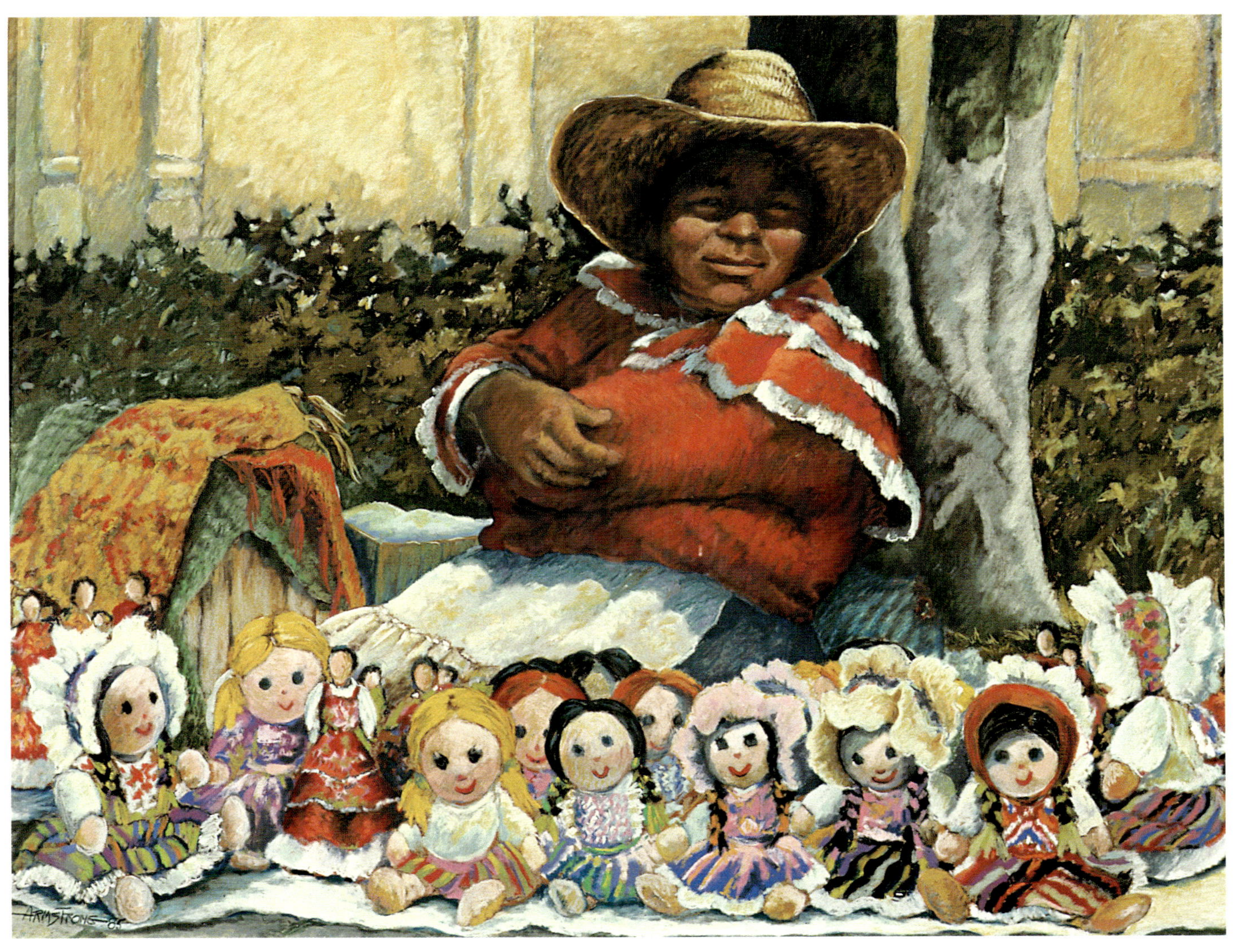

Max Stiebel

Metroglide

25" x 36"
Pastel paper

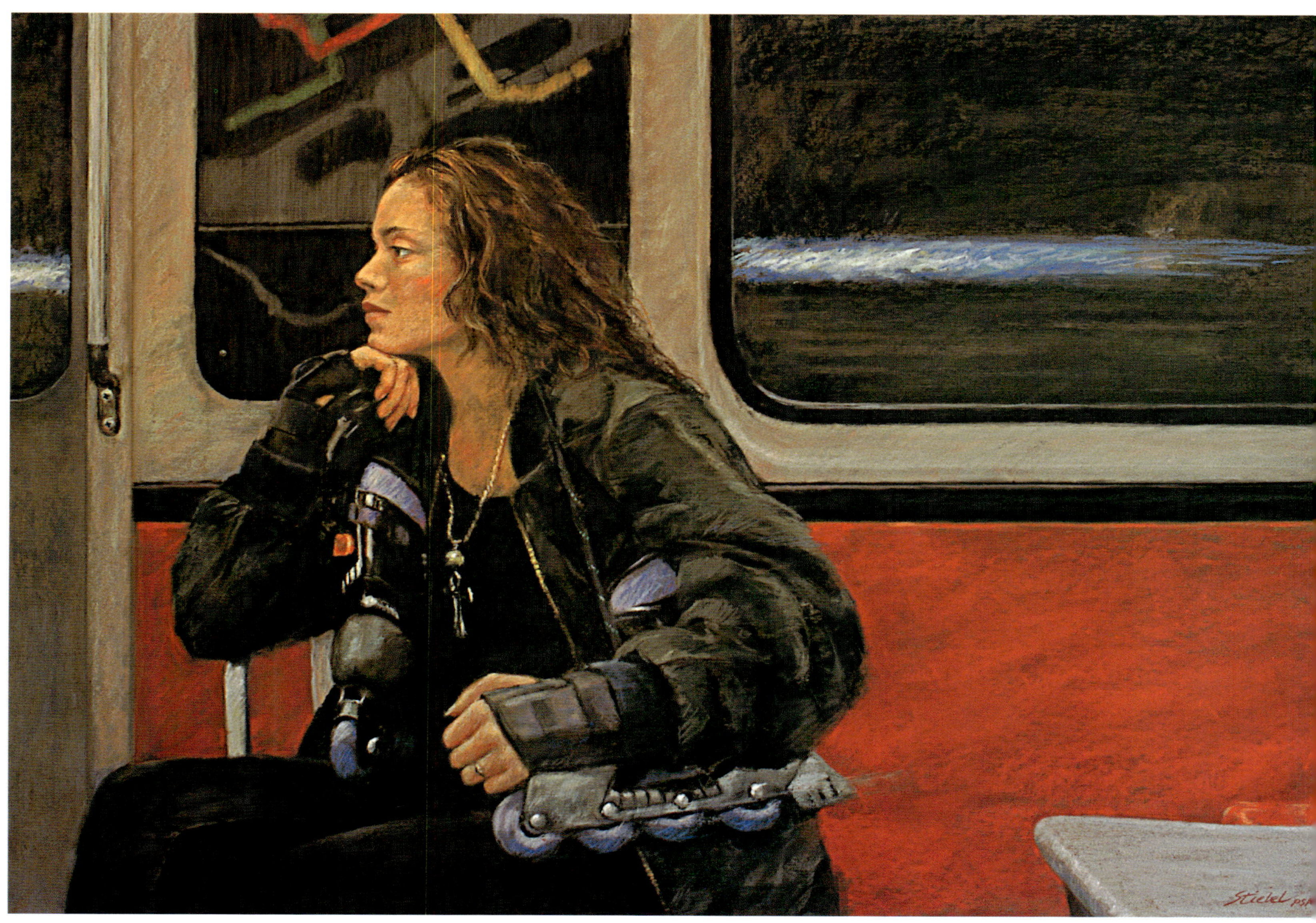

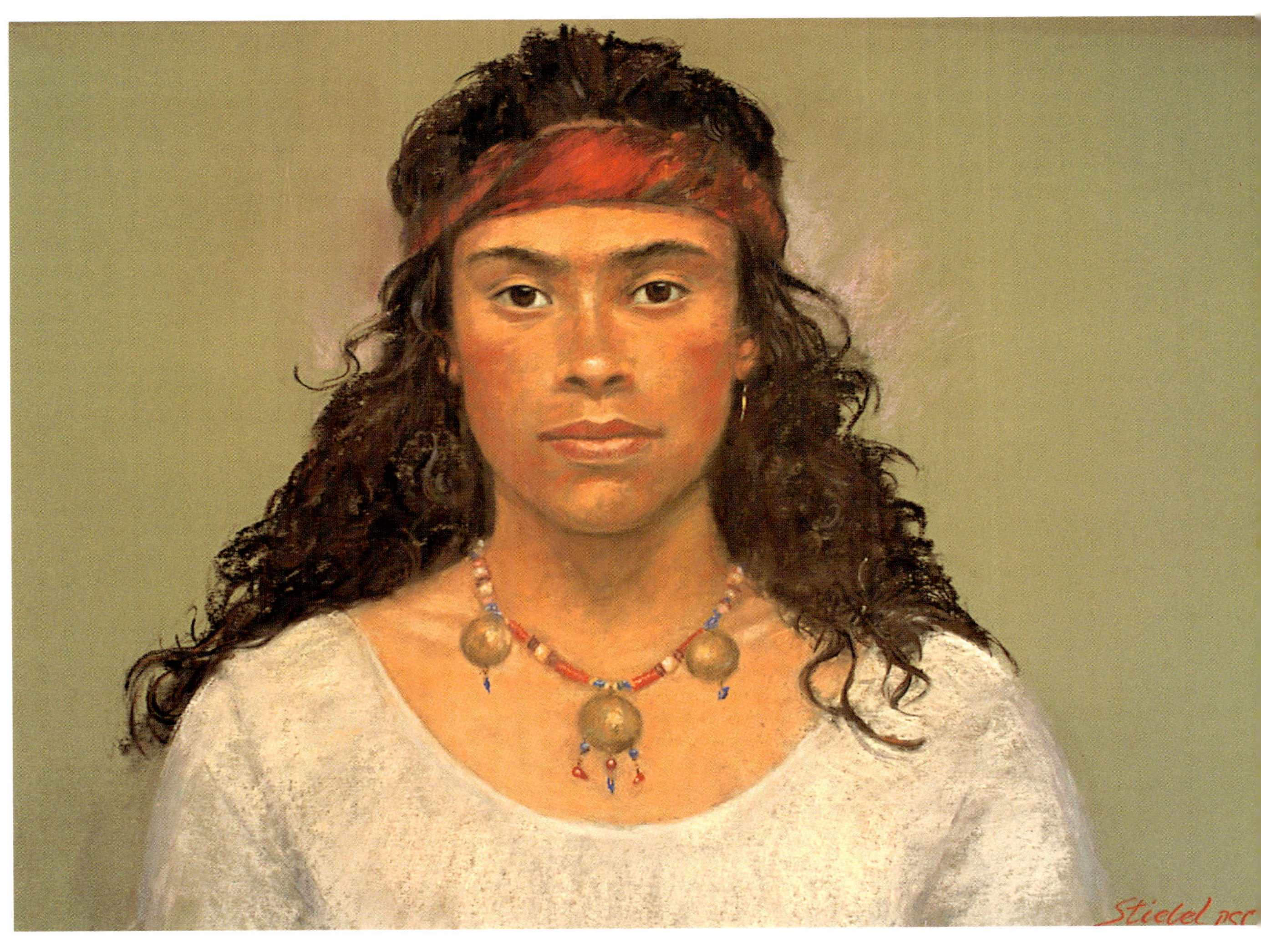

M.J. Head-On

19" x 26"
Canson Mi-Teintes

Max Stiebel

Gay

16" x 23"
Canson Mi-Teintes

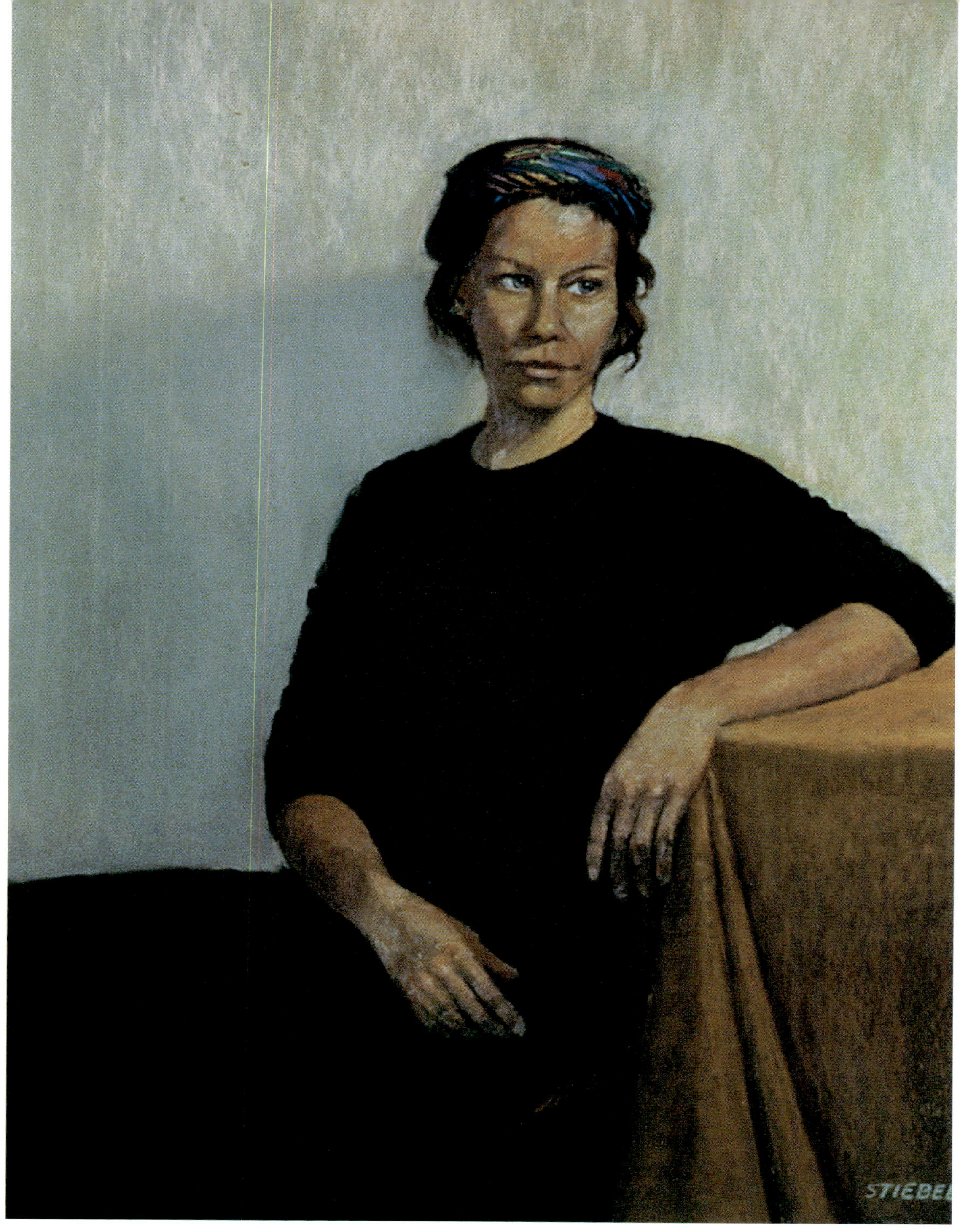

Jeanette McClelland

I use 32 colors of pastels sticks. This includes black and white. My experience is using pastels in a way that one color stroked over another or beside the other achieves the making of the color you need, rather than searching for a wide variety of shades and tints. My very first set of pastels was made by Grumbacher, an introductory assortment. I also love the soft pastels from Rowney (England) and Sennelier (France). The brand I especially like, and the largest selection for the bulk of my work, is the set that's made in Holland by Rembrandt. In the line of hard pastels, I prefer Conte a Paris, in narrow-hard sticks, and Carb-Othello pastel pencils. I use the hard pastels for initial drawing and refining details.

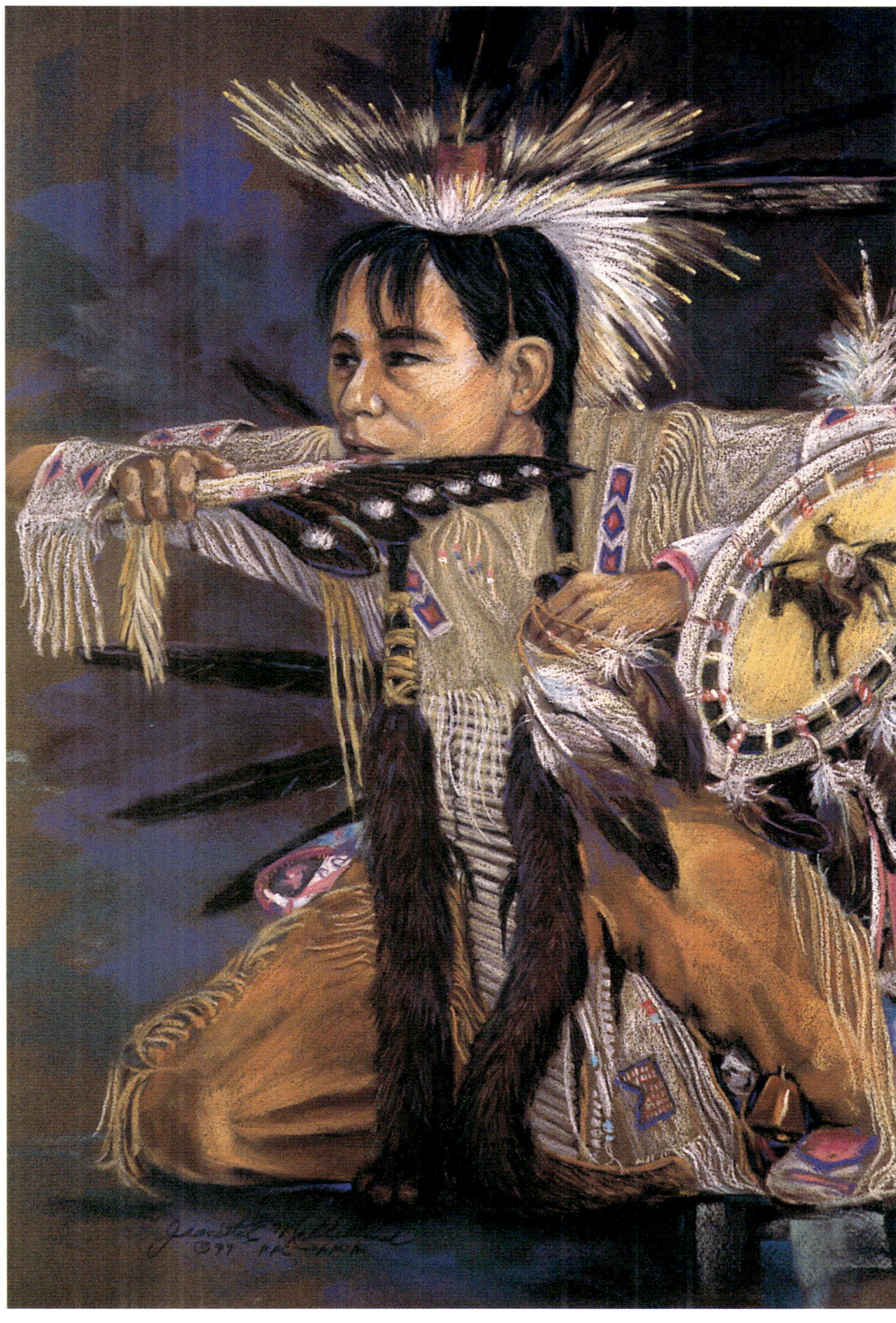

Honoring the Eagle
16" x 24"
Canson Mi-Teintes
(chocolate brown)

Ghada Fasho

I begin a painting with a sketch in pastel pencils, starting with the harder pastels and finishing the painting and details with the softer pastels. I use layers of pastel, blending the colors into the paper (Canson Mi-Teintes) to achieve a three-dimensional image. As I approach the completion of a painting, I blend the colors less and less in order to preserve the pure, vibrant quality of the pastel colors.

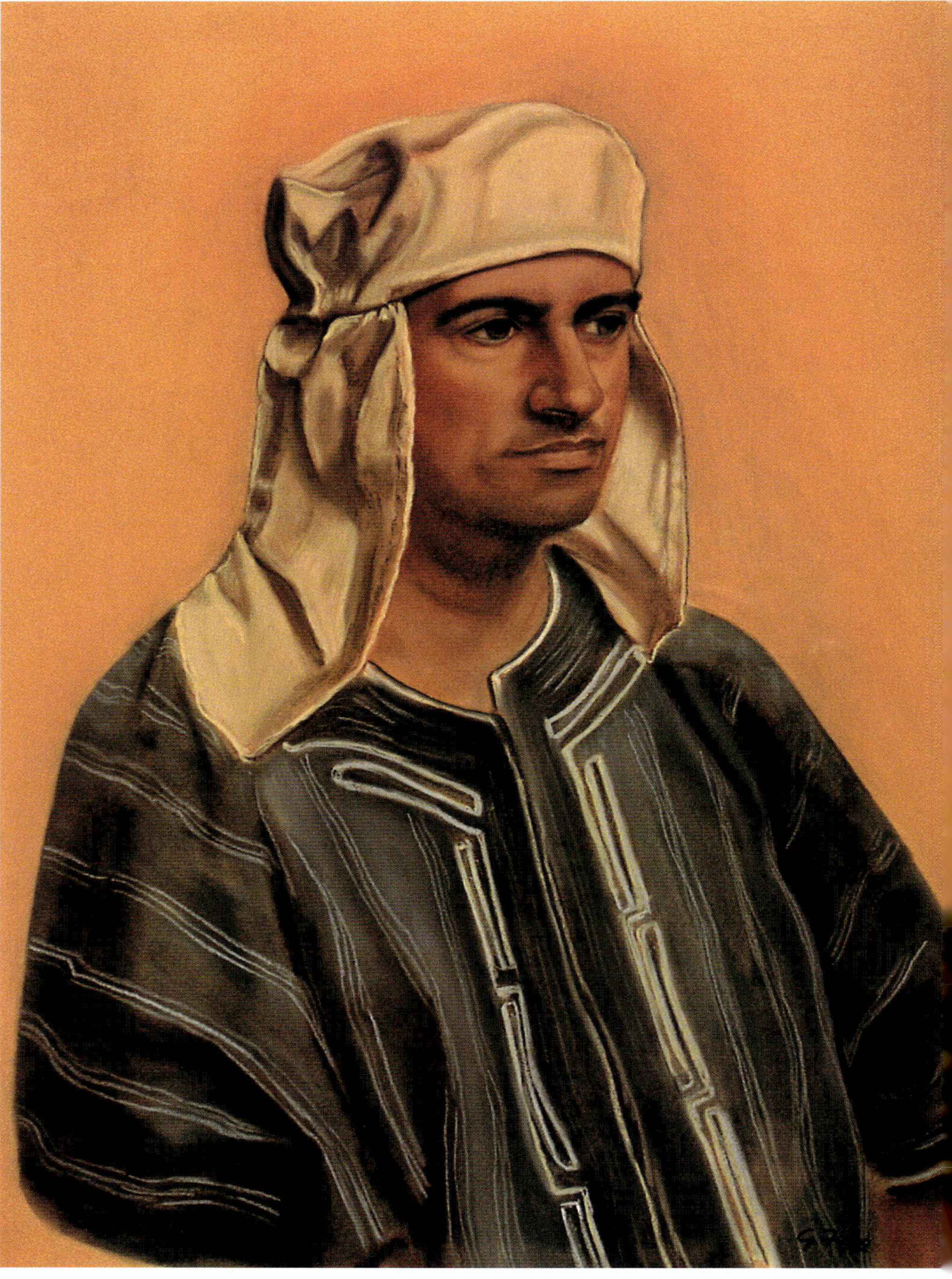

Pharaoh

28 ½" x 34 ½"
Canson Mi-Teintes

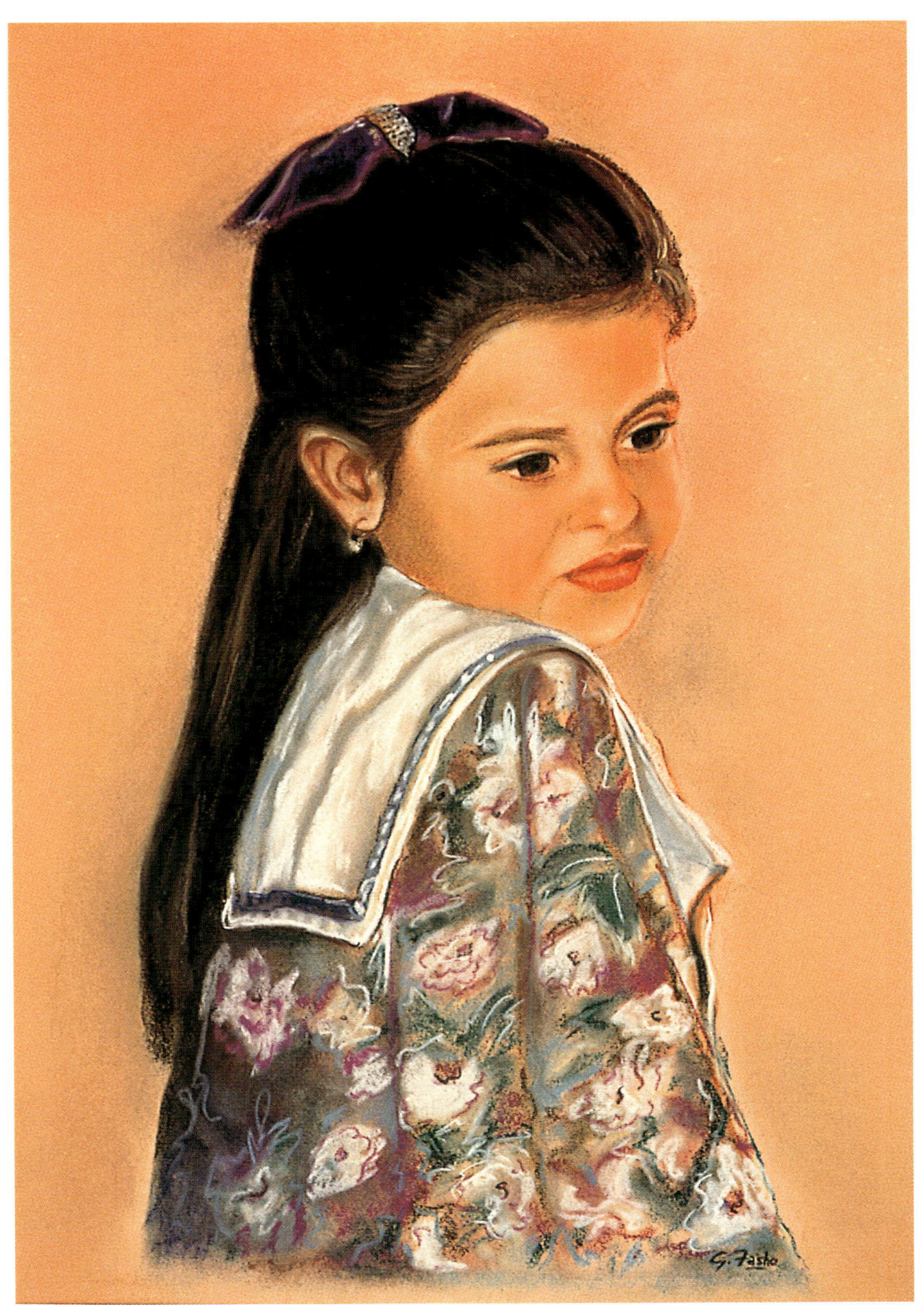

Michele Relaxing

34 ½" x 44 ½"
Pastel paper

Charles Couper

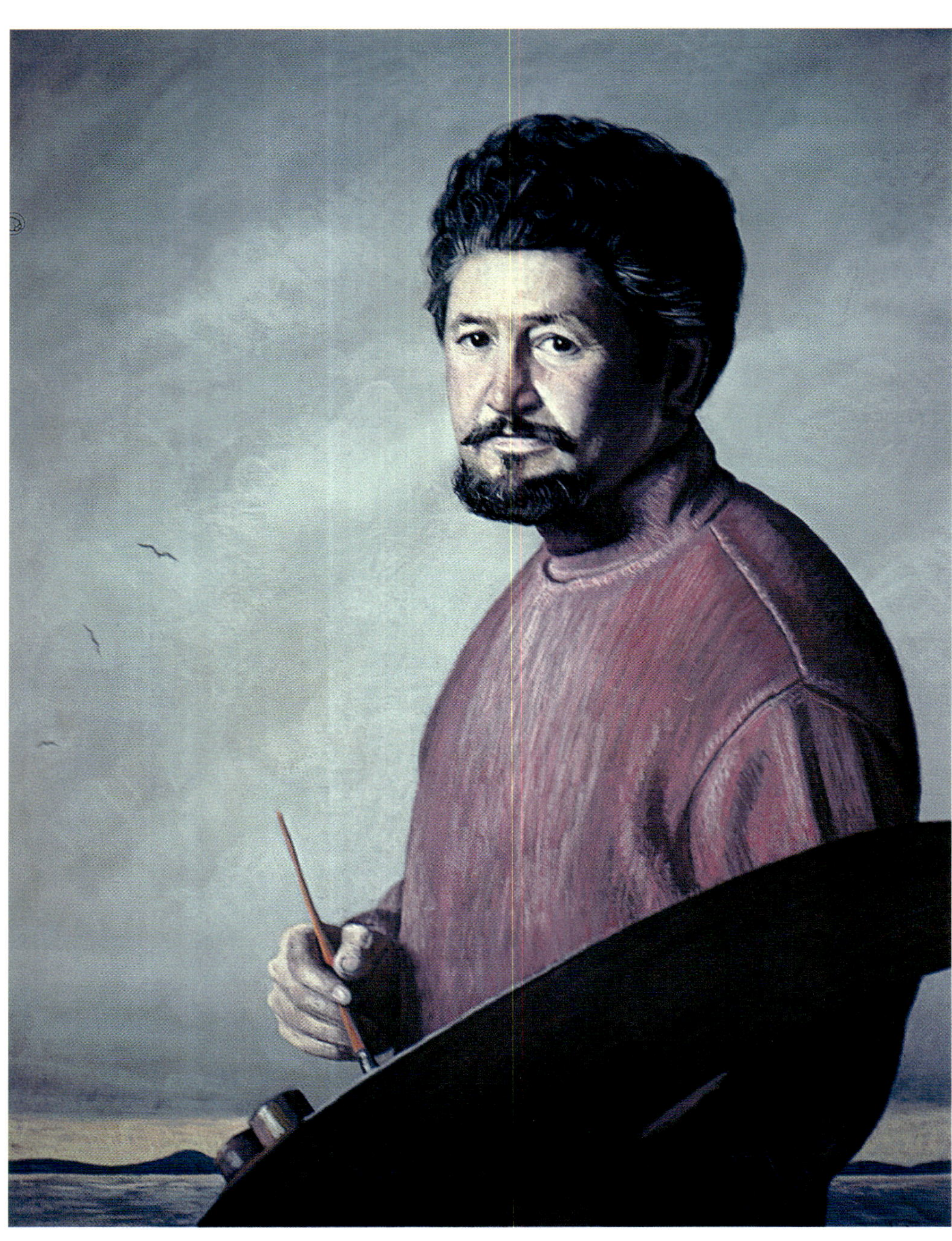

Portrait of an Artist Friend

(Salvatore Del Deo)
24" x 30"
Sandpaper panel

Andrew McDermott

Head of a Fisherman

7 ½" x 8"

Neutral colored pastel paper

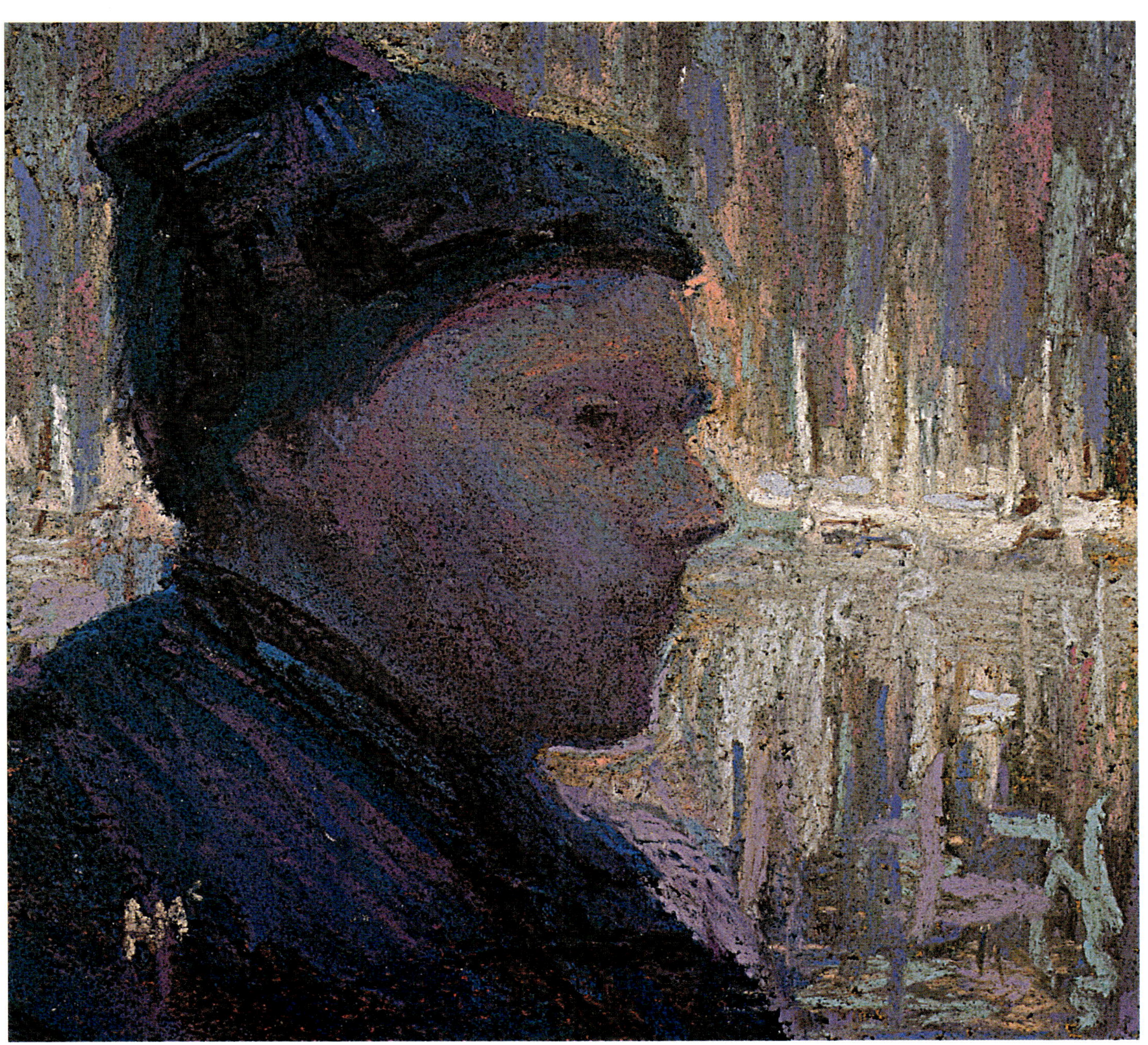

Anne Lemieux

As a figurative painter, I work from live models and/or from photographs. I find that pastel highlights human emotions. For me, painting with pastel is tremendously rewarding because of its spontaneity, sensuality and clear freshness.

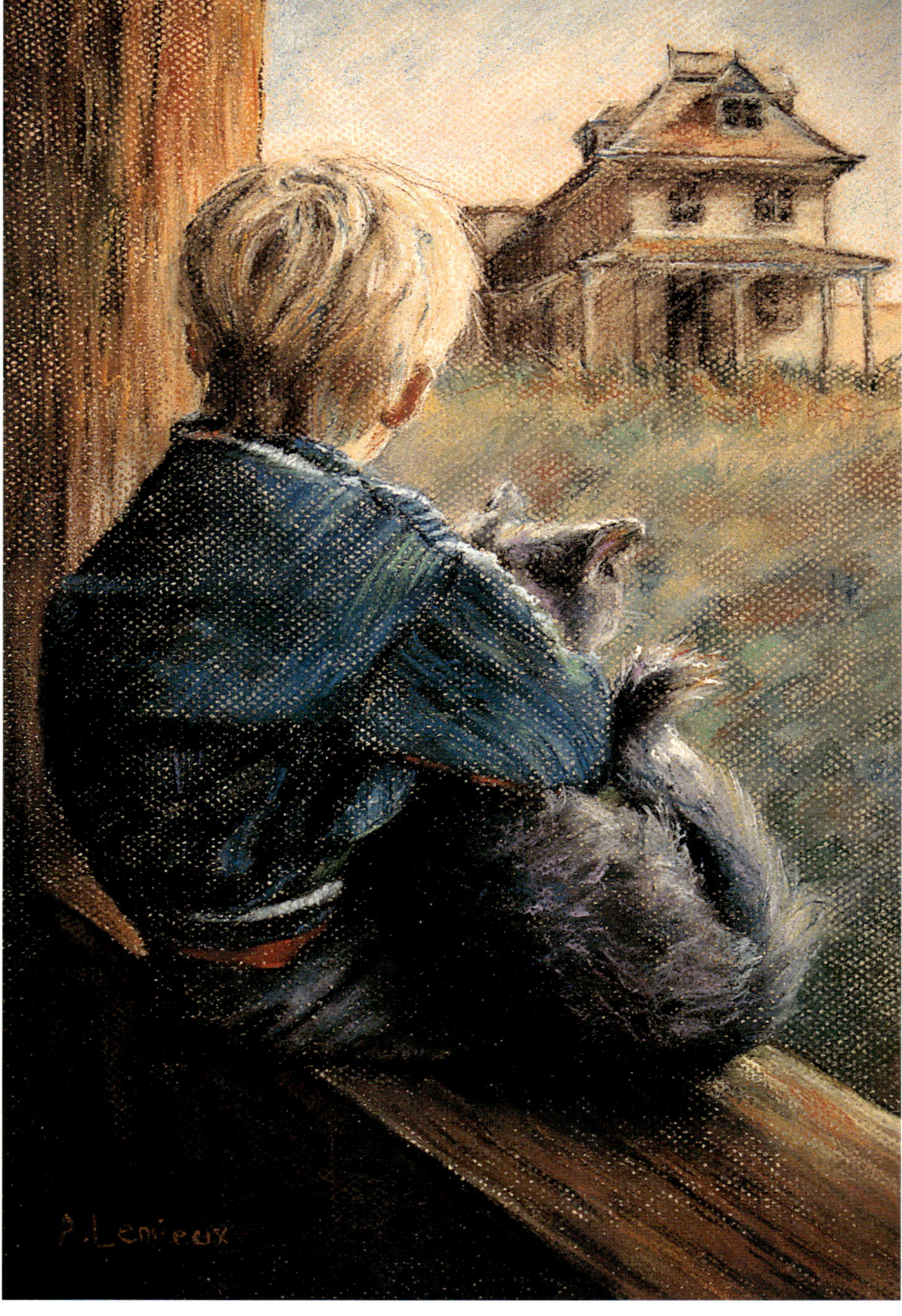

Marie-Ange

12" x 20"
Pastel paper

Nita Flick

From the time that I first experienced working with pastel, many years ago, I have never been able to do without it. I had been working in oil, acrylic and mixed media when I decided to try pastel. I first used the material on a portrait of a child. The child just blossomed under the soft texture and vibrant color of the pastel sticks. I decided to devote more of my time to working with this medium. For the past 15 years or more I've gradually adopted pastel as my medium. It is responsive, sensitive, vibrant and exhilarating to work with. No liquids, brushes, leftover paint to clean up.

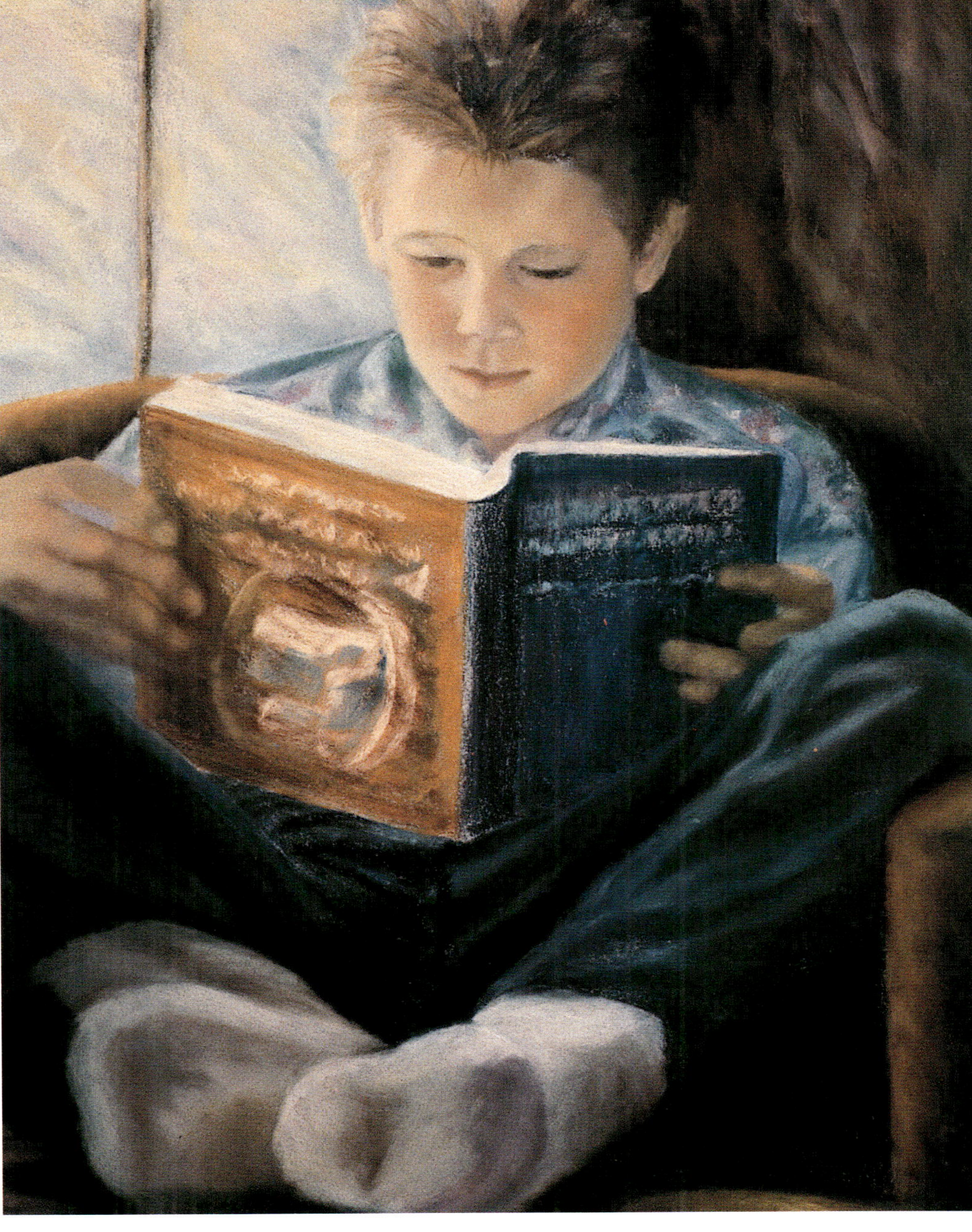

Morgan
19" x 25"
Sky blue velour

Maryse Proulx

In order to express and develop the themes of past and present life, I portray in my work the romanticism of people and the poetry of their surroundings. Generally, my paintings of men, women and children portray peace, tranquility and happiness within a specific life span.

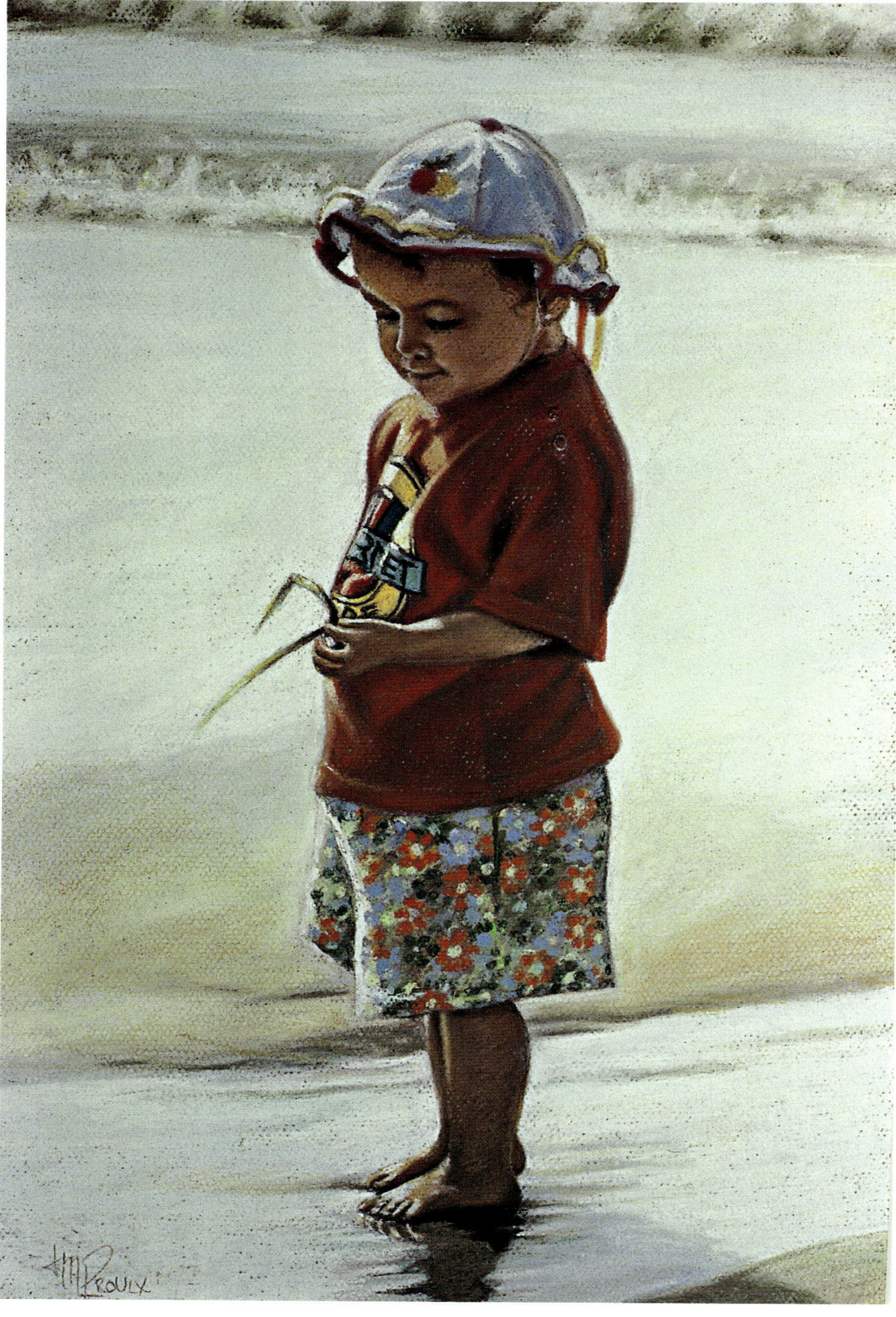

La Decouverte (The Discovery)
18" x 24"
Pastel paper

Jean Pilch

Sharing

13 ½" x 18 ½"
Pastel pencils on beige pastel paper

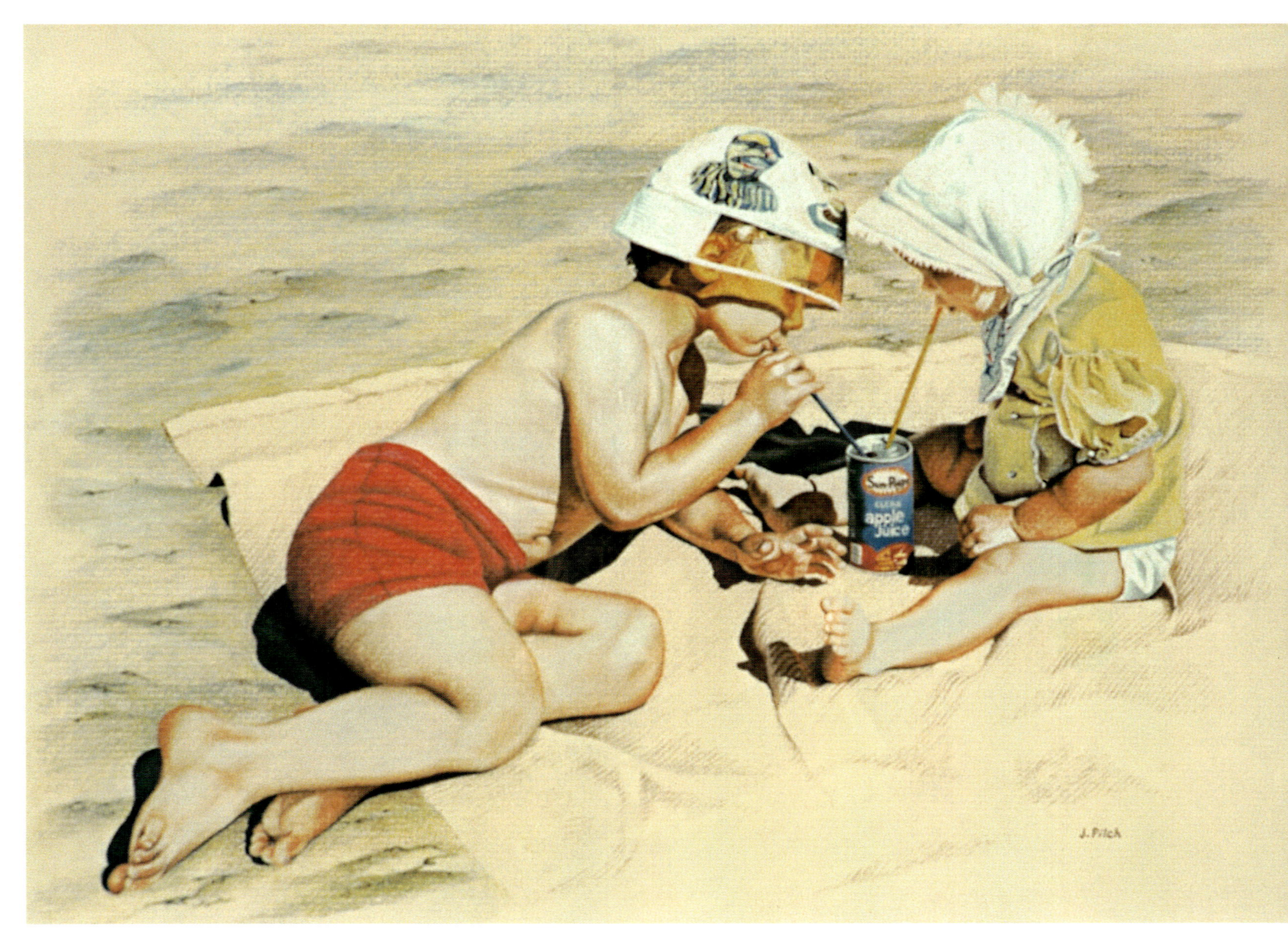

MISCELLANEOUS

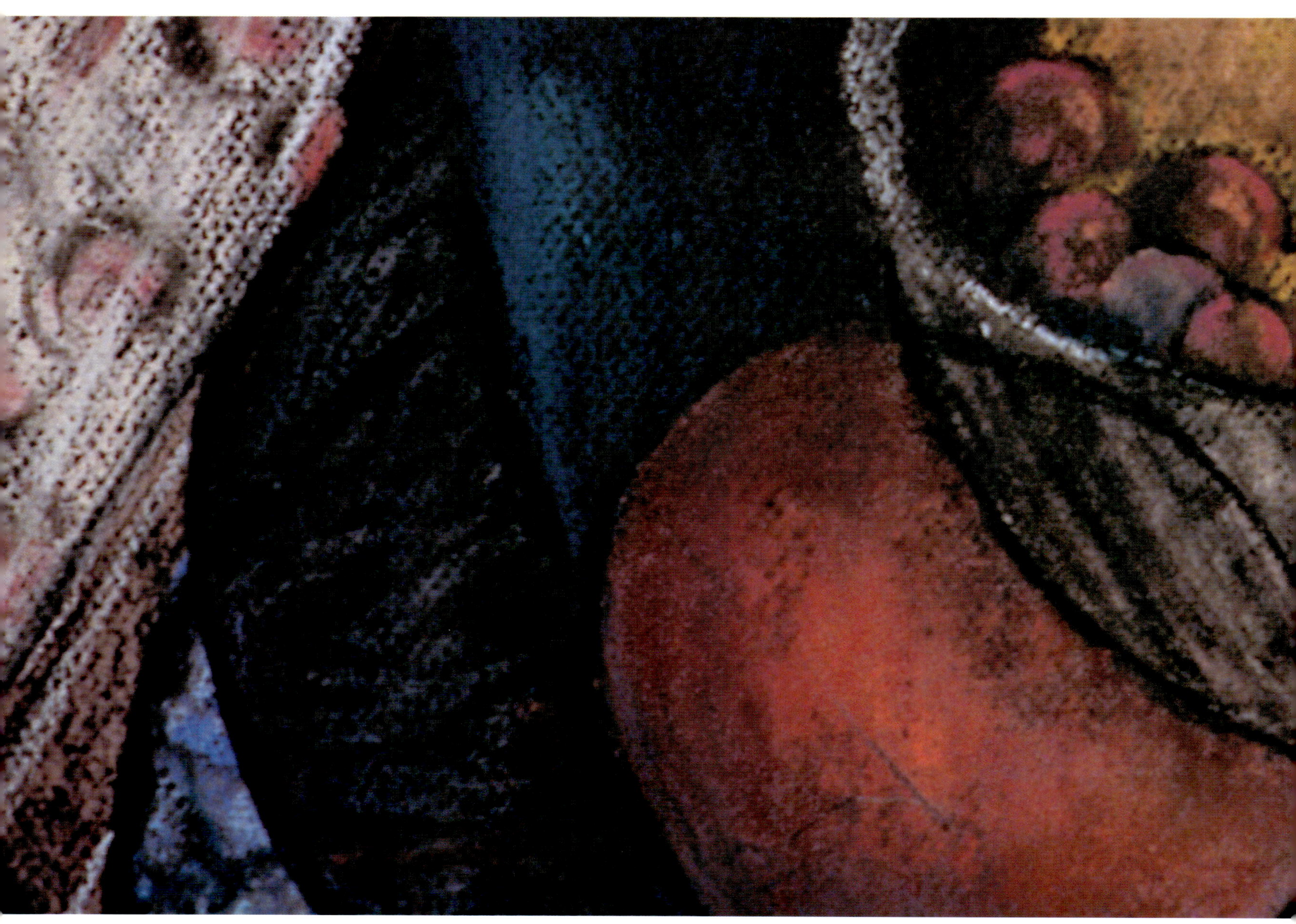

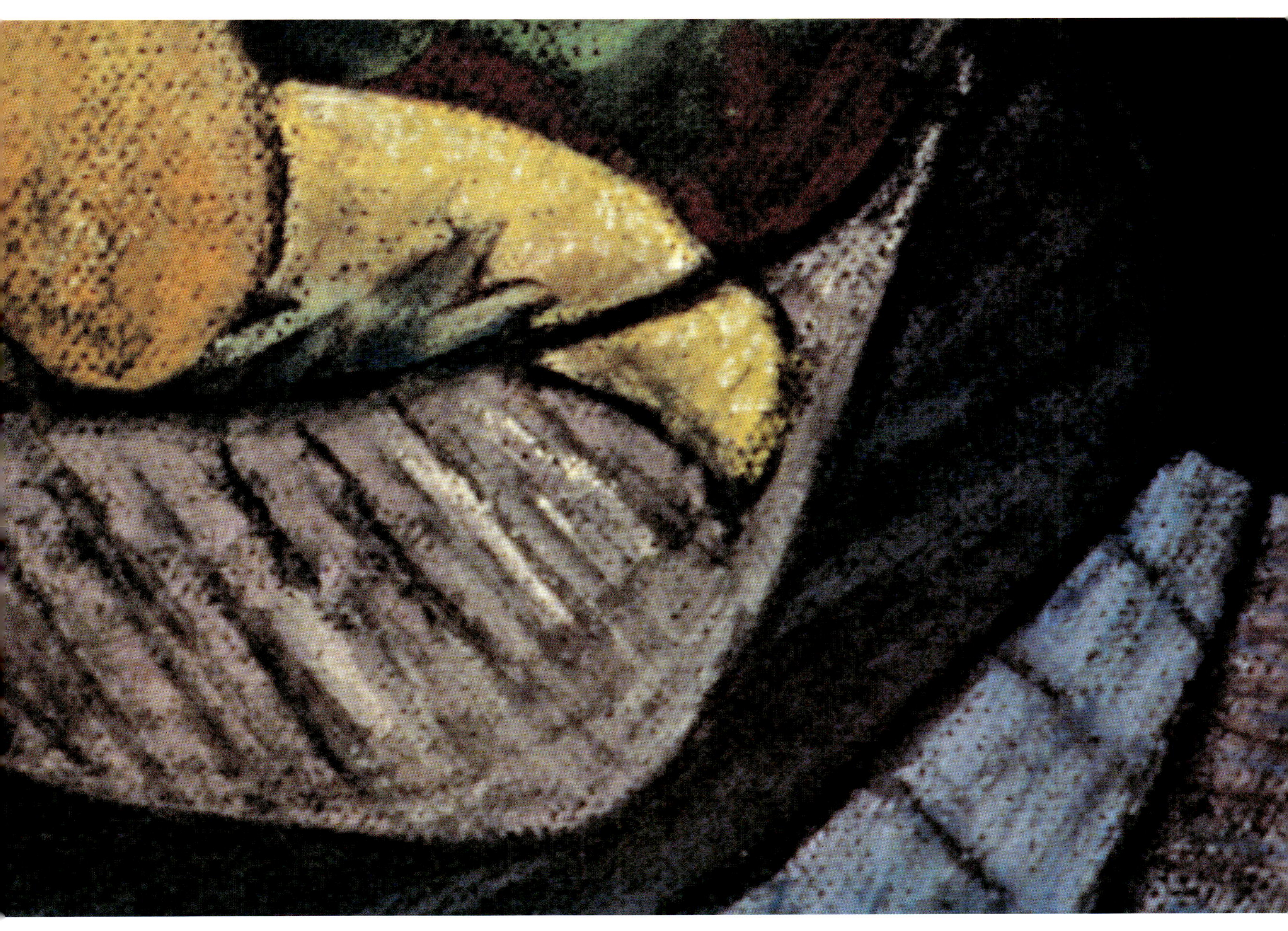

Douglas Manning

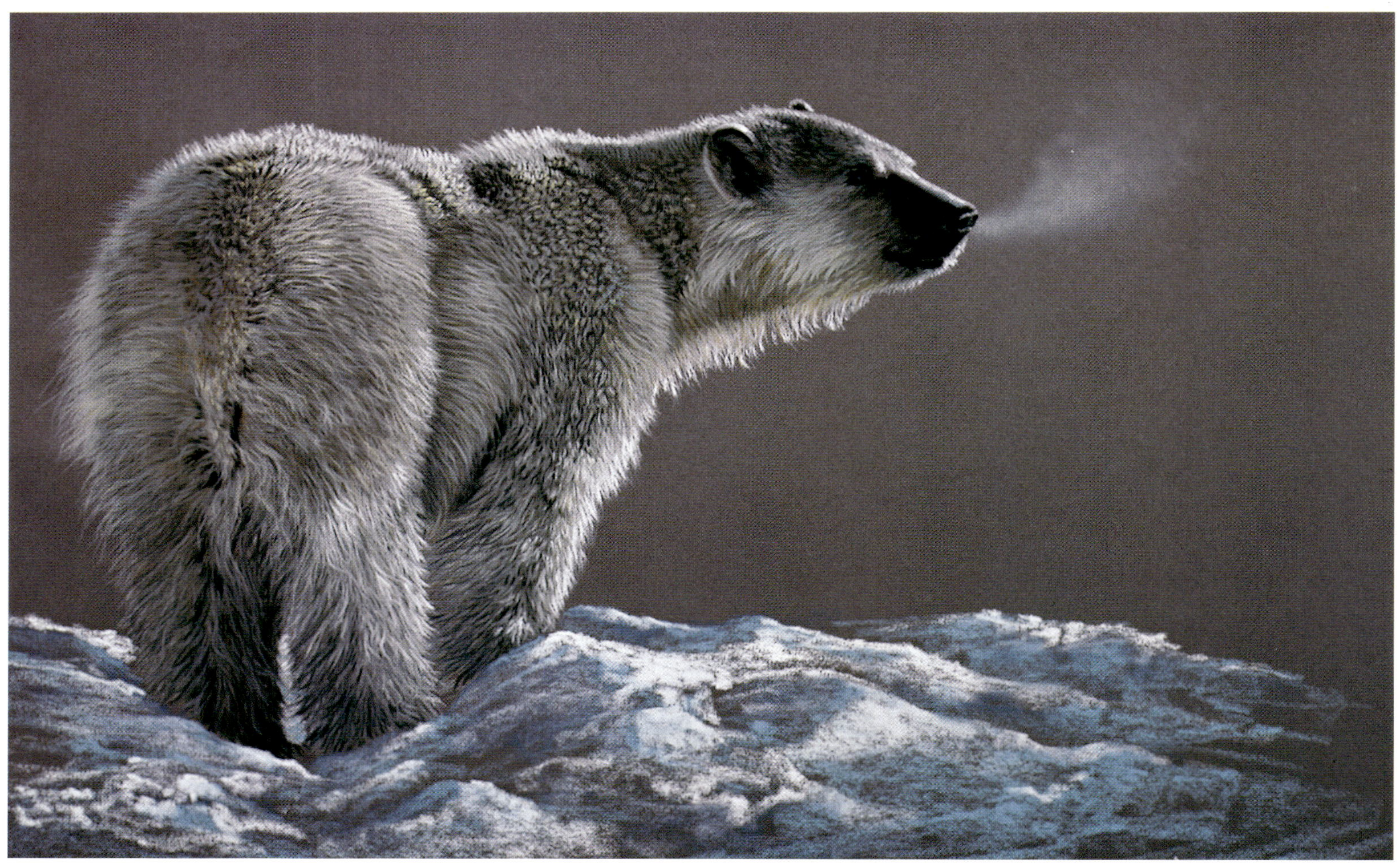

Polar Bear Study

21" × 29"
Canson Mi-Teintes

African Ivory

21" × 29"
Canson Mi-Teintes

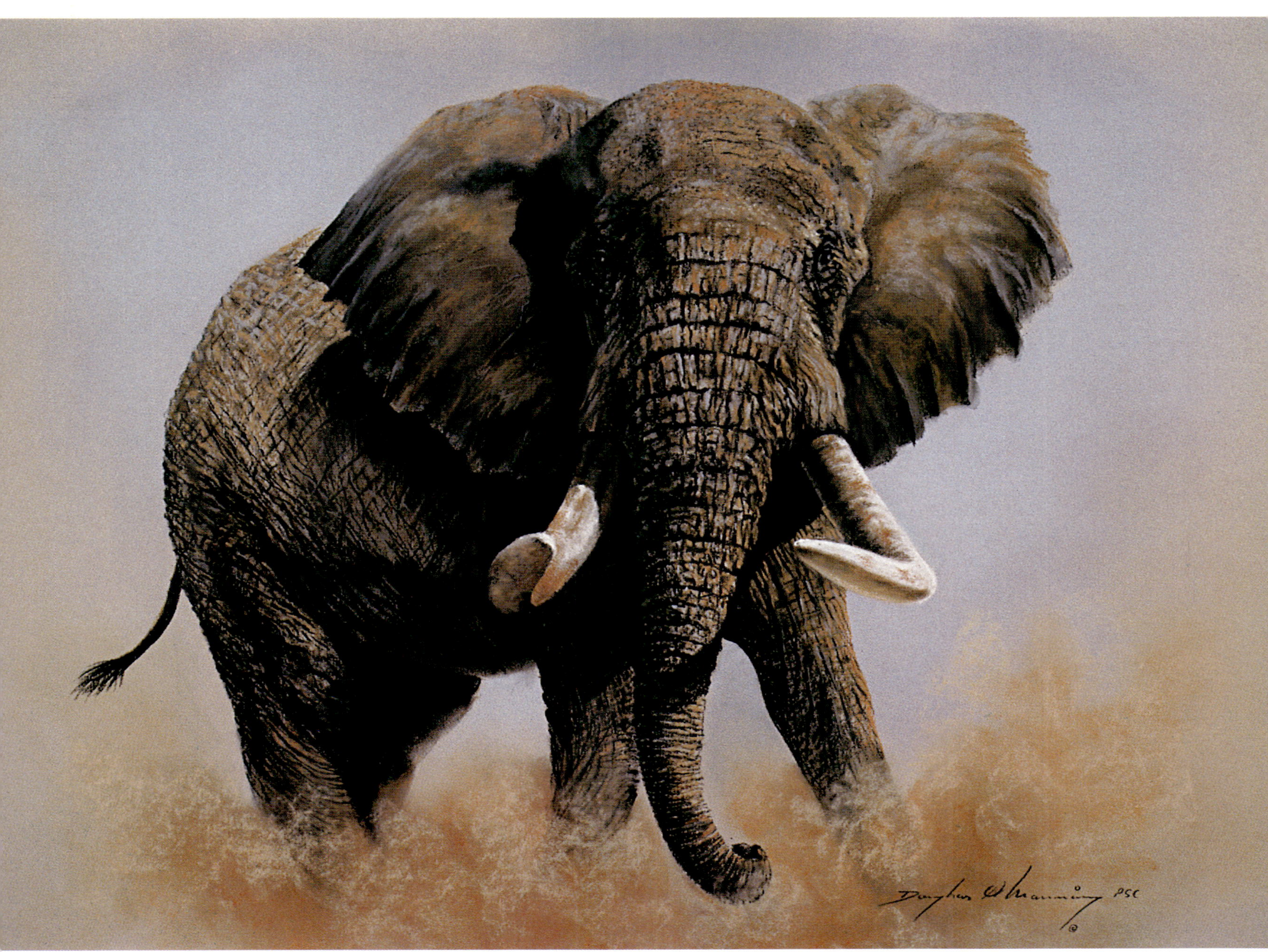

Douglas Manning

Winter Shadows

21" × 29"
Canson Mi-Teintes

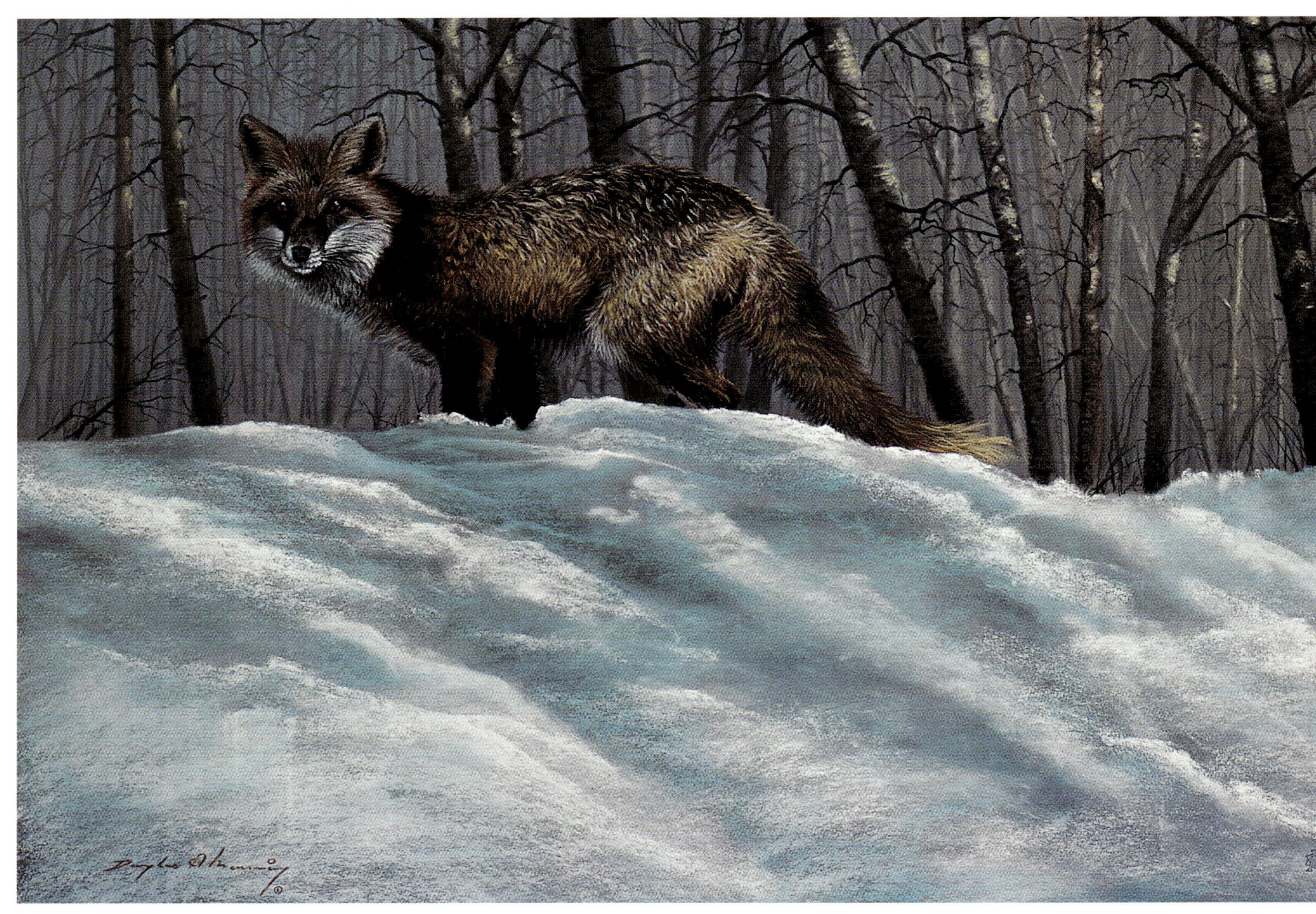

Geoffrey Jamieson

The paper I selected was medium gray. This choice allowed me to expose and use it as the shadowed side of the swan and also here and there in the water. Using the textured side of the paper, I lightly outlined the swan, using a pastel pencil that's darker than the paper. This would be covered and lost under softer pastel as the painting progressed.

Swan

21 ½" x 29 ½"
Canson Mi-Teintes paper

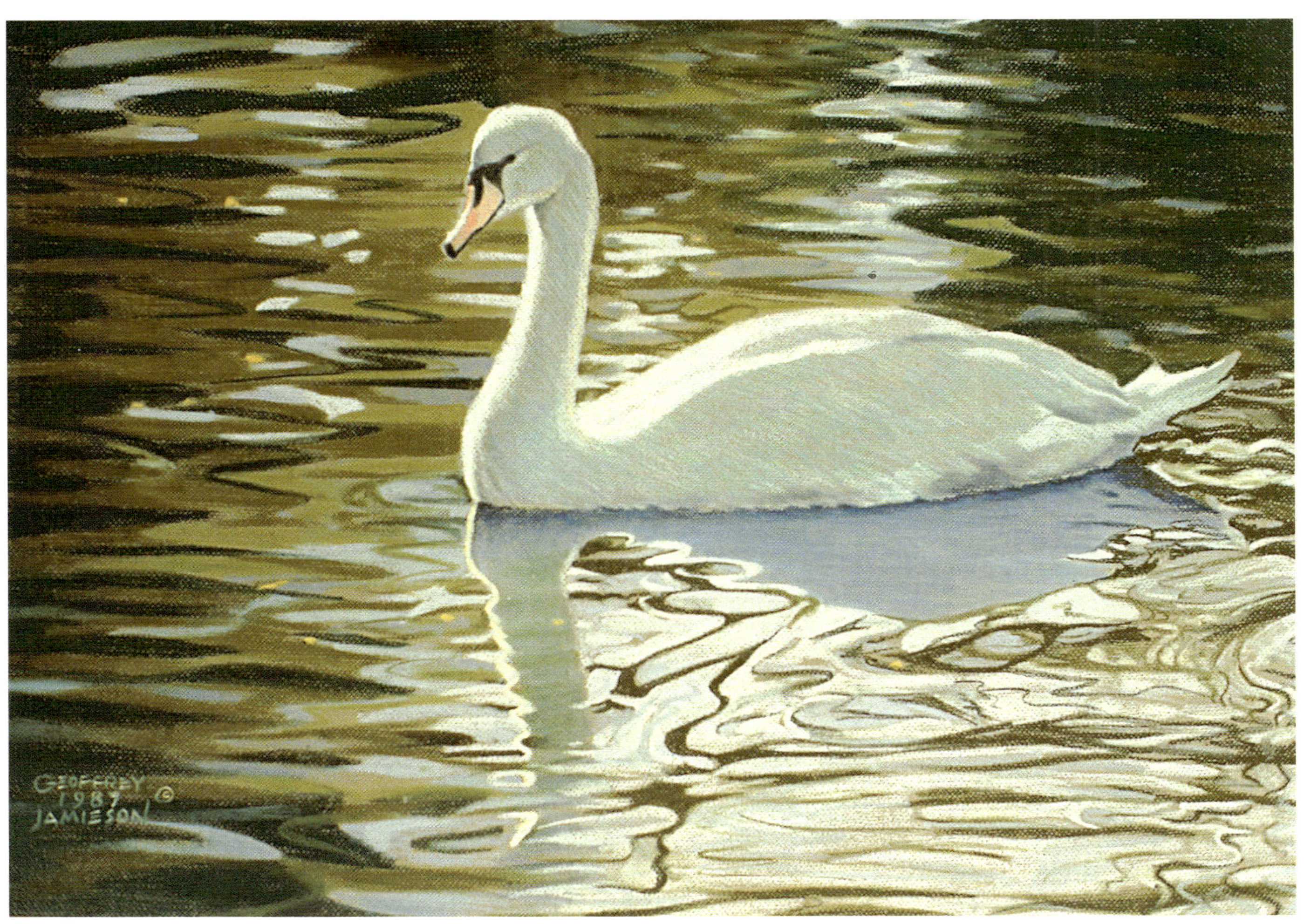

Nita Flick

I painted this picture with a new set of oil pastels I had just purchased. I didn't spend time on sketches; I wanted to see what I could produce. It was joyful; so quickly achieved.

Fun with Oil Pastel

23 ¾" x 25 ¾"
Canson Mi-Teintes (black) paper

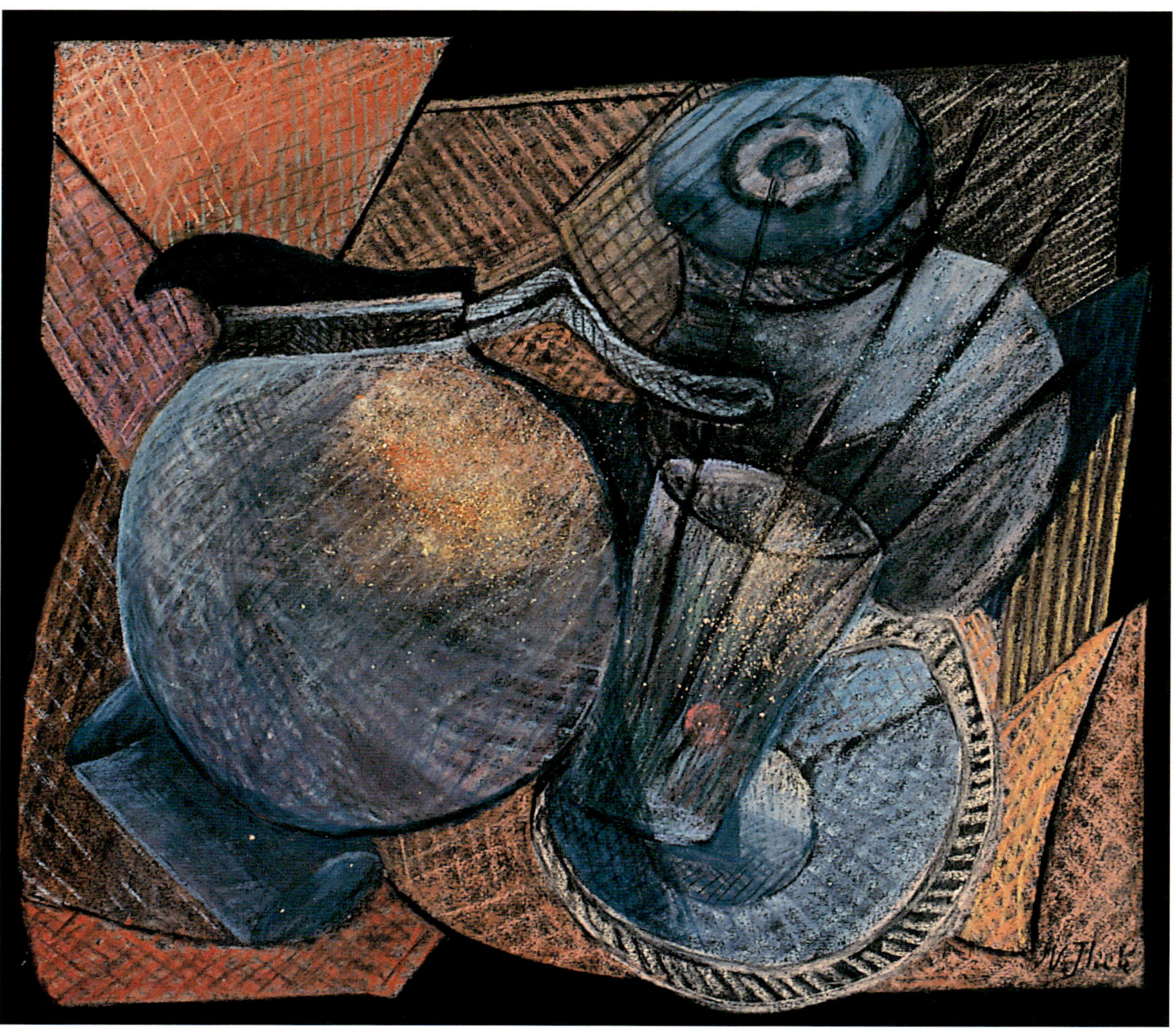

Still Life with Fruit

17" x 22 ½"
Canson Mi-Teintes
(black) paper

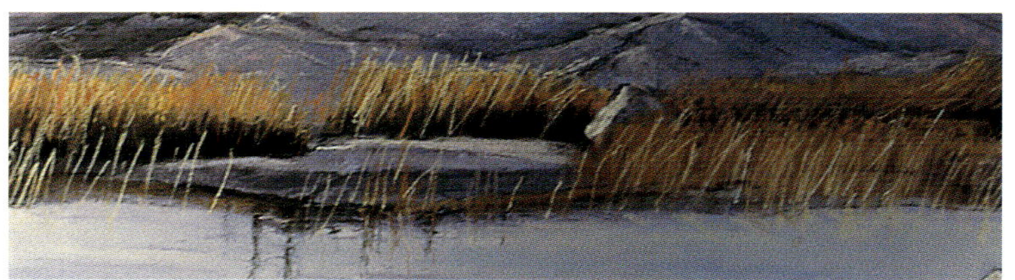

Artists' Biographies

The artists in this book are all members of the Pastel Society of Canada; they could not have made an appearance on these pages without having been selected for membership. It is for this obvious reason that we have eliminated the initials "PSC" (Pastel Society of Canada) from each name on the list that follows, and which each artist so richly deserves to have affixed to his or her name. We have, though, added the initials "PPC" (Premier Pastellist of Canada) to the names of those artists who have been honored by this award. The covetous appellation PPC is selected by a jury that meets each year to determine who, if any, will be the Premier Pastellist(s) for that particular year. It goes without saying that all of the artists whose paintings appear in this book are a source of pride to the publisher of this book. We take extra pride in choosing to honor the Premier Pastellists who have been identified for your attention.

Barbara Amos
Calgary, Alberta
Barbara Amos's work has been exhibited in a number of group shows, notably the Celebration of Women in the Arts. Her art education includes a study of the work of Degas at the Ottawa National Gallery in 1988. Barbara is represented in many public and private collections in Alberta, Ontario and Quebec.

Eileen Armstrong
Ottawa, Ontario
Eileen studied portraiture with Daniel Greene and Albert Handel, still life with Charles Reid, and watercolor with Don Getz, all U. S. painters and teachers. She has shown in group exhibitions in Ontario, Quebec and at the Hilton Leech Studio and Gallery in Sarasota, Florida. Eileen has had a substantial number of solo exhibitions.

George Balcan
Montreal, Quebec
Most of George Balcan's career has been devoted to radio broadcasting. After 35 years as Montreal's top radio personality, he left the field and chose the artist's studio. Having studied with Harvey Dinnerstein, well-known pastel painter, along with others, he felt ready to plunge right in. He succeeded in a large way and now his award-winning paintings can be seen in collections in Canada, the United States, France and Australia.

Robert Beaulieu
Quebec City, Quebec
Robert has had a lengthy seafaring career on the Great Lakes as well as in the deep sea. His marine paintings hang in the offices and boardrooms of many Canadian shipping companies. Largely self taught, Robert had the "help" of famous artists, whose works he studied extensively.

Dave Beckett, P.P.C.
Orillia, Ontario
An admirer of American painter Andrew Wyeth and of fellow Ontarian Ken Danby, Dave Beckett is a master in his own right of landscape painting. More than 25 years have passed since he first tried pastel at age 12. Today, after having left a successful career in corporate Canada for the life of an artist, Dave Beckett's pastel interpretations are in great demand across Canada.

John Brezinskis
Scarborough, Ontario
A native of Latvia and a graduate of the Latvian University, Brezinskis settled in Canada in 1951 and has been a resident of Scarborough since 1957. His pastels have been shown in a number of Canadian exhibitions where he has been honored to receive a bevy of awards.

Horace Champagne, P.P.C.
Ile d'Orleans, Quebec
After an extensive career in graphic design, Horace Champagne decided to devote all of his time to fine art painting in the medium of pastels. Born in Montreal, he traveled throughout Canada, from the coast of the Pacific to the shores of the Canadian Atlantic provinces. He now maintains a studio on the Island of Orleans. Horace has exhibited in shows in Vancouver, Calgary, Edmonton, Winnipeg, and in the United States in Palo Alto, California, and Kennebunkport, Maine, to name a few.

Alice Christenson
Salmon Arm, British Columbia
Born in New York City, Alice was educated both in the U.S. and Canada. She has exhibited in numerous group displays and many solo exhibitions. Alice's paintings are in several public and private collections.

Mireille Ducreux Collet
Quebec City, Quebec
Born in Paris, France, Mireille has been a resident of Quebec City since 1967. She has exhibited her pastel painting in France (1996, 1997), Sweden (1996), Miami, Florida (1995), Osaka, Japan (1994), winning awards in the European Art Group show in France and the Third International Female Artists exhibition in Stockholm.

Charles Couper, P.P.C.
Bear River, Nova Scotia
A native of Portsmouth, New Hampshire, Charles has been a Canadian citizen for the past nine years. He received his art education in New England schools and took private lessons from Ernest L. Major at the Santa Monica School in California. Charles has won prizes for his pastel paintings in important shows in the U.S. and in Canada.

J. Margo Cuthbert
North Vancouver, British Columbia
Drawing and painting have always been a part of Margo's lifestyle. Whether painting passengers while traveling on a train or ferry, or doing local landscapes and street scenes, she is content to be drawing and painting, even with subject matter that is dictated by the many commissions of her clients. Margo has been represented in countless shows, including those in Mexico and Australia.

Joyce Dessert
Golden, British Columbia
Born and raised in the U.S., Joyce is now a Canadian citizen and has lived in British Columbia since 1974. She says she is "more or less self taught" except for a commercial art course she took about 30 years ago while still in the U.S. She paints exclusively with pastels.

Lorna Dockstader
Calgary, Alberta
Though largely self-taught, Lorna did attend workshops through the Federation of Canadian Artists. A pastellist, Lorna is equally proficient with watercolor, winning awards in both media.

Barbara Elmslie
Harrington, Quebec
Born and raised in Montreal, Barbara now lives in the Laurentian Mountains, inspiration for many of her paintings. She has been represented in several juried group shows, winning awards in a few. Her paintings are in many private and corporate collections, among them Gulf Canada.

Ghada Fasho
Thornhill, Ontario
Ghada has been painting portraits with soft pastels for more than 18 years.

Nita I. Flick
Victoria, British Columbia
A correspondence art course offered by the Famous Artists School in Connecticut set in motion Nita's career in art. She followed that course (receiving excellent grades) with further study at the University of British Columbia and the Chapell School in New Westminster, also in British Columbia. Nita's pastel pieces have been shown in juried shows in Ottawa; Hull, Quebec; Miami, Florida and Seattle, Washington.

Dan Gray, P.P.C.
Errington, British Columbia
Dan Gray always paints on location because he believes in working from life. A self-taught artist, he was designated in 1996 as Premier Pastellist of Canada (PPC). Dan has received a coveted honor through the awards he has garnered. He gives painting demonstrations and conducts workshops across Canada.

Dick Griffin
Scarborough, Ontario
Inspired to paint with pastels by his father, a prominent pastel painter, Dick finally got to paint full time at the easel after a career in advertising. A member of various Canadian art clubs, Dick has participated in group shows throughout Ontario.

Bert Huizinga, P.P.C.
Scarborough, Ontario
Bert, a native of The Netherlands, came to Canada in 1954. He first used pastels in 1951 and after switching off to watercolors for a good length of time, he returned to pastels and now uses the medium exclusively. Aside from exhibiting throughout Canada, he has also shown his work in juried exhibitions in The Netherlands, Indonesia, and in Bradenton and Ft. Lauderdale, both in Florida.

Guylaine Jacques, P.P.C.
Saint Joseph de Beauce, Quebec
A Premier Pastellist of Canada honoree in 1983, Guylaine has participated in more than 30 group exhibitions and ten solo shows. Many of her paintings are in private and corporate collections in Quebec, Ontario and the U.S.

Geoffrey Jamieson, P.P.C.
Calgary, Alberta
Throughout his careers as a soldier and physician, Dr. Jamieson has drawn and painted. The Montreal-born artist-doctor studied with prominent American and Canadian pastellists, chief among them Daniel Greene of New York and Horace Champagne of Quebec. Most of Dr. Jamieson's works are commissioned and are to be found in corporate and private collections as well as those of Canadian army regiments. Thirty of his pictures are owned by the Canadian War Museum. Geoffrey was recognized as a Premier Pastellist of Canada in 1996.

Anita Elizabeth Kertzer, P.P.C.
Ottawa, Ontario
Anita, founding president of the Pastel Society of Canada, summers in Ottawa and winters in Longboat Key, Florida. She is a busy portrait painter, her latest, commissioned by the Government of Canada, is of former prime minister L.B.Pearson. A recipient of numerous awards, Anita is most proud of the Commemorative Medal which honors Canada's 125th Anniversary, approved by Her Majesty Queen Elizabeth and conferred by the Governor General of Canada. Listed in *Who's Who in American Art* , her paintings are represented in many private and corporate collections in both countries.

Tony Lee, P.P.C.
London, Ontario
When Tony Lee was 18 years of age, he emigrated to Canada from his native China. He received his schooling in London, Canada; Chicago, Illinois; and San Miguel, Mexico. In 1965, Tony was hired as a graphic designer by London Life and in 1972 he joined Fanshawe College in that same city as a professor of design. His pastel paintings are exhibited throughout Canada, the U.S. and France.

Anne Lemieux
St. Charles sur Richelieu, Quebec
From the moment that Anne Lemieux first viewed paintings by Degas and Cassatt, her inspiration flowed. She was rewarded for her hard work and dedication with a number of prizes in the Province of Quebec, mainly with a bronze medal in 1994 and a gold in 1995.

Rita MacKenzie, P.P.C.
Kingston, Ontario
Born in Brisbane, Australia, Rita settled in Canada in 1965. Since then, she has exhibited all over Canada and parts of northern U.S. From 1976 through 1980, she had ten paintings accepted by juries for exhibition at the British Pastel Society in London, England. Rita holds many honors, especially prized is the Grumbacher Award that she won in 1987.

Gilles Mailloux
Hull, Quebec
Gilles is represented in Quebec and Ontario by several prominent galleries. In exhibitions across Canada, his paintings have won many awards, principally a silver medal in a show under the auspices of the Circle of Artists, Painters and Sculptors of Quebec. His works can be found in private and public Canadian collections.

Jeanette E. McClelland, P.P.C.
Calgary, Alberta
Jeanette McClelland's encyclopedic knowledge of pastel as a medium for painting, which includes the various papers and textures that are most sympathetic, has prepared her well to capture the Canadian Native Indians that predominate as subject matter for her paintings.

Andrew McDermott
Vancouver, British Columbia
Andrew McDermott was born in Bolton, England, and at the age of 15, came to Canada. After a trip to New York's Metropolitan Museum of Art, where he viewed original pastel paintings by Degas, Andrew became inspired to establish his own style. He describes this style as a development from Degas and other "Impressionist influences."

Lois R. McKercher
Ottawa, Ontario
Lois exhibits regularly in shows around Ottawa and has won several top awards. She has studied with well-known Canadian artists and holds a teaching certificate for adult education from the Ottawa Board of Education.

Douglas Manning, P.P.C.
Perth, Ontario
Born in England, Douglas Manning served in North Africa with the British 8th Army from 1940 to 1945. Upon his return, he joined M.G.M. British Studios as an artist until 1957 when he emigrated to Canada. He continued his work at the film studios up to 1976 to concentrate full time on fine art painting, particularly in the field of wildlife. Douglas has participated in 15 group exhibitions and has had 12 solo shows. His work, ever in demand, hangs in many private and corporate collections, including the one of Queen Elizabeth, the Queen Mother.

Loredana May-Brind
Pointe-Claire, Quebec
Born and educated in Italy, Loredana moved in1967 with her husband to Quebec. Since 1970, she has taught art and exhibited in galleries and shows in Montreal, Beirut and Vienna.

Dorothy Marie Oxborough, P.P.C.
Victoria, British Columbia
Born in Calgary, Dorothy attended the Institute of Technology and Art in Calgary, and the Vancouver (B.C.) School of Art. Working with pastels all of her professional life, she has been represented in numerous group shows. Dorothy holds many awards, principally a Gold Medal in 1996. She specializes in portraits of Canadian Indian people.

Pierre Petel
Montreal, Quebec
A man of many interests and talents—poetry, television, song writing, and, of course, painting—Pierre likes to paint people and most of all, he tries to inject humor in his paintings. He has won several awards for his pastel paintings and is also in private and public collections.

Marija Petricevic
Calgary, Alberta
Marija arrived in Calgary in 1968 from Croatia, where she was born. She has since appeared in many group exhibitions and garnered awards in a few of them. Her work is in collections around the world, notably in Croatia, Switzerland, Israel, Australia and the United States.

Audrey Pfannmuller
Camrose, Alberta
Audrey's paintings are in corporate, public and private collections, among them the Westin Hotel in Edmonton. She has exhibited widely and has been honored with several awards. Audrey opened, in 1975, the Candler Art Gallery, where she is in constant contact with people sharing her concepts on the enjoyment of visual arts.

Jean Pilch
Calgary, Alberta
Jean is basically self-taught. After having worked in oils, acrylics and colored pencils, her medium today is pastels. She has earned a degree at the University of Alberta, and has participated in many juried group exhibitions. Jean's work is well represented in corporate and private collections.

Christiane Plante
Macamic, Quebec
Christiane has exhibited in quite a number of juried group shows in Canada as well as in cities of the U.S., and she has had several solo shows. She has studied with Max Stiebel and Dave Beckett of Canada and Daniel Greene and Ben Konis of the U.S., all highly regarded painters and teachers.

Maryse Proulx
Quebec City, Quebec
Maryse's paintings have been accepted in more than 20 group exhibitions and she has had more than eight solo shows. Predominantly a portrait painter, she has completed a number of commissions. Along with the Pastel Society of Canada, she is a proud member of several other painting organizations.

Marilyn-Ann Ranco
Montreal, Quebec
A commercial artist for ten years--Bell Canada, Canadair, Air Canada, some of her clients—Marilyn-Ann left to paint exclusively at the easel. It was a life-long dream, inculcated in her by her artist mother, Paulette Tanguay-Ranco. Having employed all media and tried every technique as an illustrator, she was not faithful to any one in particular until she had a *coup-de-coeur* (a falling in love) with pastel. Marilyn-Ann's honors are more than 50 group and solo shows in Canada and abroad; numerous awards, prominently the Howard Chandler Christy Award in 1993; representation in two books, "The Best of Portrait Painting" and "The Best of Pastels 2"; and several popular videos.

Rene St. Jean, P.P.C.
Waterloo, Quebec
Rene has been painting for 35 years. Her subject matter is varied: landscape, still life and abstract, but she's always excited to go back to portraits, choosing to paint them from life instead of from photographs.

Albertina Steinbock
Kitimat, British Columbia
Albertina arrived in Canada in 1966 with husband and children from Vienna, Austria. In 1995 she attended classes with instructor Daniel Greene after having painted for more than 25 years. She first became acquainted with pastels at a workshop in 1979.

Max Stiebel, P.P.C.
Montreal, Quebec
Max's first encounter with pastel was in 1980 at Albert Handel's workshop in Woodstock, N.Y. Instantly captivated, Max went on with the medium to win, in various group shows, a multitude of awards, including Premier Pastellist of Canada and the Grumbacher Gold Medal in 1994.

Wendy Trethewey
Ottawa, Ontario
From 1964 to 1996, Wendy was commissioned to paint portraits in Canada, the U.S., Australia and Germany. In 1995, her exhibition, "Wendy Trethewey, Portraits of the Artists," was mounted in Dartmouth Heritage Museum in Nova Scotia. Wendy has participated in a wide number of group and solo shows. She is represented in private and public collections throughout Canada, the U.S., Australia and England.

David Whitzman, P.P.C.
Halifax, Nova Scotia
Upon graduation from Nova Scotia College of Art, David became an instructor in portrait and composition at the college. He exhibited portraits for many years in Montreal, the Nova Scotia Artists Exhibits and the Maritime Art Exhibits. He has had one-man shows in galleries in Halifax. Whitzman, an octogenarian, has been designated a Premier Pastellist of Canada. His pastels have won prizes in international shows.

Lucienne Zegray, P.P.C.
Montreal, Quebec
Lucienne has been represented in group and solo shows throughout Quebec and Ontario. Her paintings have appeared in print in Canadian magazines and greeting cards, UNICEF among them. Amoco Petroleum Canada Ltd. and other corporations are proud to number Lucienne's paintings in their collections. Galleries all over the country show and sell her pastel interpretations of nature.

Rose Zivot, P.P.C.
Calgary, Alberta
Rose holds a number of awards, notably one as finalist in *Artists Magazine's* 1986 Floral Competition. She has exhibited in art shows across Canada and the U.S. and has her paintings in collections in Calgary, Vancouver and, in the U.S., Palm Springs, California, and Scottsdale, Arizona.

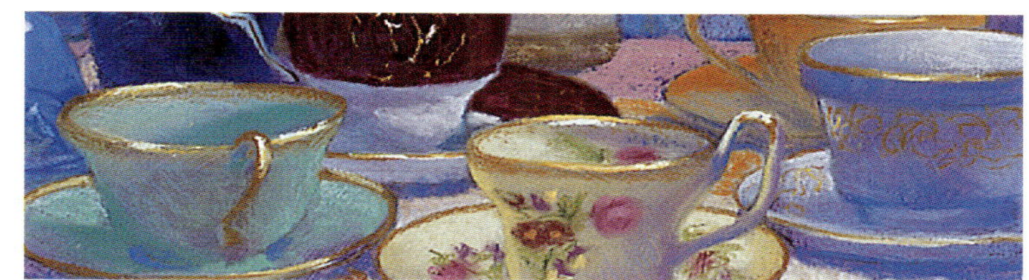

Index

Barbara Amos 14–17
Eileen Armstrong 83, 99
George Balcan 27, 76, 98
Robert Beaulieu 46–47
Dave Beckett, P.P.C. 6, 19, 38–40
John Brezinskis 78–80
Horace Champagne, P.P.C. 18, 62–64
Alice Christenson 51
Mireille Ducreux Collet 30–31, 74, 91
Charles Couper, P.P.C. 24–25, 108
J. Margo Cuthbert 107
Joyce Dessert 26, 75
Lorna Dockstader 69
Barbara Elmslie 60, 97
Ghada Fasho. 104–105
Nita I. Flick 111, 120–121
Dan Gray, P.P.C. 65
Dick Griffin 82
Bert Huizinga, P.P.C.. 70–72
Guylaine Jacques, P.P.C.. 55
Geoffrey Jamieson, P.P.C. 21, 44, 119
Anita Elizabeth Kertzer, P.P.C. 28–29, 94–95
Tony Lee, P.P.C.. 106
Anne Lemieux. 110
Rita MacKenzie, P.P.C. 48–50
Gilles Mailloux 81
Jeanette E. McClelland, P.P.C. 103
Andrew McDermott. 66–68, 109
Lois R. McKercher 32, 84
Douglas Manning, P.P.C.. . . . . 61, 116–118
Loredana May-Brind 33
Dorothy Marie Oxborough, P.P.C. 88–90
Pierre Petel. 45, 96
Marija Petricevic 20
Audrey Pfannmuller 52–54, 73
Jean Pilch 41–43, 113
Christiane Plante 57
Maryse Proulx. 112
Marilyn-Ann Ranco 22–23, 92
Rene St. Jean, P.P.C.. 93
Albertina Steinbock 85
Max Stiebel, P.P.C. 77, 100–102
Wendy Trethewey 34–35
David Whitzman, P.P.C. 58–59, 73
Lucienne Zegray, P.P.C.. 56
Rose Zivot, P.P.C. 10–13